Why We HATE

Understanding, Curbing, and Eliminating Hate in Ourselves and Our World

RUSH W. DOZIER, JR.

Contemporary Books

Chicago   New York   San Francisco   Lisbon   London   Madrid   Mexico City
Milan   New Delhi   San Juan   Seoul   Singapore   Sydney   Toronto

Library of Congress Cataloging-in-Publication Data

Dozier, Rush W.
  Why we hate : understanding, curbing, and eliminating hate in ourselves
and our world / Rush W. Dozier, Jr.
      p.   cm.
  Includes bibliographical references and index.
  ISBN 0-8092-2483-6
  1. Hate.   I. Title

  BF575.H3 D69   2002
  179'.8—dc21   2002067304

Contemporary Books

A Division of The McGraw·Hill Companies

1 2 3 4 5 6 7 8 9 0   AGM/AGM   1 0 9 8 7 6 5 4 3 2

ISBN 0-8092-2483-6

This book was set in Monotype Fournier
Printed and bound by Quebecor Martinsburg

Cover design by Nick Panos
Interior design by Monica Baziuk

This book is printed on acid-free paper.

For peacemakers everywhere

CONTENTS

PREFACE

ONE OF THE STORIES OF writer and humorist Sholom Aleichem tells of the court-martial of a young soldier charged with failing to fire his weapon during a battle. The soldier freely admits that he was ordered to shoot when he saw the enemy. "Then why didn't you?" someone asks. "But I never saw the enemy," he explains. "I just saw people." I thought of that story many times after the devastating attacks of September 11, 2001. Why did the terrorists see only enemies among the thousands of innocent men, women, and children who were killed on that terrible day? Why couldn't they see that their victims were just people?

Sadly, the answer to these questions is: hate. For those infected by this ghastly emotion, no violence is too extreme. Hate has a nearly limitless ability to dehumanize its victims, shutting down the most basic human capacities for sympathy and compassion. This is not the problem of just a few fanatical terrorists. It is a problem of human nature generally that threatens the well-being of all of us in an era of proliferating weapons of mass destruction. For hate can arise in an infinite number of forms: religious hatred, racial hatred, national hatred, ethnic hatred, class hatred, political hatred, and on and on. In the twentieth century, countless millions died on the altar of hate in a worldwide outbreak of wars and genocides. Can we stop this cycle from beginning again? *Why We Hate* argues that the problem of the twenty-first century is the problem of hate.

This book will explore hate—and its companion, self-hatred—from the perspective of a wide variety of disciplines and fields of study, including neuroscience, psychology, evolutionary biology, archaeology, paleontology, the history of warfare, and the rise of civilization. We will probe how hate perpetuates itself, generation after generation, in the vulnerable minds of children. We will examine the relationship of hate to conflicts around the world as well as to a broad range of issues including school shootings, bullying, media violence, the Internet, terrorism, genocide, racism, sexism, love, marriage, sexuality, violence in the workplace, depression, suicide, and eating disorders.

For at least three thousand years, philosophers have debated the origin of the darker human impulses. One venerable and popular line of thinking is that civilization corrupts human nature, perverting its innate goodness. But the findings of modern neuroscience and behavioral biology lead to the opposite conclusion. Powerful destructive and self-destructive tendencies appear to be built into the human brain by evolution. Left unchecked, these individual impulses can be amplified by the scope and power of civilization into a global threat. Yet we are also discovering that although civilization can make these tendencies worse, it can also serve to control them.

Over the past two decades, neuroscience has begun unraveling how specific structures and neurochemicals in the human brain generate negative emotions such as hate and fear. New imaging technologies can watch the living brain as it thinks and feels, allowing scientists to see which areas of the brain interconnect to create the more complex mental capacities. This revolution is revealing the basic mechanisms of human emotion hidden deep within the brain. Combining this knowledge with our growing understanding of the evolutionary and cultural aspects of hate gives us for the first time the hope of curbing its terrible influence.

A book of this nature could never be completed without the help of many people. I would first like to thank my wife, Patricia June Dozier, whose encouragement and assistance were essential to this project. I would also like to thank John Nolan, former vice president and publisher of Contemporary Books, who shared my vision; Denise Betts, my editor, who saw this vision through to reality; copyeditor Dawn Shoemaker, who perfected the vision; and the many others at Contemporary Books who pitched in. In addition, I gratefully acknowledge Denise Houffe, computer consultant, for her expertise and support.

Many groups around the world monitor the effects of hate. Some of the most important work has been done by Rabbi Marvin Hier, founder of the Simon Wiesenthal Center and the Museum of Tolerance in Los Angeles; and Morris Dees and Mark Potok of the Southern Poverty Law Center in Montgomery, Alabama. Over the years, I have benefited from the wisdom of many outstanding scientists and thinkers. Some of these include Nobel laureate Eric R. Kandel, professor, Columbia University; Joseph LeDoux, Henry and Lucy Moses Professor of Science, New York University; Antonio Damasio, M. W. Van Allen Distinguished Professor and head of the department of neurology at the University of Iowa College of Medicine; the late Jonas Salk, founder of the Salk Institute for Biological Studies in San Diego; Thomas Albright, professor and director of the Sloan Center for Theoretical Neurobiology at the Salk Institute; James McGaugh, director of the Center for the Neurobiology of Learning and Memory at the University of California at Irvine; and Richard M. Restak, M.D., expert in neurology and the author of many outstanding books on the brain. Although I have absorbed the insights of many gifted individuals, responsibility for the analysis and conclusions of *Why We Hate* is mine alone.

I hope that within these pages you too will find insights into what makes human beings do what we do to each other and, ultimately, hope for a more peaceful future.

"*If we have suffered or expect to suffer some willful injury from a man, or if he is in any way offensive to us, we dislike him; and dislike easily rises into hatred.*"

—CHARLES DARWIN in
The Expression of Emotions in Man and Animals

1

SCIENTIFIC INSIGHTS INTO THE NATURE OF OUR EMOTIONS

HATE IS THE NUCLEAR WEAPON of the mind. Its detonation can blow apart the social order and plunge nations into war and genocide. It shatters relationships, leading people who once loved each other into bitterness, violence, even murder. Blasts of hate sweep away civility and tolerance, spurring individuals to commit acts of savagery and pitting group against group in combat that can grow vicious and deadly. Hate poisons the workplace. It warps the minds of children, who are defenseless against its destructive influence, and this allows it to reproduce itself generation after generation. Hate can undermine our health by stressing the heart, raising blood pressure, suppressing the immune system, and damaging the brain. As self-hatred, it can insidiously create a negative self-perception that robs life of its pleasure, leading to depression and even suicide.

In the name of hate, human beings carry out the most shocking and repulsive acts imaginable. These unspeakable acts go by many different names: *oppression*, *torture*, *genocide*—and *terrorism*. What the entire world witnessed on September 11, 2001, was only the latest horrific episode of hate-inspired violence. Like all such acts, hate-filled terrorism emerges from primitive areas of the human brain buried deep beneath the more recently evolved outer layers and from years of cultural conditioning that pits groups in an us-versus-them battle for survival.

Over the past five centuries, hate has periodically ravaged Western civilization, leading to bloodier and bloodier conflicts. At the end of the Renaissance, wars of religion ripped Europe apart. At the end of the Enlightenment, the Napoleonic Wars spread across large parts of the globe. The twentieth century was disfigured by seventy-five years of ferocious hot and cold world wars that began in Sarajevo on June 28, 1914, with a terrorist's assassination of Archduke Francis Ferdinand and his wife, Sophie, of the Austro-Hungarian Empire, and did not end until the Berlin Wall fell on November 9, 1989. Now, after a lull of fewer than twelve years, this hideous cycle may be starting again. It is not enough to root hatred out of the caves of Afghanistan, we must also root it out of the human mind.

Our focus on the underlying cause of the kind of brutality we saw on September 11 must be unwavering. "Can it be explained?" asked Elie Wiesel, Holocaust survivor and Nobel Peace Prize winner, of the horror of that day. "Yes," he said, "by hatred. Hatred is at the root of evil everywhere. Racial hatred, ethnic hatred, political hatred, religious hatred. In its name, all seems permitted. For those who glorify hatred, as terrorists do, the end justifies all means, including the most despicable ones."[1]

Terrorism cannot be understood solely by exploring political, religious, and cultural conflicts or the personalities of individual terrorists. It is part of the darker emotional tapestry of the brain. Terrorism's motive is hate, and its weapon is fear. On the most primitive level, the brain has evolved a response to threats that encompasses two basic behaviors: fight and flight. Hatred arises from the fight response, while fear and terror are generated by the flight response.

Hate can be so overwhelming that it can motivate terrorist attacks. But hate can also turn inward, which is an important reason that we are the only species in which significant numbers of individuals intentionally commit violent suicide. Suicidal self-hatred takes an especially heartbreaking toll on young people. Suicide is the leading cause of nonaccidental death among U.S. teenagers. On average, a young person commits suicide in this country at least every ninety minutes and probably much more frequently. Many young deaths classified as accidents are actually suicides. Over the past half century, the teenage suicide rate has tripled.

Fifteen-year-old Kip Kinkel, looking more like Huck Finn than Charles Manson, strode into the cafeteria of his crowded Springfield, Oregon, high school shortly before 8:00 A.M. on May 21, 1998, and opened fire with a .22-caliber Ruger semiautomatic rifle. Two students were killed and twenty-two others wounded before Kinkel was tackled by a varsity wrestler while he paused to reload. As Kinkel was pinned to the floor by the wrestler and other students, he shouted, "Just shoot me. Shoot me now." When authorities went to his house, they found Kinkel's journal. In it, he wrote: "Hate drives me. . . . I am so full of rage. . . . Everyone is against me. . . . As soon as my hope is gone, people die." They also found the bodies of his parents, whom he had shot to death the day before.[2]

Kip Kinkel, of course, is the exception. Despite the massive publicity they receive, school shootings are rare. But tendrils of hate and violence can penetrate almost anywhere. When I was in college, I worked for a time as the assistant director of an evening program for teens and preteens at a community center in east Cambridge, Massachusetts, just across the Charles River from Boston. This was a working-class neighborhood, and the kids who came to the center were mostly from Italian-American families. They were lively and bright, but I glimpsed the bleaker undercurrents that parents and teachers often see.

Besides the occasional bullying and teasing that one finds in any schoolyard—which made some kids miserable and depressed—I saw signs of racial and ethnic intolerance. The kids I talked to knew this was unfair, but they couldn't help being influenced by the attitudes and stereotypes that were being expressed by some in the larger community. Thus, I was not totally surprised when Boston—a remarkable town that is home to some of the most accomplished minds in the world—later went through horrendous turmoil as it tried to use busing to integrate its schools. Racial and ethnic tensions became superheated. Much of the anger was directed against African-Americans, and people chose sides. A vocal minority boiled over with hate, and the result was violence, riots, and killings. For years, hatred tore the city apart until moderation finally prevailed. Yet in its agony, Boston was simply a microcosm of the world at large, where the problem of hate has yet to be solved.

Human beings are the most volatile product of evolution imaginable: a fantastically adept toolmaking species with an enormous brain capable of generating the most powerful and destructive forms of hate and self-hate. As our tools have evolved over the past hundred thousand years from stone axes and spears to firearms, hydrogen bombs, and intercontinental ballistic missiles, the consequences of this darkest part of our nature have become infinitely more ominous. And so we strive to answer these questions: What exactly is hate? Why does it lead not only to the most irrational acts of violence but also the most extreme forms of cruelty and torture? What is the unique quality of human beings that allows us to hate ourselves? Why does love sometimes lead to hate? How can hate be stopped?

We can for the first time begin to answer these questions because of a revolution in our understanding of this deadliest of emotions that draws on a wide range of scientific research—from anthropology to zoology. Not only can this knowledge transform our own lives, it also can transform the world at large.

Researchers have discovered that hate emerges from an ancient survival instinct that combines intense dislike, anger, stereotyping, and us-versus-them distinctions. Surprisingly, hate and self-hate (exhibited by depression and suicide) appear to engage different areas of the brain. This discovery has provided fundamental insights into how hate affects our behavior and how we can control it—

insights that are crucial to every one of us. Using these scientific insights, I will propose specific strategies for curbing hate (see Chapter 2). These strategies can be used both in our everyday lives and in our efforts as a society to heal the hatred within our nation and among the peoples of the world. They presuppose that tolerance must be taught, especially to children, not only explicitly but implicitly—by example. Although we are born with the capacity to cooperate and love, we also have an innate ability to stereotype and hate. To enhance the former capacity rather than the latter, the strategies to curb hate require the replacement of our primitive tendency to adopt an us-versus-them orientation with an us-us perspective, in which we steadfastly focus on the common humanity and unique individuality of members of other groups rather than dehumanizing them.

THE ANATOMY OF HATE

Within the ancient emotional centers of the brain, neuroscientists have discovered a key area responsible for orchestrating our emotional and motivational reactions to the outside world: the amygdala. Like many structures in the brain, the amygdala is twinned, with one in the right cerebral hemisphere (which fills the right half of the skull) and another in the left. Much brain activity occurs through parallel processing that takes place in both hemispheres simultaneously. Your right amygdala is slightly more than an inch beneath your right temple, while the left amygdala occupies the same position beneath the left temple. For convenience, I will normally refer to twinned brain areas in the singular. When I discuss the amygdala, for example, I am actually referring to both the right and left amygdala. If it is important to distinguish between twin brain areas, I will specify either the right or left.

The amygdala—along with the hypothalamus and the hippocampus—is one part of the limbic system, which is the area of the

brain concerned with emotion and motivation. Each amygdala—
about the size of a grape—is linked to your sensory systems and
constantly scans the information flowing through them, looking for
any sign of threat or pain, whether physical or mental. The amygdala plays an important role in many emotions, including hate,
anger, fear, joy, and love, and serves as an emotional and behavioral
trip wire, capable of automatically triggering a response before we
consciously realize what is happening. This preconscious response
is almost instantaneous and selects from a repertoire of innate
behaviors that all of us share. We may stare wide-eyed, flinch, duck,
jump, bolt, freeze, brace, or scream.

I once served as chairman of the management committee of a
federal economic development agency, which required me to be in
Washington several times a month. Usually I stayed at the Washington Hilton, just down Connecticut Avenue from the agency's
offices. In the early morning, I would go out the side door of the
Hilton for a jog through the surrounding neighborhoods. It was
from a door at this side entrance that President Ronald Reagan and
a group of aides and Secret Service agents emerged on March 30,
1981, after Reagan had made an appearance before a group at the
Hilton. And it was here that a twenty-five-year-old drifter named
John W. Hinckley Jr. tried to kill the president, gravely wounding
him and several others. Whenever I passed this eerie spot, I couldn't
help thinking about that terrible attack. There is a famous videotape
showing the assassination attempt. The shots are fired as Reagan,
just about to enter his limousine, waves to a small group of onlook-
ers, including Hinckley. If you watch closely, you see everyone—
including the president—instinctively duck almost simultaneously
as their limbic systems detect the sound of gunfire.

The function of the amygdala in hate and related emotions has
been highlighted by the study of a rare disorder called episodic
dyscontrol or intermittent explosive disorder. Some victims of this
disorder suddenly, with little or no warning, experience overwhelming feelings of terror and hatred, accompanied by violent

rages. During these rages, a victim of the disorder may attack or even try to kill anyone who happens to be around. The episodes end as suddenly as they begin, leaving sufferers at a loss to explain why they acted so violently. The feelings of hatred are usually temporary: once the episode has passed, individuals often express profound sorrow for how they behaved. Some studies have found evidence of abnormal activation of the amygdala during these episodes—a sort of localized epileptic seizure. In one case, microelectrodes that could be turned on by radio control were inserted into the amygdala of a woman with episodic dyscontrol who had stabbed and almost killed a complete stranger. Sure enough, when these electrodes were activated without the patient's knowledge, she immediately flew into a violent rage.

Scientists have known for more than half a century that the amygdala plays a role in the emotions of other species. Monkeys that were uncontrollably aggressive when approached by humans became completely tame and easily handled after their amygdala was removed. Animals with natural enemies completely changed their behavior after an amygdala operation. Aggressive dogs suddenly coexisted peacefully with cats, and cats did the same with mice. But this sudden passivity comes at a severe cost. Animals without an amygdala lose the ability to interact normally with others of their species because they no longer give off or receive appropriate emotional signals. In humans, the right amygdala seems to play a primary role in hate and rage. This is consistent with the suggestion of many studies that, in most people, the right cerebral hemisphere appears to have a dominant role in expressing negative emotions, while the left hemisphere is primarily responsible for positive emotions. Although the amygdala is extremely important in humans, it is not overwhelmingly dominant as it appears to be in species such as monkeys and apes. The human emotional system is much more complex, and the amygdala is just one part of this neural system. Destruction of the amygdala alone diminishes but normally does not completely destroy human emotional responsiveness. The specifics of the emotional systems of the human brain are still being worked out, and there remain many controversies and unanswered questions. In the case of the woman who had microelectrodes inserted into her amygdala, it was the electrical stimulation of her right amygdala that appeared to cause her violent rage. After an operation to have areas of her right amygdala surgically destroyed, her sudden emotional outbursts completely disappeared.

Decades of research indicate that the amygdala performs a key role in both human aggression and the brain's response to aggression. It seems likely that John Hinckley's amygdala played an important part in his assassination attempt. And it is also likely that the automatic defensive reaction of the president's limbic system may have played a role in saving his life.

The amygdala is interconnected with many parts of the brain. It is closely linked to another region intimately associated with aggression and defense: the hypothalamus. This tiny area—about the size of a lima bean—has an enormous role in regulating the body's basic systems, including many automatic responses. Hanging just below the hypothalamus and connected to it by a slender stalk is the pituitary, which is the master gland that controls the body's hormones. When the amygdala signals danger or anger, it is the hypothalamus that, in turn, activates the pituitary. The pituitary—located above the roof of the mouth—then releases an emergency hormone into the bloodstream that flows to the adrenal glands and instructs them to immediately release stress hormones, including the adrenaline and noradrenaline that galvanize the body. This is just one of a wide range of connections between the hypothalamus and other areas of the brain. Electrical stimulation of specific parts of the hypothalamus of animals can trigger stereotyped aggressive and defensive behaviors.

The amygdala is also wired to one particular area in the brain's speech centers that seems to control obscenities as well as other forms of emotional sounds and language. These are the kinds of words and sounds we tend to automatically utter when under physical or mental stress—as when we accidentally hit our thumb with a hammer while trying to drive a nail. Researchers have closely examined this speech area in the course of studying a disorder called Tourette's syndrome. Victims of Tourette's usually display a variety of tics. Sometimes a patient with Tourette's, in addition to physical tics, will experience a kind of verbal tic that takes the form of involuntary torrents of obscenities. Imaging studies have shown that this symptom is precipitated by abnormal activation of this primitive speech area, which is part of the limbic system. The amygdala's connection with the same area may explain why outbursts of hatred are so often accompanied by a flood of obscenities.[3]

The cerebral cortex is the wrinkled outer skin of the brain. It is the seat of our most advanced abilities, including self-awareness. The cortex is divided into several different parts. The neocortex ("new" cortex) is the most recently evolved and complex area of the cortex. It covers the top and sides of the right and left cerebral hemispheres. The frontal lobes are the areas of the human brain that have expanded most and constitute roughly the front 40 percent of the cerebral hemispheres. Each frontal lobe is made up of two parts: neocortex on its top and sides as well as a more ancient type of cortex on its bottom and inner surface. This more ancient part of the frontal lobes is called the orbitofrontal cortex. It curls under the front of the brain, resting on top of the eye sockets. It also spreads into the fissure between the hemispheres that runs from the middle of the forehead to the back of the brain—called the interhemispheric fissure. The orbitofrontal cortex is one of the most sophisticated parts of the limbic system and serves as a bridge between the advanced areas of the neocortex and the more primitive emotional centers deeper in the brain, including the amygdala. It is the orbitofrontal cortex that appears to play an important part in deflecting the hate response of the amygdala away from an external threat and onto the self. So central to self-hatred is the orbitofrontal cortex that patients who have suffered certain kinds of damage to this area seem to largely lose their ability to experience most kinds of embarrassment, humiliation, and shame.

Another insight about the nature of hate comes from studies of these seemingly unrelated emotions (embarrassment, humiliation, and shame). As it turns out, many of the physiological reactions generated by these emotions are virtually identical to fear or anger: the flushed face, rapid heart rate, adrenaline surge, perspiration, tensing of the body, and even the urge to swear. In addition, embarrassment, humiliation, and shame usually include a powerful aggression response that tends to be directed not at others but at oneself: self-hatred. Forgetting someone's name, bungling a speech, or otherwise making yourself look ridiculous can be painfully embarrassing. It is common for people enduring a humiliating experience to wish they could sink into the floor—even wish they were dead. In the most catastrophic circumstances, the self-hatred manifested by shame and humiliation can actually lead to suicide.

THE SIGNIFICANCE OF MEANING

The human limbic system poses a special danger because of its extensive connections to the neocortex, allowing us to fuse hatred and violence with the highest capacity of the human mind: meaning. Hate can override the fear of death in individual cases, but hate-oriented meaning systems can make such behavior systematic and widespread. Meaning is uniquely significant to human beings because, unlike virtually every other species, we are not born with specific instincts that tell us what to eat, where to live, how to organize our social groups, what tools to make, or whom to hate. The vast majority of our thoughts, emotions, and behaviors are shaped by meaning systems of our own creation. Much of this knowledge is contained within cultural meaning systems that the young spend years mastering. "Beavers build dams, birds build nests, bees locate food, baboons organize social groups, and mice mate on the basis of forms of learning that rest predominantly on the instructions encoded in their genes," observed Princeton University anthropologist Clifford Geertz. "But men build dams or shelters, locate food, organize their social groups, or find sexual partners under the guidance of instructions encoded in flowcharts and blueprints, hunting lore, moral systems and aesthetic judgments; conceptual structures molding formless talents."

Humans have remnants of the kinds of specific instincts that guide other species. We jump when we hear a loud noise or flinch when an object flies at us not because we have learned to do so but because these responses have been genetically wired into our nervous systems. Evolution has taught our genes the significance of these events and how to respond to them. We don't have to think about it. But there is another category of instinctive tendencies that psychologists call "prepared fears," which include fear of snakes, spiders, heights, and enclosed spaces. We are not born with these fears but with a tendency to quickly develop them, and they are common in all cultures. Experts believe that they represent phenomena that were especially dangerous to our early hominid ancestors. But these kinds of innate responses play a relatively small part in the human psyche.

Meaning rather than instinct is so overwhelmingly important to our species—and to our distinctive toolmaking cultures—that our limbic system has evolved a powerful tendency to blindly interpret any meaning system that we deeply believe in as substantially enhancing our survival and reproduction. Someone who wholeheartedly converts to a particular religion or political ideology, for example, is likely to experience strong primal feelings of joy and well-being coupled with an exciting new sense of purpose. This is true even if the belief system has elements that are bizarre or self-destructive. Because of this unusual feature of the human brain, strongly held meaning systems are capable of decoupling our behavior from the objective criteria of survival and reproduction. If a par-

ticular group's strongly held meaning system calls on its members
to be celibate and suicidal, their primitive brain areas will tend to
presume that this is the best way to ensure their survival and reproduction, even though rationally, of course, it is not. At the end of
World War II, there was no lack of kamikaze pilots willing to die by
crashing their explosives-laden aircraft into American warships.
These young Japanese airmen were guided by a meaning system
centered on emperor-worship, which placed a high value on dying
for the emperor.

The immense significance of meaning to human beings and its
distinctive link in our species to the primitive emotional centers of
the brain lay the groundwork for a primary source of hatred: fanaticism and intolerance. Lacking specific instincts, humans have no
innate identity. It is meaning systems that provide us with our personal sense of meaning and purpose. The tremendous emotional
commitment we tend to make to these systems leaves us vulnerable
to interpreting differences in meaning as threats to our survival and
reproduction. Many of the most savage conflicts in history have
involved quarrels over religious, political, and cultural systems of
meaning.

Islamic terrorists of the kind we witnessed on September 11,
2001, have an elaborately rationalized fanatical meaning system—
based on a misguided religious interpretation—which holds that
committing a suicidal attack as an act of holy war, or "jihad," will
ensure the survival of their souls at the top of the hierarchy in an
eternal paradise. Thus, the objectively irrational becomes perfectly
rational in the mind of the terrorist, at both the conscious and primitive levels. To this person's limbic system, suicide is ensuring the
individual's eternal survival—even reproduction (some interpretations of paradise include sexual activity). In fact, within this frame
of reference the act of dying is not even defined as suicide but rather
as martyrdom for a higher cause. The brain's capacity for mixing the
rational and the irrational makes the conquest of hate urgently
important but exceptionally challenging. Some analysts of human

behavior overlook the delusional capacity of the human mind and the power of meaning systems to create values and emotions that contradict and override the objective conditions for survival and reproduction.

Meaning systems naturally proliferate in any large human population. Conflicting meaning systems can not only be the source of violent strife, they can create clashing worldviews that make agreement on even the most basic issues difficult as well. Terrorism is a perfect example. Differences in worldview make this concept slippery and controversial. Terrorism is a form of psychological warfare in which the object is not to destroy an enemy—the way a conventional army would—but to use selective acts of violence to demoralize, intimidate, and manipulate. Some of his supporters argued that Osama bin Laden, as they perceived him, was not a terrorist but a freedom fighter, because he struck nations that are enemies of Islam. Others admitted that he was a terrorist but made a distinction between bin Laden and groups such as Hezbollah, Hamas, and Islamic Jihad that attack Israelis, even though Hamas and Islamic Jihad explicitly target civilians. Terms such as *terrorism* must be specifically defined if they are to retain their usefulness. Here, one of the better definitions comes straight from federal law: "The term terrorism means premeditated, politically motivated violence perpetrated against noncombatant targets." Using this definition, bin Laden, Hamas, and Islamic Jihad have clearly engaged in terrorist activities.

History makes it painfully apparent that when hate pervades a meaning system, there is virtually no limit to the atrocities an individual, group, or society can perpetrate. And the structure of the human mind provides no assurance that people will behave rationally. This is why hate is such an urgent problem in the post–cold war era, when weapons of mass destruction are spreading. If a group or nation with a hate-filled meaning system that exalts martyrdom obtains such weapons, it may well be willing to use them and face—even welcome—the ghastly consequences.

Robert McNamara was secretary of defense during the October 1962 Cuban missile crisis when the United States discovered that the Soviet Union was positioning nuclear-armed ballistic missiles in Cuba. He reported that Fidel Castro told him at a historical conference years later that Castro and Ernesto "Che" Guevara had fervently urged the Soviets to use nuclear weapons against the United States during the thirteen-day confrontation. Such an attack might have cost eighty million American lives. McNamara asked if Castro understood what this would have meant for Cuba. Castro, who has never disguised his hatred for the "Yankees," told McNamara that he and Guevara were perfectly willing to make martyrs of themselves and the Cuban people. At the time, Guevara expressed his desire "to walk by the path of liberation even when it may cost millions of atomic victims." The Soviets reportedly called this a "beautiful gesture" but backed away from starting World War III. President Kennedy was able to negotiate an end to the crisis, and the ballistic missiles were withdrawn.[4]

The power of meaning over the human mind is both a curse and a blessing. Some genetic determinists believe that our genes make war, racism, sexism, class conflict, and other forms of bigotry and violence inevitable. Yet this pessimistic conclusion ignores the power of meaning systems to modify our innate tendencies. If meaning systems are capable of submerging the fear of death, they certainly have the potential to reshape other basic attitudes and behaviors in a positive way. However, human behavior under the influence of a meaning system is not infinitely plastic. The role of meaning is exceedingly complicated. The instinct for self-preservation, for instance, doesn't just disappear under the influence of radical Islamic fundamentalism and may reassert itself if such a meaning system loses its hold. This is why the competition of ideas can have a profound effect. If the fanatical interpretation of *jihad* can be undermined, potential terrorists will be less willing to sacrifice their lives. One important reason for the widespread collapse of Communist regimes in the late twentieth century was disillusionment with the

Marxist-Leninist meaning system. The hope of the twenty-first century is that meaning systems that discourage primitive, irrational behavior and minimize the influence of hate-oriented doctrines can be crafted and disseminated. The spread of concepts such as the rule of law, human rights, democracy, and freedom of thought over the past five thousand years provides at least a glimmer of optimism.

AN EVOLUTIONARY VIEW OF HATE: THE FIGHT-OR-FLIGHT RESPONSE

Why do we hate? From an evolutionary standpoint the answer is straightforward. Hate is a primitive emotion that marks for attack or avoidance those things that we perceive as a threat to our survival or reproduction, which are the prime directives of evolution. Many of the most important insights about hate come from studies of another powerful emotion: fear. Hate is an extreme form of aggressive dislike that mirrors an extreme form of fear—the phobia. Someone with a serious snake phobia, for example, experiences an instantaneous fear reaction whenever he or she sees any kind of snake, from a garter snake to a rattlesnake. The fear is irrational. It makes no difference that the garter snake is harmless. The reaction is automatic and stereotyped. Similarly, someone filled with racial or ethnic hatred experiences immediate, irrational hostility whenever he or she encounters any member of the hated class—Arab or Jew, Serb or Croat, black or white—irrespective of that particular individual's unique qualities or beliefs.

Fear is often described as the fight-or-flight response. But it would be more accurate to call it the flight-or-fight response. The first reaction to fear is to flee, not fight, and this is reflected in our biological response. When someone with a snake phobia spies a snake, blood is automatically channeled to the large muscles of the legs in preparation for running or jumping back. Oxygen-rich blood may be shifted from the upper to the lower body so fast that, as it drains away, the face turns pale. The oxygen-starved brain may even temporarily shut down, causing the person to faint. Anger, on the other hand, is the true fight-or-flight response. When we experience a surge of anger, adrenaline-rich blood is automatically shifted to the upper body for fighting. The face flushes as blood is shunted upward, and the muscles in the arms and chest tense. Thus, we tend to pale with fear but flush with anger, including hate-inspired anger. People who are extremely angry may strike out, slapping or punching, before they realize what they have done. In the hate response, the automatic impulse is to fight—that is, respond aggressively. But if the opponent is too intimidating, then the secondary impulse is to flee—that is, respond defensively. In humans, this defensive response may be expressed in many complex ways, including hiding one's feelings until the time is right to be more aggressive. Conversely, in the fear response the automatic impulse is to escape the threat in some way. This may involve not only fleeing but freezing to avoid detection. And it may also involve more complex behaviors, such as appeasement, to defuse an adversary. If escape is impossible, however, the secondary impulse is to fight.

In his classic book *The Expression of Emotions in Man and Animals*, published originally in 1872, Charles Darwin explicitly identified the fight-or-flight response. Humans "during numberless generations," he wrote, have dealt with their enemies by "headlong flight" or "violently struggling with them." He vividly described the characteristics of rage: "The respiration is laboured, the chest heaves, and the dilated nostrils quiver. The whole body often trembles. The voice is affected. The teeth are clenched or ground together, and the muscular system is commonly stimulated to violent, almost frantic action. But the gestures of a man in this state usually differ from the purposeless writhings and struggles of one suffering from an agony of pain; for they represent more or less plainly the act of striking or fighting with an enemy." The tenth chapter of Darwin's book, entitled "Hatred and Anger," shows how closely he linked these two emotions.[5]

Hate is a product of the limbic system, which has been pro-grammed to carry out the prime evolutionary imperatives of sur-vival and reproduction. The amygdala and related limbic structures are responsible for detecting both danger and opportunity—the snake in the grass and the quickest way to escape from it. Once the amygdala marks something like snakes as a serious threat, its reac-tion is difficult to change because the limbic system is the seat of our most primitive survival responses. People with a severe snake pho-bia who know full well that garter snakes are harmless still can't help being afraid. The limbic system has seized control of their behav-ior, and the rational mind can't make it let go. The architecture of the limbic system is, in general, more primitive than the advanced areas of the cortex and, as a result, the limbic system tends to think in a radically different way. In particular, amygdala-driven areas of the limbic system have difficulty conceptualizing uniqueness. Let's call the more ancient areas of the brain, including the limbic system, the "primitive neural system," in contrast to the circuitry dominated by the more sophisticated neocortex, which we will call the "ad-vanced neural system." Not only is the neocortex the most recent evolutionary addition to the brain, it is the seat of consciousness as well, and, thus, the only system in the brain that is fully self-aware.

The primitive neural system's less sophisticated architecture allows it—with some exceptions—to think only in generalizations and stereotypes. It can grasp a general category such as "animals," or a middle-level category such as "snakes," but it has extreme dif-ficulty conceptualizing a specific category such as "garter snakes." This is why someone with a fear of snakes is equally afraid of a garter snake and a rattlesnake. The primitive neural system is unable to tell the difference.

The primitive neural system and advanced neural system are not neatly packaged entities. They have bewilderingly complicated interactions and a huge number of subsidiary systems that we are only beginning to understand. The primitive neural system can use elements of the advanced neural system to accomplish some of its functions, and vice versa. The advanced neural system registers and refines the output of the primitive neural system, including primitive emotional responses.

One important subsidiary system of the primitive neural system is what we might call the "preconscious alerting system," which is coordinated by the amygdala and other older areas of the brain. It not only serves as our fast-acting alarm for pain and danger but also as our alerting system for opportunities to enhance our survival and reproduction. Whenever you turn your head automatically as you catch a glimpse of an attractive member of the opposite sex, your preconscious alerting system is at work. And it is the preconscious alerting system that causes a highly phobic individual to instinctively jump back and scream at the sight of a spider. This alerting system is called "preconscious" because it often acts—making us flinch, duck, or jump, for example—before we are fully conscious of what is going on. The key here is speed. The preconscious alerting system can respond in a fraction of a second: far faster than consciousness. This can be the difference between life and death if the amygdala has detected a truck speeding toward you or a snake about to strike. But such fast processing is also quick-and-dirty processing involving primitive cues such as the twisted shape of a snake. These cues constitute a kind of cartoon sketch encompassing a general category (animal) and a middle-level category (snake). Why didn't the amygdala evolve the capacity to process the more detailed cues necessary to identify a specific category (such as garter snake)? Probably because this would take too much time.

With severe phobias, the primitive neural system preempts another major element of the human mind—what we will call "advanced neural choice." This is the rational choice that the advanced neural system allows us to make, based on all our knowledge and experience. Unlike the preconscious alerting system, which generally completes its work in a tenth of a second, there is no time limit on advanced neural choice. We can ponder a problem for minutes, hours, or years. Through institutions such as science, we can collectively use our advanced neural systems to consider problems for centuries. It is advanced neural choice that gives us the capacity—though often with great difficulty—to rein in our limbic impulses. Within the mind of the snake phobic, there is a struggle between the primitive neural system and advanced neural choice over how to respond to a garter snake: fearfully or calmly. Because the primitive neural system deals directly with the immediate evolutionary needs of survival and reproduction, however, its commands tend to override all other brain systems in circumstances that are perceived to be an immediate threat. But as we shall see, therapy techniques have been developed to bolster the advanced neural system and restrain the primitive, irrational responses of the limbic system. With these techniques, phobias can often be greatly improved, even cured. Variations of these techniques can be used to counter hatred as well.

Hate is a kind of anger phobia. And like all phobias in the modern world, hate is obsolete. For early humans in a primitive environment, phobias probably served a useful purpose. They crudely but powerfully signaled the danger of things such as spiders, snakes, and heights, which is why they evolved. Today, however, a phobia is treated as a mental health problem if it significantly interferes with normal functioning. Using this comparison, hate should be treated the same way. In fact, it might be wise to expand the concept of phobia to encompass not only persistent, irrational fear but also persistent, irrational hatred.

Like fear, hate has a strong tendency to create stereotypes. In the hate response, the primitive neural system negatively prejudges some portion of experience, just as the phobic prejudges snakes, or insects, or heights. People who are intensely afraid of spiders or cockroaches, for example, will tend to avoid them. If they see a cockroach in their kitchen, they will try to have someone else get rid of it. But there are others who simply hate cockroaches. They have no fear of them; they just detest them. When these people see a cockroach in their kitchen, they will obsessively search high and low until they find it and kill it. The destructive power of hate comes from its fusion of primitive prejudice with aggression and anger. Generalized categorization, which comes straight out of the primitive neural system, is one of hate's characteristic features. The racist hates all blacks, all whites, all Jews, all Arabs, all Christians, all Serbs, all Croats, depending on his particular prejudice. The hater sees someone, first and foremost, as a stereotype. Unique individual qualities are of little or no importance.

Unlike hate, anger can be selective. We may be angry at our children for something they have done, but we still love them—hate is unthinkable. Transient anger is capable of being kept under rational control and doesn't necessarily have the phobic quality of hate. Similarly, nonphobic fear can serve many useful purposes, as when we learn to fear and avoid only poisonous snakes.

Because hate involves the primitive nervous system, which has difficulty distinguishing between a garter snake and a rattlesnake, how do we manage to hate an individual? Again, primitive generalizing comes into play. The limbic system understands stereotypes, so when we reject a person, our primitive neural system tends to stereotype him or her as a threat and is typically unable to distinguish between the individual's good and bad qualities.

But Darwin recognized that hate is more complex than emotions such as fear, disgust, anger, joy, and sadness, which Darwin's own research and subsequent modern work strongly suggest are innately manifested by facial expressions that are recognized in all cultures. Hate, however, does not have a characteristic form of expression. As Darwin noted, hate is not always accompanied by overt anger. "Few individuals," he wrote, "can long reflect about a hated person, without feeling and exhibiting signs of indignation or rage. But if the offending person be quite insignificant, we experience merely disdain or contempt. If, on the other hand, he is all-powerful, then hatred passes into terror, as when a slave thinks about a cruel master, or a savage about a bloodthirsty malignant deity." Hatred can be expressed in many ways, depending on the circumstances:

through anger, rage, contempt, mockery, disgust, avoidance, indignation, or stony silence. Hate can turn positive emotions into negative ones, as with cruel laughter. But the underlying theme of all these emotions, and what we experience internally with hate, even if we express no outward sign of our feelings, is hostility. Hate is the most intense and long-lasting form of primal hostility.

Why do we react to someone with hate instead of fear? If a mouse encounters a cat, it will instantly respond with fear and run away. But if the cat traps the mouse in a corner, the mouse will often attack the cat in a last, desperate attempt to save its life. Within the simplistic fight-or-flight repertoire of the primitive neural system, being hopelessly trapped by a threat usually triggers the fight response. A sense of being trapped is a common precursor to the development of a hate reaction. When we feel trapped in a situation that threatens us, there is a tendency for our reaction to shift to the limbic system and to a primitive aggressive response that can evolve into hate. For human beings, this sense of being trapped plays out in many complex ways. Frustration is one important manifestation of a sense of being trapped, whether by a person's actions or in a situation in which the individual feels that he or she has no control. We can also feel trapped if we are physically attacked by someone and there is no escape. When one country attacks another, as when Iraq attacked Kuwait to begin the Persian Gulf War, people in the country that is attacked often develop a potent sense of hatred for their adversary.

Some of the most virulent, violent, and intransigent forms of hate surface when competing groups are trapped together in the same geographical area: the Middle East, Northern Ireland, the Balkans, the Indian subcontinent, for example. Similarly, some of the most extreme forms of racism and violent hatred in America have emerged from the multiple ethnicities of the struggling inner cities and from prisons, with their volatile racial mix. Inner-city gangs represent a particularly unadulterated form of hate. These gangs usually detest and indiscriminately kill each other simply because they are wearing the wrong colors or are on the wrong turf. Similarly, many bitter domestic disputes emerge when the parties perceive themselves as being trapped in a marriage or other relationship.

SELF-HATRED

Perhaps the most profound experience of being trapped is the sense of being trapped within oneself. This can create self-hatred. With this kind of hate, the limbic system marks and stereotypes aspects of the self, such as looks or intelligence, as a threat to one's survival or reproduction. Rational dislike of some attribute of our own behavior ("I'm not studying hard enough") can be a useful guide to self-improvement. But when we become frustrated with ourselves, the specific problems we are having can shift into a categorical rejection of our being, in whole or in part. The primitive neural system may grossly overreact to discrete personal difficulties—doing poorly in school, being overweight, experiencing emotional or financial setbacks—and develop feelings of self-hatred that are expressed in a generalized way: "I'm stupid," "I'm ugly," or "I'm worthless." Intense self-hatred can create a damaging feedback loop within the brain that leads to self-destructive behavior. Children are particularly susceptible to these kinds of self-esteem problems because their limbic systems mature far earlier—by about age five—than the rational centers of their cerebral cortex, especially the frontal lobes, which continue maturing into the early twenties. The mature frontal lobes are the areas of the cortex best able to suppress incipient feelings of hate and self-hate.

The orbitofrontal cortex plays a rich and complex role in the formation of a sense of self. Damage to the orbitofrontal cortex can lead to a dramatic reduction of feelings of self-hatred. Why? Studies by a number of researchers, including the noted husband-and-wife neuroscientists Antonio and Hanna Damasio, have found that this part of the brain controls our ability to vicariously experience emotions. This ability is at the core of empathy, which allows us to imaginatively place ourselves in the position of others and experience their thoughts and feelings. But the orbitofrontal cortex is central to our personal experience of emotion as well. It is this area of the brain that allows us to recall the emotions we experienced during some past event. If you told a joke that fell flat during an important speech ten years ago, your orbitofrontal cortex allows you to recall your stinging embarrassment. Although this is unpleasant, it makes us better able to learn from the mistakes of the past. Of equal importance, this brain area, working with other parts of the frontal lobes, gives us the capacity to imagine alternative scenarios in our lives and experience the emotions we would feel in those scenarios.

One important source of self-hatred is regret: our disappointment at not having directly experienced the positive emotions we might have if things had gone differently. We may begin to hate the person we are because we can imagine the person we might have been. If you strike out with the bases loaded during a championship baseball game, your emotional suffering is intensified by vicariously experiencing what you would have felt if you had hit a home run. Patients with severe orbitofrontal damage lose this capacity. They are no longer able to recall the emotions they felt in past situations and cannot imagine the emotions they would have felt if things had gone differently. Without this ability, they seem to shed their self-hatred.

The Damasios report that many patients with certain kinds of orbitofrontal damage not only have trouble empathizing with others, they can calmly discuss in clinical detail all their past failures, humiliations, and embarrassments with little or no sense of emotion. Antonio Damasio described one patient, whom he called Elliot. "I found myself suffering more when listening to Elliot's stories than Elliot himself," said Damasio. "In fact, I felt that I suffered more than he did just by *thinking* of those stories." Such patients generally feel good about themselves and tend to show little regret about anything that has ever happened to them, including their brain damage. This injury to the emotional system is dramatic but quite discrete. The patients' intelligence usually remains the same as it always was, and they score in the normal range on most psychological tests. This kind of brain injury may not sound serious, but the impact on these individuals' lives is disastrous. Without the appropriate emotional cues, they lose the capacity to make sound decisions, principally in the personal and social domain. They tend to fritter away their money. They often lose their jobs and sometimes their families, too. Their emotional compass has been destroyed.[6] If you or I were to envision a scenario in which we went on a gambling spree, for instance, we would probably be deterred from actually doing it by imaginatively experiencing the emotions we would feel if we lost a huge amount of money. Someone with orbitofrontal damage does not imaginatively feel these emotions and thus may decide to go on the spree. And if he actually loses his money, he will experience little or no regret.

This marked reduction in the ability to recall one's past emotions or to empathetically experience one's potential emotions in different scenarios is an important clue to the nature of self-hate. And the reduction in these patients of the ability to vicariously empathize with others is also a clue to the general nature of hatred. One of the most striking aspects of hate is how it cuts off the ability to empathize with those who are hated. The Nazis who administered the death camps cared nothing for the thousands of men, women, and children they were slaughtering. Hate is blind to the suffering of others. Oklahoma City bomber Timothy McVeigh described as "collateral damage" the heartbreaking deaths of nineteen children among the 168 victims of the 1995 blast. Osama bin Laden had only the highest praise for the September 11 hijackers who destroyed the lives of thousands of innocent people. This lack of sympathy for victims is a hallmark of hate that has been repeatedly evident through countless massacres and genocides. It allows the most terrible cruelty and torture to take place without the slightest pity. The primi-

tive neural system has the power to modulate our capacity for empathy—turning it up or down. We may be exquisitely sensitive to the
feelings of our family and friends and totally insensitive to the feelings of our enemies. The primitive neural system can even pervert
normal empathy, allowing us to take great pleasure in others' suffering. In the case of empathy, there is a competition between
advanced neural choice and the primitive neural system for control
of the orbitofrontal cortex. By rationally and systematically exercising our will, we can resist the primitive tendency to dehumanize
our adversaries.

2

PREVENTING AND ELIMINATING HATE

HATE-DRIVEN ATROCITIES are a tragic and all-too-common feature of history. The venomous racial hatred of Nazi Germany led to the gas chambers and ovens of the Holocaust, which swallowed up six million Jews and millions of others including Slavs, Gypsies, and individuals with physical and mental disabilities. The class hatred and lethal paranoia of Stalinism led to the extermination of millions of Soviet citizens. Similar kinds of hate triggered mass killings in the 1960s during the cultural revolution in China and sparked the slaughter of nearly two million men, women, and children by the Khmer Rouge in the killing fields of Cambodia in the 1970s.

In the post–cold war era there remains one overwhelming threat to peace: hate. The major trouble spots of the world are infused with hatred. Fighting between Protestant and Catholic extremists in Northern Ireland—an example of how a cycle of violence with strikes and counterstrikes enormously intensifies hate—is being kept in check by a fragile negotiated settlement. The 1990s witnessed genocidal episodes of "ethnic cleansing" among the peoples of the former Yugoslavia fueled by long-standing hatreds that continue to cause instability. The rivalry between Hutu and Tutsi ethnic groups in Rwanda and nearby countries threatens the peace of sub-Saharan Africa and has resulted in periodic episodes of mass murder. The enmity between India and Pakistan, both of which have nuclear weapons, has led to an endless succession of skirmishes along their border and three all-out wars. All this hatred in so many regions of the world leads inevitably to terrorism, mass murder, and arms races among adversaries, accelerating the proliferation of nuclear, chemical, and biological weapons. The post–September 11 mailing of anthrax-laced letters to U.S. politicians and journalists—killing five people and alarming a nation—has raised the specter of biological warfare that uses far worse weapons, such as smallpox, to kill millions.

Hate not only exacts a devastating human cost but inflicts staggering economic losses as well. The September 11 attacks alone have cost the world economy countless jobs and untold billions of dollars. And to this must be added the gargantuan sums that are lavished on arms and arms races year in and year out—money that, in a more peaceful world, could be spent far more productively.

Aside from international terrorism and increased world tension, the damage done by hate in the United States alone is unacceptable: the bombing of the federal building in Oklahoma City, the burning and vandalism of synagogues and black churches, violent attacks on abortion clinics and the murder of doctors who work in them, and persecution and discrimination in many forms. Hate plus guns turn our children into killers. Too often, our schools have become places where people fear for their lives, not just from urban gang violence, but from seemingly ordinary kids such as Kip Kinkel who live in suburbia and small towns in places such as Colorado, Arkansas, Mississippi, Kentucky, Oregon, and California. Thousands of hate crimes are committed each year that target victims solely because of their race, gender, religion, ethnicity, or sexual orientation. Racial hatred, in particular, has been a plague on America for nearly four centuries. It continues to take a terrible toll.

Shortly after 2:00 A.M. on June 7, 1998, a forty-nine-year-old African-American man was walking along a winding country road on the outskirts of a small east Texas town. A pickup truck passed him, then began to slow. The truck stopped and, as he walked past, one of the three young white men in the truck offered him a ride. But when James Byrd Jr. got into the truck, the men grabbed him and began hitting him. After he was beaten senseless, the men carried Byrd behind the truck, chained his ankles together, and tied the other end of the chain to the pickup. Byrd was then dragged at high speed for nearly three miles before the men dumped what was left of his body in a ditch. Sickened Jasper, Texas, police investigators later collected body parts from seventy-five places along the roadway. When three men were arrested and charged with the murder, they were found to have ties to white supremacist groups, including the Ku Klux Klan and the Aryan Nation. The first of the men to be tried in a Jasper courtroom was John William King. Among his many tattoos was one of a swastika and another of a lynching. Of the three men, two—including King—were sentenced to death, and one received a life sentence.

This unspeakable act echoed many hideous events in American history. Between 1882 and 1919 more than three thousand African-Americans were lynched, mostly in the South, an average of almost one person every four days. In some places, lynchings were considered popular social events, commemorated in photographs that were sometimes made into postcards. This was the cruel reality facing black Americans of that era, including the brilliant scholar W. E. B. DuBois. Not long after receiving the first doctorate ever awarded to an African-American by Harvard University, DuBois settled in Atlanta, accepting a position as a professor of sociology at a black college. DuBois had decided to devote himself to academia and leave the political struggle for equal rights to others. But one day while taking a walk, DuBois was horrified to see the dismembered remains of a lynched black man on display in a storefront window. This was 1900 and that day transformed DuBois's life. He began a relentless campaign to win equal treatment for African-Americans, a campaign that led him to become a founder of the NAACP. DuBois wrote: "The problem of race is the problem of the twentieth century." Despite the enormous strides that have been made over the past century, racial prejudice remains a central challenge for America and the world.

This may be humanity's last chance to solve this daunting problem. The most irrational, violent, and cruel forms of aggression are motivated by hate, and this poses an extraordinary danger in an age in which weapons of mass destruction are proliferating. The terrifying reality is that rational deterrence may not be sufficient to maintain world peace in the long run. Hate unquestionably has the potential to blow apart the evolving globalized world system. Some experts predict that within a decade terrorists will obtain and use a nuclear weapon. Any attack using weapons of mass destruction could set off the most tragic chain of events imaginable. Yet the first thing we must realize is that the most terrible of all weapons of mass destruction lurks within our own primitive psyches, and we must find a way to deactivate it.[1]

This task, of course, is far from simple. Within the massive human brain, hate becomes an extremely complex emotion. In some cases, we love to hate. Hollywood knows this and uses it to attract millions of people to its films. We not only love the good guys but love hating the bad guys. And we often relish the hideous destruction of an uncommonly diabolical villain, from the Wicked Witch of the West in *The Wizard of Oz* to the loathsome monsters Sigourney Weaver kills again and again in the Alien movies. Whether it is Darth Vader of the Star Wars series or Hannibal "the Cannibal" Lecter of *Silence of the Lambs* and its sequel, there is nothing like a memorable villain to draw a crowd.

Hate can do strange things to our natural sympathy for others. It is capable of producing a perverse empathy. Normally, when you affectionately empathize with others, their joy is your joy and their pain is your pain. But hate can reverse this. If you bitterly hate someone, his joy can become your pain and his pain, your joy. In a captured videotape released by the U.S. government in December 2001, Osama bin Laden and his associates are seen repeatedly talking about how overjoyed they were when the hijacked airliners destroyed the World Trade Center, killing far more people than they had expected. This sort of perverse joy is also quite evident in hate-related emotions such as envy. If you envy someone's success, then news that he has suffered a career setback may make you feel good. Though enjoying the demise of a Hollywood villain can be perfectly harmless, when perverse empathy takes root in a violent psychopath or sadistic torturer, the result is real horror. To avoid this horror, we need to find ways to minimize hatred.

STRATEGIES TO PREVENT AND ELIMINATE HATE

The flood of recent scientific insights into the nature of our emotions suggests a set of ten strategies that, when used in tandem, could prevent hate from ever developing and minimize or eliminate hate where it has taken hold. The strategies are be specific, empathize, communicate, negotiate, educate, cooperate, put things in perspective, avoid feeling trapped, immerse yourself, and seek justice not revenge. Each of these strategies is designed to maintain the advanced neural system's control over the darker forces of the primitive neural system and end the vicious cycle of hate.

First, be specific—in other words, identify any source of anger, pain, or threat with as much specificity and detail as possible. This tends to keep things in the rational areas of the advanced neural system, which are designed to handle uniqueness, and outside the primitive neural system, including the amygdala, with its relentless tendency to overgeneralize and stereotype. This approach is critically important with children. If a child does poorly on a test, a parent might say, "Let's go over these math problems together and see what you didn't understand." But if, instead, a parent makes a general negative comment ("You really let me down"), the stereotyping centers of the primitive neural system are activated, which, over time, can lead to both hate and self-hate ("I'm terrible at math and I hate it"). This step harnesses our virtually unlimited capacity to categorize existence in specific and interrelated categories—an almost miraculous attribute of the enormous human brain that has allowed us to build global civilizations based on the most sophisticated and powerful social, spiritual, and scientific systems.

Second, develop an us-us orientation, which requires you to try to empathize with others, even those with whom you have little or no natural sympathy. Empathy is not the same as sympathy. Through empathy we seek to understand—not justify—another person's thoughts and feelings. It makes good sense to try to put yourself in the shoes of even your deadliest enemies. If you can understand what specifically motivates them, you stand a much better chance of reaching an accord with them, or at least coming up with the best possible strategy for outwitting or defeating them. As long as we can empathize, we are unlikely to fall into mindless hostility and demonization. This keeps us from slipping under the control of the primitive portions of our brain, where dislike is easily transmuted into hatred, empathy is obliterated, and opponents are transformed into a dehumanized "them" subject to ruthless extermination. There is a growing body of evidence that the brain is remarkably like a muscle. The more its capacities are exercised, the more they strengthen. Children who, starting at an early age, are consistently encouraged to empathize with others tend to develop a robust capacity for empathy that can last a lifetime.

When violence or war is unavoidable, an empathetic us-us perspective promotes reconciliation afterward. One of the most striking examples of the superiority of an us-us to an us-them approach came at the end of World War II. After the Allies achieved total victory over the Axis powers, Nazi Germany and Imperial Japan were purged of the leaders who had directed the commission of crimes against humanity, their societies were restructured as democracies, and these nations were quickly brought back into the international community as equals. Though each country had made terrible mistakes and perpetrated unimaginable atrocities, we nevertheless recognized our common humanity and refused to ostracize, stigmatize, or demonize all Germans and Japanese. Consequently, Germany and Japan have become two of the most peaceful and prosperous nations in the world. This was in stark contrast to the punitive attitude embodied in the Treaty of Versailles that ended World War I, which laid the groundwork for the rise of Adolf Hitler and an even more destructive war little more than two decades later.

Third, simply communicating the specific reasons that you feel angry or threatened can help dissipate negative emotions. The important point, again, is to be specific. One of the more dangerous aspects of hate is that if you talk about it using only the generalizations and stereotypes of the primitive neural system—what is often called "hate speech"—anger can be intensified and hatred inflamed.

Fourth, beyond simple communication, whenever possible seek to negotiate constructively and specifically to resolve sources of conflict and anger.

Fifth, educate yourself and others. An enormous amount of hatred and prejudice come from sheer ignorance. The more specific the knowledge you have about an individual, group, or culture, for example, the less likely you are to fall into stereotypes, which are the breeding ground of hate. In general, sophisticated and rigorous education of any type tends to be good for the brain. It enormously strengthens the advanced neural system, allowing it to serve as a bulwark against primitive urges and impulses. But education itself is not enough unless it incorporates empathy, specificity, and the other elements of this strategy. When Hitler came to power, Germany was probably the best-educated nation in the world.

Sixth, try to cooperate with others in mutually beneficial ways whenever possible. This builds bonds of trust that can replace feelings of hate. In a profoundly important finding, social psychologists have discovered that cooperating with others to achieve a common goal tends to activate subconscious mechanisms in the primitive neural system that can erase us-them divisions. This is why, when a nation is attacked and sets about to repel the attackers, internal divisions often disappear. The tidal wave of patriotism and national unity that followed the September 11 attacks was a dramatic example of this phenomenon.

Seventh, try to put things into perspective rather than overreact. You might ask, for example, whether your anger is worth it or whether a threat is really that important. Just going through this kind of analytical exercise tends to engage the advanced neural centers and suppress the primitive neural system.

Eighth, make every effort to avoid a sense of being trapped. This may require the application of all previous steps, particularly communication and negotiation. If you are unhappy in your job, for example, let people know in a constructive way and, if possible, negotiate some changes. If you find that there is nothing you can do to change things, you might start exploring opportunities elsewhere. Or you might try to put things in a different perspective by viewing the frustrations you feel as creative challenges that can lead you to a new level of personal growth.

Ninth, if for whatever reason the primitive neural system has taken control and you find yourself gripped by hostility, even hatred, make every effort to seek out opportunities to immerse yourself in a positive way with the source of your hate. At the height of the cold war, for instance, American presidents regularly met face-to-face with Communist leaders. These meetings usually provided a constructive antidote to the propaganda-driven stereotypes that fueled antagonism on both sides. Positive immersion, like cooperation, tends to activate subconscious mechanisms that erode us-them divisions and primitive emotions.

Immersion applies not only to yourself but to others as well, which is particularly important for children. Adults in every society have a special responsibility to seek to immerse children in an environment that is as free as possible of prejudice, bigotry, hatred, abuse, and violence. Research indicates that a child's primitive neural system is tuned by the environment—though each child varies in his or her susceptibility to this tuning. Children tend to quickly absorb the bigotry and hatred around them. There can be lifelong biological consequences of immersion in a negative environment. Some children exposed to violence, abuse, and other forms of excessive stress may develop neurochemical abnormalities in their limbic systems. They may exhibit a permanent tendency to overreact to threats, even minor threats, with fear, anger, hatred, and even violence. Other children will exhibit just the opposite condition: their limbic systems will tend to underreact to threats, including the sanctions society imposes for violating accepted norms of behavior. Some of these children will become violent sociopaths, who will do whatever they want with little or no fear of the consequences and no empathy for those they hurt.

Tenth, and finally, seek justice, not revenge. Vengeful hatred tends to lock us into the past. In areas of the world that are dominated by hate, grievances are never forgotten, and the cycle of revenge and retaliation can go on for centuries. The most recent period of mass murder and ethnic cleansing in the Balkans had its beginning in 1987 when Serbian strongman Slobodan Milosevic traveled to the Yugoslavian province of Kosovo and made an inflammatory speech at the site of the Battle of Kosovo Polje, which the Serbs lost to the Ottoman Turks in 1389. This ancient battle remains an emotionally resonant source of Serbian anger. Similarly, Osama bin Laden in his statements invariably referred to America and its Western allies as "crusaders" and called President Bush "crusader Bush"—all this in reference to the Christian crusades, which began at the end of the eleventh century and sought to wrest the Holy Land from Islamic control. Obtaining justice can be complex and difficult, but it requires a determined effort to seek a fair resolution of conflicts rather than a primitive venting of hostility and aggression.

RESISTANCE TO CHANGE

Hate is irrational. Though the initial reason for dislike may, in some cases, be perfectly reasonable, once real hatred has taken hold someone cannot be rationally talked out of it any more than you can rationally talk someone out of his or her fear of heights. To cure a phobia—say, a snake phobia—a therapist normally uses what is called behavior therapy. On a gradual, step-by-step basis and in a controlled, reassuring setting, a patient might be slowly exposed to snakes until he or she can handle a harmless snake without significant fear. Although rational discussion, or cognitive therapy, may be part of this process, the primitive neural system tends to learn best by doing. Through gradual immersion with snakes themselves, the limbic system absorbs the lesson that most snakes do not pose a threat, and eventually the phobia diminishes in strength and may even disappear altogether. Similarly, in combating racial, ethnic, religious, and other forms of us-them hatred, programs that mix people of diverse backgrounds in a positive setting in which unique individual qualities are on display can be exceptionally useful.

But hatred is often highly resistant to change because, unlike most phobias, hate can be linked to elaborate rationalizations produced by the advanced neural system. People may passionately believe these warped meaning systems and fool themselves into thinking that they are being completely reasonable when they are not. For beneath all their rational argument is intense, primitive, stereotyped hostility. This was the case with the Nazi theory of Aryan superiority—an elaborate mix of pseudoscience, selective history, and myth that concealed a core of naked hate. People with a fear of enclosed spaces generally know that their terror at the thought of going into an elevator is irrational. They realize that the phobia is distorting their behavior. Hate, however, can be delusional. In acting out their hatred, people may honestly believe they are doing the right thing.

In the aftermath of the dragging death of James Byrd Jr., the shocked citizens of Jasper, Texas, tried to follow some of the strategies and end the primitive cycle of hate. The little town of eight thousand—with roughly equal numbers of blacks and whites—went through an intense and painful period of soul-searching. There were impassioned calls for reconciliation. At the same time, both the Ku Klux Klan and the Black Panther Party held rallies in the town and sought new members. But they were ignored. Instead, a series of vigils was held in memory of Byrd that drew hundreds of citizens to the courthouse lawn. Blacks and whites talked about the barriers between them.

On January 18, 1999, in Jasper, Texas, the mayor and a large group of townspeople gathered in the city cemetery to watch as workers tore down a long, rusty, iron fence. For seventy-five years, the fence had separated the graves of blacks from the graves of whites. "This is a new day in Jasper," said the mayor. "A new day."

3

THE BINARY INSTINCT

✦

IT WAS SUPPOSED TO BE a simple homework assignment. The students in Lynn Stoldt's eighth-grade social studies class had spent three weeks prior to the 2000 presidential election holding a mock campaign of their own. Now, on election night, they were going to watch the election returns at home with a map of the United States in front of them. When George W. Bush won a state, each of the students was to color it red. When Al Gore won, each was to color it blue. Quickly, things went downhill.

"They first said Florida went to Bush. Then it went to Gore. Then it went back to Bush," said twelve-year-old Alex Parker, one of Ms. Stoldt's students at Vista Verde Middle School in Irvine, California. "Then they did a recount. We had to keep crossing it out and recolor and keep recoloring and I was just confused." It wasn't long before Ms. Stoldt began getting calls at home. "I can't finish this, it's getting late and I have to go to bed. What am I going to do?" asked one anxious student. "Can I use Wite-Out?"

And, of course, that was far from the end of it. For the next thirty-seven days the candidates slugged it out in an extraordinary seesaw battle that had virtually the whole nation choosing sides. First the candidates went to the lawyers, then to the courts. Then they battled on television. Then they went back to the courts. Then to the Florida legislature. Then to television again. Finally, by the narrowest of margins, the United States Supreme Court effectively awarded the election to Bush. It was the most divisive presidential election in modern history, and it featured flaring tempers and hard feelings—and even a residue of hate in some quarters—as the contest went back and forth. But it graphically illustrated one of the most characteristic qualities of the primitive neural system: the binary instinct, by which we tend to label people and things as good or bad, us or them, friend or enemy. There was a powerful tendency, depending on where you stood in the election, to emotionally classify the major players—the candidates, Florida Secretary of State Katherine Harris, Florida Governor Jeb Bush, the Florida Supreme Court, the U.S. Supreme Court, the Florida legislature, the various lawyers—as good or bad, one of us or one of them, friends or enemies. Despite gracious attempts by both candidates to heal the wounds, the bitterness lingered. Many Bush partisans felt Gore had tried to steal the election. Some Gore supporters argued that Bush was a usurper and his presidency illegitimate. The passionate divisions opened by this bizarre election remained a significant problem until they were overwhelmed by the surge of national unity after the September 11 terrorist attacks.[1]

Our reaction as a society to the Bush-Gore election controversy was typical of every culture ever studied. We displayed what French anthropologist Claude Lévi-Strauss and others have called the binary instinct. It is the innate tendency, according to Harvard biologist Edward O. Wilson, to use a "quick and easy mental algorithm that creates order in a world otherwise overwhelming in flux and detail." The us-them distinction is an important element of this intuitive binary process, which, said Wilson, involves "the proneness to use two-part classifications in treating socially important arrays. Societies everywhere break people into in-group versus out-group, child versus adult, kin versus nonkin, married versus single, and activities into sacred and profane, good and evil. They fortify the boundaries of each division with taboo and ritual. To change from one division to the other requires initiation ceremonies, weddings, blessings, ordinations, and other rites of passage."

US VERSUS THEM

In the context of hate, us-versus-them divisions are deeply felt and sometimes lethal. The distinction between us and them, however, does not completely coincide with hate. We can label someone or something as "them" yet not respond with hate. Prior to September 11, most people who were even aware of Afghanistan classified its Taliban government as part of the vast benign category of "them," meaning "not like us," and viewed the Taliban with indifference or, perhaps, vague hostility. Yet virtually all primitive us-them distinctions have the potential to detonate into anger or hate during times of stress or conflict. After September 11, many Americans expressed virulent hatred of the Taliban members. Every big-city mayor in America is aware that racial us-them divisions are particularly explosive, as was painfully evident in the massive 1992 Los Angeles riots and the civil disturbances that occurred in Cincinnati in the spring of 2001—both triggered by charges of police misconduct against African-Americans.

Even when hate is not involved, the us-them binary division has a formidable ability to turn off our empathy. Meat eaters, for example, consider cows "them" and willingly acquiesce in these animals' slaughter for food. People who eat meat don't hate cows, but they generally do not concern themselves with cows' existence; they are indifferent. The "them" designation allows meat eaters to block whatever suffering these animals experience at the slaughterhouse.

Most people probably would not treat an executive from a meat-packing company any differently than they would treat anyone else.

When humans combine this kind of us-them indifference with hate, however, the results can be appalling. As with the Nazis, assembly lines for killing other humans classified as "them" can be constructed. And workers at these hellish slaughterhouses—guards, supervisors—can put in their shifts and go home every night to their wives and children. The primitive neural system thoroughly dehumanizes "them." Hate promotes habituation to this unimaginable world of death, just as a new young worker will eventually habituate to a cattle slaughterhouse. Some vegetarians, on the other hand, might identify the cows as part of "us" and meat eaters as "them." Similarly, antiabortion groups tend to identify unborn fetuses with "us" and those in favor of abortion as "them." Given this definition of terms, many in the antiabortion movement consider those who operate abortion clinics as setting up the same kinds of human slaughterhouses as the Nazis did. The dispute tends to become extremely emotional on both sides, with strong us-them divisions among the protagonists. As long as the abortion debate is carried on primarily at this emotional level, there is little hope for compromise and—as we have seen for more than twenty-five years—a strong tendency for discord, even murder.

Unexpected conflicts can highlight and deepen simmering divisions. We saw this phenomenon in April 2001 when a Chinese jet and a U.S. Navy reconnaissance plane collided over the South China Sea. The aftermath—a dead Chinese pilot and an eleven-day detention for the twenty-four-member Navy crew at the Chinese military base where their crippled plane was forced to land—immediately raised tensions and outright hostility between the two countries already experiencing strained relations.

Of course, us-them divisions can lead to violence that is not based on hate. Such aggression may be motivated by many different things, including greed, envy, bullying, humiliation, and even rational calculation. But once a conflict begins, it can easily escalate into hatred on both sides. And hate-fueled violence tends to be the most destructive.

Us-them stereotyping emerges directly from the primitive neural system's basic survival response. It is a form of categorical thinking in which the categories are mutually exclusive. To the primitive areas of the brain, one is either "us" or "them." One cannot be both. It appears that this kind of either-or analysis results from the preconscious alerting system's need for extremely rapid processing, which requires that phenomena be simplified as much as possible and placed in unambiguous categories. It is beneficial to have the brain wired so that a hiker instantly jumps back from a curved stick that the alerting system has suddenly detected. This time it was only a stick. Next time it might be a rattlesnake. From an evolutionary point of view, better to jump back from ten sticks than miss one rattlesnake. As neuroscientist Joseph LeDoux put it: "Failing to respond to danger is more costly than responding inappropriately to a benign stimulus. . . . We do not need to go through a detailed analysis of whether or not what we are seeing is a snake. . . . The brain simply needs to be able to store primitive cues and detect them." The problem, however, is that we are stuck with a primitive neural system that tends to see everything as black or white, good or bad, friend or enemy. This served us well living in the unforgiving African savanna of a hundred thousand years ago. It serves us less well today.[2]

OTHER BINARY CATEGORIES

Us-them distinctions are just one example of the many binary categories that permeate human thought. These binary distinctions can sometimes serve as a useful analytical tool, as long as we recognize that such divisions are not unequivocal and there are often complex connections between them. In physics, the wave-particle debate over the nature of light led to an understanding that light—and all forms

of matter and energy—has both wavelike and particle-like qualities. The nature-nurture controversy in the behavioral sciences
resulted in a better understanding of the intimate interaction
between the two. Binary distinctions cause problems when there is
a primitive insistence that they are mutually exclusive, as is the case
with most forms of bigotry.

The negative, binary stereotyping that accompanies hate trans-
lates the hated phenomenon into the general or middle-level categories that the primitive neural system understands and can quickly
process. This permits the rapid activation of the preconscious alerting system. The mechanics of negative, binary stereotyping include
two separate steps. Initially, a general or middle-level simplification
and categorization take place. A snake, for example, is categorized—
among other ways—by its shape, which is stored as a primitive cue.
This is why the preconscious alerting system may initially react to
a curved stick (or a crude rubber snake) as if it were an actual snake.
This type of simplified categorization is not necessarily negative—
we might momentarily confuse a curved stick with a snake even if
we aren't especially afraid of snakes. In the second step of creating
a hate response, however, the simplified categorization (primitive
cue) is given a permanent or semipermanent negative, binary label.
There are many different kinds of such primitive characterizations.
Fears (and phobias) generally use the binary distinction of safe versus dangerous. The object of a phobia (snakes) is given the rigid
binary label of "dangerous." Safe versus dangerous probably derives
from the basic binary division between good and bad, as do most
value-laden binary characterizations. Good-bad may, in turn, derive
from the primal pleasure-pain distinction, which sorts phenomena
into those that produce pleasure and those that produce pain. Pain
is associated with a threat to survival and reproduction; pleasure is
associated with enhancing these basic evolutionary goals. Like an
object of fear, an object of hate might also receive the negative,
binary label of "dangerous," which identifies it as a threat to survival and/or reproduction. But in addition to good-bad and safe-

dangerous, there are many other possible binary classifications. And within the primitive neural system, these binary classifications can overlap. In the hate response, which itself embodies a like-dislike distinction, us versus them (with "them" having a negative connotation) may overlap such binary pairs as friend-enemy, superior-inferior, and right-wrong. The superior-inferior classification, in particular, is central to most forms of prejudice and bigotry, including those involving race, religion, gender, ethnicity, national origin, and sexual orientation.

Serious threats, such as the attacks on September 11, strongly sensitize the limbic system. This tends to shift society as a whole toward primitive limbic reasoning with its hasty generalizations, stereotyping, us-them distinctions, and raw emotions—particularly anger and hate. Thus, after September 11, many people began to be suspicious of and angry at all Muslims. There was a sharp rise in threats against Muslim-Americans that included some attacks on property and several murders. The primitive nature of this stereotyping was evidenced by its superficial quality. Sikhs, for example, were lumped into this threat category because of their turbans and beards, though they are not Muslims. National leaders quickly moved to quell this irrational fear and anger. In retrospect, such stereotyping and hostility seem ridiculous and tragic, but the primitive power of the brain's survival response is undeniable. Even today, some enlightened air travelers—no matter how hard they try not to—report taking special notice of any Arab-looking men who board their plane. This primitive stereotyping response was also activated after several anthrax-laced letters were sent to politicians and journalists, killing five people and infecting more than a dozen others. Though only a relatively tiny number of people were affected, there was an immediate tendency by many Americans not only to view their mail with suspicion but also to regard any unidentified white powder as anthrax, even though it almost invariably turned out to be something harmless such as spilled sugar, talcum powder, or coffee creamer.

The us-them dynamic can be quite complex and unpredictable, as can the human brain that produces it. The terrorism of September 11, rather than demoralizing Americans, had the effect of unifying them. There was a tremendous burst of patriotism. Flags were everywhere. We are a social species and have evolved to experience a strong sense of comfort and security in emotionally bonding with an us-group—in this case, the nation. The primitive neural system tends to interpret us-group bonding as an enhancement of survival and reproduction: the group protects its individual members and their families. "Disasters can pull people together," said Carol North, professor of psychiatry at Washington University in St. Louis. "A community outpouring of support can make an enormous difference." But within the complicated human mind there are many potential us-groups besides the nation-state. These groups can be formed based on kinship ties, ethnicity, race, religion, political affiliation, economic status—to name just a few. Exactly how us-groups will actually coalesce under stress depends on specific circumstances.

The binary instinct tends to operate within all human social groups. It promotes shifting alliances for offensive and defensive purposes: to gain power and influence or to keep it. We see it in the operation of political parties in a democracy and the factions that compete in all forms of government—from tribal societies to authoritarian empires. This constant jockeying for position among us-group alliances, and the divisions this can create, is part of both the dynamism and instability of human social organizations. The human us-them instinct is extremely flexible and can go far beyond mere kinship. Though binary divisions can cause deep disagreements and sometimes bloody strife, they also allow an enormous variety of human organizations to form, fusing strangers or even former enemies into close collaborators and even friends. This is the kind of healing that unifying rituals such as the inauguration of a new American president are designed to promote. For hate, the binary instinct is both the problem and a significant element of the solution—when rationally employed by advanced neural choice.

SHIFTING TO AN US-US PERSPECTIVE

Clearly, the modern danger of us-them hatred is that the bitter divisions it creates regularly explode into all forms of violence—including terrorism, war, and genocide—which employ the frightening tools of modern civilization. By understanding the binary us-them mechanism so characteristic of hate, we may be able to prevent or defuse these distinctions and intelligently broaden our perception of "us" to encompass all humanity. The goal of the civilized world must be to shift from the ancient us-them orientation of our primitive neural system to an us-us orientation orchestrated by our advanced neural system. An us-us approach rationally recognizes that there will always be a shifting mosaic of human groups (us-groups), many of which will compete. But by using the positive, hate-combating strategies presented in this book, one of which is empathizing with others, we can keep our primitive binary instincts in check. Though we may fundamentally and inalterably disagree with other groups, an us-us perspective allows us to maintain our basic empathy and recognize the common humanity and unique individuality we share with those we oppose. This perspective tends to restrain us from slipping under the control of the primitive portions of our brain, where dislike is transmuted into hatred, empathy vanishes, and opponents are transformed into dehumanized "them" subject to ruthless extermination. Shifting from us-them to us-us will not end all conflict. But it will tend to minimize it. It will not end all violence. But it will tend to diminish the most callous forms of cruelty by ceaselessly reminding us that our opponents are fellow human beings, not stereotypes. And when hostilities are at an end, it will tend to promote genuine reconciliation. In the long run, an us-us perspective will tend to prompt all of us to vigorously search, wherever possible, for nonviolent solutions to our problems through constructive and informed communication, negotiation, and mutual empathy—not hatred and violence.[3]

For a variety of complicated reasons, the outcome of World War II embodied this us-us approach. Germany, Japan, and Italy were restructured and brought back into the community of nations, not ostracized and permanently condemned. The peace of the world has been greatly enhanced by this wise choice. In the span of human history, however, this is a rare exception. But there is hope that somehow this example can be reproduced in post-Soviet Russia, post-Taliban Afghanistan, and the Balkans, post-Milosevic.

Obviously, changing such a deeply entrenched primitive tendency as making us-them distinctions will be extraordinarily difficult. In fact, it will require nothing less than a new age of enlightenment in the globalizing world civilization in which we all seek to eliminate hate. But this shift is urgently needed if we are to avoid the periodic hate-inspired catastrophes that have befallen humanity. In an era of weapons of mass destruction, the next catastrophe may be our last.

4

THE REPTILE WITHIN

A PRIMITIVE ANIMAL lives in your mind and brain. It is aware but not self-aware. It knows it must feed, have sex, and fight or flee if threatened. When a phobia grips you—when you feel a fear of heights, of spiders, of snakes—you are overwhelmed by its presence and its raw emotion. When you panic, it takes over, often leaving you with only a blurred memory of your wild effort to escape danger. When you instinctively jump or flinch because of something you have barely glimpsed out of the corner of your eye, it is there. It continuously monitors your surroundings, even while you sleep. If something goes crash or bump in the night, it rouses you. If your child or your spouse is suddenly and violently attacked in front of you, it will very likely emerge instantly and you will attack: punching, kicking, clawing, and screaming. This primitive animal can love with obsessive devotion; it can hate with violent fury. To describe it, we use the term *reptomammal*, and it represents a descendant of a kind of reptile-mammal hybrid—a living fossil of ancient structures that

reside in your brain and have descended from the very first reptomammals: the therapsids.

Around 350 million years ago, large animals began emerging
from the oceans onto the land in the form of amphibians. From the
amphibians evolved the first vertebrate animals fully adapted to living on land: the reptiles. And it was from the reptiles that two other
notable forms of life evolved between about 300 million and 250 million years ago: first, the therapsids and then, the dinosaurs. Therapsids were reptomammals and the direct ancestors of all modern
mammals, including ourselves. Dinosaurs were a different sort of
reptile variation and may be the ancestors of modern birds. These
two kinds of creatures were to spend 200 million years in a war for
control of the Earth. At first it looked as if the therapsids would win.
They proliferated into many species and grew to giant size, rele-
gating the dinosaurs, which were generally small, to the periphery
of the ecosystem. But then something unexpected happened.
Around 200 million years ago, there was a great amount of death. It
may have been caused by one of the huge comets or asteroids that
seem to have struck the Earth periodically over the eons. Or colossal volcanic eruptions may have drastically changed the climate of
the planet. The larger therapsids died off along with many other
forms of life, and the reptomammals' relationship with the dinosaurs
was reversed. The remaining therapsids stayed small, while the
dinosaurs became huge and dominated the land. For well over a hundred million years thereafter, dinosaurs ruled the Earth. But the
therapsids had two surprises ahead of them: one in the form of evolution, the other in the form of chance.

Reptiles have no emotions, as we understand the term. They feel
only pain and pleasure. Reptiles operate primarily from instinct.
They do not generally bond with each other and, except in rare
cases, they do not care for their young. Neither are they social. They
have a crude territorial instinct and can sense intruders. Their neural equipment consists of a brain stem and basal ganglia, which control their movements and innate behaviors. They have only the most

rudimentary amygdala and hippocampus and very little cortex. Therapsids were mammal-like reptiles. But their architecture, both physical and mental, represented some striking evolutionary advances. Their legs were relocated underneath their bodies instead of to the sides, as is the case with the reptile body plan. This allowed them to run long distances much more efficiently. There were advances in the structure of the ears, indicating the beginning of intricate vocal communication, which doesn't exist among reptiles. A snake hisses a warning, but it doesn't use sound to engage in complex communication with other snakes. Reptomammals probably employed an array of calls that allowed them to communicate not only a certain amount of information, but their feelings as well. Cries of pain, anger, hate, and joy evolved. With therapsids, we have the first emotions. They cared for their young, and many species seemed to have been social. All this was reflected by advances in the architecture of their brain.[1]

The therapsids had all the old structures of the reptile brain governing the instinctive drives for feeding, fighting, fleeing, and reproducing. But they added additional structures as well in the form of an advanced limbic system. The amygdala and hippocampus became more sophisticated, along with other limbic structures that formed a ring around the brain stem. All these were elaborately connected to the structures of the diencephalon: the thalamus and hypothalamus. Even more momentous was the development of additional layers of cortex that could integrate sensory data and memory into relatively complicated cognitive and emotional patterns. The limbic system and all the advanced structures of the brain, including the human neocortex, evolved from the primitive organs of smell. The olfactory system detects chemical traces of the world around it and seeks to categorize these different chemical signatures, from the scent of a mate to the scent of prey. This categorization of the world through smell was elaborated by evolution and became the basis of all the more complex structures of the brain that process data from all the senses. The limbic system is sometimes called the olfactory

brain because the amygdala, hippocampus, and other limbic structures evolved from the primitive olfactory system. The therapsid
could categorize the world in a much more sophisticated way than
a reptile could. And emotions supplied a far more elaborate motivational system. Raw pleasure and pain still existed, but these could
be transformed by the advanced limbic structures and limbic association cortex into emotions. In primates, the pain of a stubbed toe
would be supplemented with the pain of a broken heart. But for reptomammals, emotional responses were more basic, often ferocious
and cruel, reflecting the harsh reality of the dinosaur-dominated
world in which these creatures struggled to survive. And the mental categories, emotional and cognitive, of the reptomammals were
generalized. Like the phobic of today, a reptomammal could identify a snake but probably could not distinguish in any detailed way
between one type of snake and another.

Dinosaurs, too, may have cared for their young, and some
species of dinosaurs might have been social. They represented an
advance over reptiles, but their brains were relatively unimpressive
and did not have the potential of the reptomammal brain. Nevertheless, dinosaurs continued to dominate the Earth while reptomammals remained small and were relegated to the margins. But
then came a momentous evolutionary change. Between a hundred
million and seventy-five million years ago, true mammals evolved
from reptomammals. The brain became much larger and more intri-
cately interconnected in mammals. To the limbic system and the limbic association cortex of the reptomammals was added the
neocortex, which allowed a far more sophisticated and detailed categorization and modeling of the world. Both communication and
behavior became more complex and nuanced. Yet it is not clear that
this alone would have been enough to overthrow the dinosaurs. But
then came the second surprise in the form of the Earth's chance
encounter with another giant comet or asteroid—or perhaps several of them—that seemed to have taken place sixty-five million
years ago. The result was a violent collision that created a maelstrom

of destruction, especially for land creatures. The remnants of a large impact crater still exist in the Gulf of Mexico near the Yucatán peninsula of Mexico. In another reversal, the dinosaurs died off and the smaller mammals that survived were able to come out of hiding and take their place. The age of dinosaurs was succeeded by the age of mammals, and this time the victory was total. Dinosaurs completely disappeared. Their only living descendants, some scientists believe, are modern birds. The mammalian neocortex continued to evolve, spreading over the entire outer surface of the brain, becoming conscious, and burying the brain stem, diencephalon, basal ganglia, limbic system, and limbic association cortex deep within its folds. But the reptomammal is still there, and sometimes it comes out.

THE REPTOMAMMALIAN IMPULSE TO KILL

The North Valley Jewish Community Center is situated in a quiet, prosperous neighborhood of Los Angeles, dotted with palms and roses. Located next to a church in an area of the San Fernando Valley called Granada Hills, the center consists of several tan stucco buildings with a large outdoor swimming pool and other athletic facilities. It was a perfect, sunny August day in 1999, and sixty-eight-year-old Isabelle Shalometh, the friendly receptionist at the center, was at her desk, which faced the front door of the center's main building. A hundred children were enrolled in the community center's summer camp. Another forty-three attended the center's nursery school. At about 10:45 A.M., Shalometh noticed a heavyset man with a mustache walking into the lobby through the open front door. She would learn later that his name was Buford O. Furrow. At that moment, however, she was focusing on the man's nine-millimeter assault rifle. Furrow calmly raised the rifle and began firing. Shalometh dived behind the counter, yelling for people in the nearby offices to get down. Her back and arm were grazed by gunfire. Bullets shredded a stack of papers on the lobby desk. "The girls in the back offices were screaming," Shalometh recalled later.[2]

Furrow kept firing. He walked down a short hallway, shooting at anyone he happened to see. "At first, I thought it was just a jackhammer," said Rhea Nagel, a student in one of the center's classrooms. "I looked out and saw a man shooting down the hallways and at the reception desk." Mindy Finkelstein, a sixteen-year-old camp counselor, ran into one of the classrooms, bleeding from a wound in her leg. Furrow fired seventy rounds before he fled. Besides Shalometh and Finkelstein, two six-year-old boys and a five-year-old were wounded. The five-year-old boy suffered the most serious injuries, sustaining bullet wounds to the abdomen and left thigh. All survived.

Police, paramedics, and terrified parents soon swarmed the community center along with an army of media. Live television pictures of police officers leading long lines of small children from the center were beamed around the world. Some of the children were smiling, totally oblivious to the hate that almost swallowed them up. One of the frantic parents, Katey Pianko, was clutching her two-year-old daughter, Zoe, who had been playing inside the center when the shots were fired. She was waiting to be reunited with her five-year-old son, Sam. "Why are all these people here?" Zoe asked her mother. "Because they are trying to catch a bad guy," Pianko said. "Is he a monster?" asked Zoe. "Yes," said Pianko. "He's a monster." Furrow was gone. But he wasn't far away.

In the nearby community of Chatsworth, postal worker Joseph Ileto was delivering mail. Ileto was born in the Philippines and had come to the United States when he was fourteen. He loved working for the Postal Service and often wore his post office T-shirts on his days off. The thirty-nine-year-old Ileto was an excellent chess player, and everyone described him as easygoing. When Buford Furrow walked up to him, Ileto apparently hadn't heard about the Granada Hills shooting an hour earlier. Furrow asked Ileto to mail a letter for him then suddenly drew a handgun and began firing. Residents of the area said Furrow chased Ileto down a driveway and shot him at close range. Ileto was killed. At first, police didn't think Ileto's death and the Granada Hills shooting were connected. They were puzzled by the seemingly motiveless crime. Long after the attack on Ileto, his postal van full of undelivered mail stood on the street with its emergency lights blinking as police scoured the area for clues.

Furrow, a classic lone wolf (see Chapter 9), was a resident of Washington state who had a history of mental problems. He continued to wander the streets of Los Angeles as police mounted a major manhunt. He had abandoned his van full of firearms, hand grenades, and ammunition. At 8:00 that night he hailed a cab and paid the driver to take him to Las Vegas. On arriving, he looked up the names of synagogues in the local telephone book and considered another attack. But the next day, after seeing his picture on television, he went to the Las Vegas FBI office and turned himself in. "You're looking for me. I killed the kids in Los Angeles," he said. Authorities later learned that Furrow had been associated with the white supremacist group Aryan Nation. He reportedly became seriously interested in the white supremacist movement after attending the 1989 Aryan World Congress in Hayden Lake, Idaho. Furrow once served as a volunteer guard at the Aryan Nation's compound in Idaho. He told the FBI that he attacked the Granada Hills community center because he wanted to send a "wake-up call for Americans to kill Jews." When asked about Ileto, Furrow said he shot the postal worker because "he looked Asian or Latino."

Buford Furrow was spared the death penalty when federal prosecutors learned of his history of mental illness. For a decade prior to the Los Angeles attacks, he had tried to get treatment for suicidal and homicidal tendencies, according to U.S. Attorney Alejandro N. Mayorkas. Two government psychiatrists reviewed Furrow's medical history and found that he had checked himself into psychiatric hospitals three different times and frequently went to hospital emergency rooms complaining of panic attacks and powerful impulses to kill himself and others. Less than a year before his attack on the Jewish community center, he tried to commit himself to a private psychiatric facility. During an interview with staff members, he became angry and threatened them with a knife. He was arrested and sentenced to six months in jail. Even while he was being held on murder and assault charges in Los Angeles, Furrow continued to have violent outbursts, threatening to kill nonwhites, including a Latino inmate and several guards. He also reportedly became angry at his ex-wife, threatening to kill her son. Furrow began taking five different medications to control his aggressive behavior.

In March 2001, Furrow pleaded guilty and received five life terms for killing Joseph Ileto and wounding the five people at the Jewish community center—a sentence that will keep him in jail for the rest of his life. At his sentencing, Furrow was calm but remorseful. He expressed "deep sorrow" for the killing of Ileto. As for the attack on the community center, he said: "I hold myself responsible for what happened. . . . I wish I had been kept in the [psychiatric] hospital I was previously in. I think about what happened every day and I will grieve for it every day for the rest of my life."

But the victims and their families were unmoved. His hate-motivated act had caused them ineradicable pain. Some of them were upset that he hadn't received the death penalty. Their suffering came pouring out during the sentencing. "I feel deep inside that he knows the difference between right and wrong," said Joseph Ileto's mother, Lillian. "When he killed my son, he killed a part of me. My son was gunned down like an animal, not shot just once or twice but nine times. My heart aches every day knowing he was suffering. . . . Just saying he's sorry doesn't bring back my son. I was brought up to always forgive. We will never go down to that level of hate. . . . I pity Buford. He has to wake up every day and see his reflection in the mirror." Mindy Finkelstein, the counselor who was wounded at the community center, said she still was suffering emo-

tional scars. "I've been to hell and back," she said, periodically sobbing. "Buford Furrow tried to kill me and he failed. But in a way,
he succeeded."[3]

UNDERSTANDING THE
EVOLUTIONARY LEVELS
OF THE BRAIN

The case of Buford Furrow tragically illustrates what can happen
when mental illness weakens the neocortex's control over our primitive core. As the instincts of the reptomammal emerged, Furrow
experienced violent impulses directed at himself and others. And
like many mentally unstable people, he was susceptible to being dan-
gerously warped by hate, which gave these impulses a target. But
this kind of primitive warping is not confined to the mentally unbal-
anced. Even apparently normal people in hate-infested areas of the
Middle East, Northern Ireland, the Balkans, Rwanda, or a thousand
other trouble spots can sometimes seem like reptomammals tearing
at each other in some Jurassic nightmare.

Paul MacLean, who for many years was the chief of the laboratory of brain evolution and behavior of the National Institute of
Mental Health, pioneered the modern formulation of the limbic system. Though the functional specifics of the human emotional system remain a matter of controversy, many neuroscientists have
found the limbic system concept useful in understanding the evolutionary structure of the brain. MacLean put the limbic system in a
larger context within what he called the triune brain. This framework conceptualizes the brain as having three interconnected evolutionary levels: the reptilian brain, the old mammalian brain, and
the new mammalian brain. The reptilian level consists of the upper
brain stem, diencephalon, basal ganglia, and rudimentary elements
of the limbic system. MacLean found that the reptilian brain con-

tains the largely instinctual programs for self-preservation: fighting, fleeing, mating, establishing territory, hunting. Many of these instincts are lodged in the basal ganglia, which are the most highly developed portions of the reptile brain. The basal ganglia are ancient motor centers that have a special responsibility for automatic movements. In humans, it is the basal ganglia that cause us to instinctively flinch, duck, jump, brace, bolt, or freeze when threatened. Reptomammals such as the therapsids were an intermediate step toward the old mammalian brain, which fully emerged with the evolution of true mammals. At this evolutionary level, the limbic system was greatly elaborated and became the most highly developed portion of the brain. In primitive mammals such as rodents and rabbits, the limbic system—including the amygdala, hippocampus, cingulate cortex, and related structures—occupies a much higher percentage of the brain than in advanced mammals such as primates. The old mammalian brain added elaborate emotional behavior to the instincts of the reptile. This included care for the young and play behavior.[4]

The most recent evolutionary level is the new mammalian brain, which reached its fullest development in primates. It is dominated by a huge neocortex. Within the neocortex of the new mammalian brain, consciousness emerged. The powers of abstraction, complex language, and planning attained their highest levels. The reptilian and old mammalian levels continue to function, however, and constitute the reptomammalian portion of the human brain—what we have previously referred to as the primitive neural system. Our version of the reptomammalian brain is more advanced than the therapsid version—because our limbic system is more highly developed—but it is still quite primitive, and its behaviors are mediated by structures such as the amygdala. As neuroscientist Eric Halgren put it: "The amygdala lies, functionally and anatomically, between these two poles, between the enormous thinking mantle that creates an objective model of external reality, and the subjective inner reality of pain and fear, of surviving to mate and ensuring that our offspring do also."[5]

Complex mental states such as love and hate as well as complex behaviors such as sexuality and aggression involve widespread networks of many specialized centers in the brain. Neuroscience is just beginning to understand how such distributed networks operate. Some of these networks operate in parallel—simultaneously extracting different kinds of information from the same stream of data—while others operate sequentially. Vision, for example, links centers specializing in the analysis of color, motion, movement, shape, and many other qualities to produce the unified sense of the visible world you experience as you look at this page. Your visual system employs both step-by-step processing of the visual data that stream into the brain through the optic nerves and parallel processing, in which different centers in the right and left hemispheres analyze the same data at the same time. This gives the brain great resiliency and redundancy.

The basic architecture of our brain helps explain why we consciously know the reptomammalian portion of our mind only indirectly—through the primitive emotions and stereotypes it signals to our consciousness. We never directly enter its primitive awareness. Like many other brain systems, it operates in parallel with the system that generates our consciousness, using a different network. "What occurs in one brain area is sometimes unintelligible to another as each has its own specializations and limitations," said psychologist Rhawn Joseph. "Some forms of information which are being processed or expressed by old limbic brain tissue may not be recognized or comprehended by the new brain, and vice versa. . . ."[6]

We can think of the brain as a self-assembling information processor that employs a kind of alphabet to create its complex functions. In this metaphor, the neurons are the letters of the alphabet. The letters form words—a vocabulary—that correspond to the brain's system of localized modules specializing in elementary operations. And just as a given word can be used in many different sentences to produce many different meanings, each localized module can be used in a number of different widespread networks that create different complex functions. Some of the same memory modules, for example, may be involved in the visual system, auditory system, and other sensory systems that require the identification of learned patterns of stimuli.

Though the reptilian, old mammalian, and new mammalian evolutionary levels of the human brain are densely interconnected, the vast numbers of modules within each of the three different levels also seem to be wired together to produce distinct types of functions. Experiments have tended to confirm MacLean's triune brain model. If the neocortex of a hamster is removed, the hamster's most advanced abilities—such as maze running—disappear. But it continues to both play and care for its young. And its instinctive behaviors are generally unaffected. All the behaviors that the decorticated hamster exhibit are contained in the reptilian and old mammalian portions of its brain. But if the hamster's old mammalian brain—the limbic system—is removed as well, maternal behavior and play cease. Its emotions seem to vanish. But its instinctive behaviors are preserved. It keeps on feeding, fighting, fleeing, and engaging in sexual behavior. Its reptilian brain continues to function.

MacLean argued that the most significant development in the history of evolution was the tremendous expansion in the human brain of the frontal lobes' prefrontal cortex. The prefrontal cortex contains both the prefrontal association cortex, which is the most advanced portion of the neocortex, and the orbitofrontal cortex, which is the most advanced portion of the limbic association cortex. These areas give us our powers of foresight and advanced empathy. "It is this new development," MacLean said, "that makes possible the insight required to plan for the needs of others as well as the self, and to use our knowledge to alleviate suffering everywhere. In creating for the first time a creature with a concern for all living things, nature accomplished a one-hundred-eighty-degree turnabout from what had previously been a reptile-eat-reptile and dog-eat-dog world."

A critical function of the frontal lobes is to serve as a massive inhibitor of the reptomammalian mind, shaping its primitive impulses into more sophisticated forms. The frontal lobes can transform visceral rage into principled outrage. Thus, the neocortex makes enlightened behavior possible. But the more primitive portions of our brain may have other ideas. The fearful reptomammal within us ceaselessly searches our perceptions and thoughts for any sign of a threat. Its intelligence is limited, and it is quick to spot danger even where none exists—in the form of a twisted stick that it interprets as a snake, for example. At the first hint of a threat, it begins to fashion primitive defensive measures. Even our complex language contains cues this primitive mind can twist into stereotypes and prejudices it can use to trigger aggression or avoidance. "The process of communication [among humans] has been over a billion years in the making and has been derived from multiple sources and species, both extant and extinct," said Rhawn Joseph. "The modern mind is a veritable museum and the manner in which we communicate reflects these multiple forces and ancestral influences."

HOW COMPLEX LANGUAGE, THOUGHT, AND EMOTION INFLUENCE THE PRIMITIVE MIND

Complex language of the human variety has three important elements: symbols, displacement, and productivity. Symbols refer to the arbitrary link between sequences of sounds and the elements of experience. The word *human* has nothing intrinsically to do with our species; it is simply an arbitrary sound label that we have linked to ourselves through mental association. Symbols by their nature are abstract, and humans excel in the communication of abstract concepts. The category of "trees" represents an abstract concept that includes everything from redwoods to dwarf pines, but not bushes. Humans can manipulate these symbols in unprecedented ways. Using the symbols embodied by language and manipulating them according to the rules of syntax, we can engage in elaborate abstract reasoning such as deduction and induction. Displacement involves the ability of human language to allow us to consider different spaces and times from the present moment, including imaginary time and space. This gives us our unique sense of time, space, and possibility, allowing us to contemplate any place and any time. Productivity refers to the capacity of human language to use a finite set of sounds to produce a potentially infinite number of new meanings. Most vocalizing animals have a limited set of calls, and each call has a relatively specific meaning.

Infinite different meanings mean unlimited new meanings. Thus complex language can generate a theoretically infinite amount of innovative thought. With our complex language, we can create complex social organizations, which allow a potentially infinite number of tasks to be accomplished. Complex language and complex organization are the core of innovative culture. Subsistence culture, whether agriculture-based or hunter-gatherer-based, tends to have a relatively simple organization that minimizes innovation and tends to operate with stereotyped tools and practices. Though our distant ancestors probably used complex language, they did not appear to have a complex social organization. We see evidence of this in the stereotyped tools used by modern humans for the first sixty thousand years or so of our species' existence.

But the nature of our complex language strongly reinforces our tendency to stereotype, generalize, and manufacture prejudices. As part of its structure, complex language abounds with general descriptive terms that represent either general categories (animals) or middle-level categories (snakes). The general and middle-level categories of complex language are essential to sophisticated neocortical language, but they are also instantly recognized by the primitive limbic system—such generalized concepts are its basic categorical framework—and represent the only way the preconscious alerting system is wired to categorize and model experience.[7]

But general and middle-level categories are capable of playing a much more complex role in neocortical language and thought than they are in primitive limbic thought processes. We can use them as part of a structure to create detailed, scientific classifications of virtually any phenomenon. We might, for example, begin with the general categories of women and men and end with the identification of the X and Y chromosomes that determine the sex of a child. The primitive neural system, however, can take any of these same descriptive terms—women, men, blacks, whites, Asians, Hispanics, Muslims, Jews, Christians, Americans, French, English, Germans, Chinese—and turn them into limbic stereotypes that then take on powerful emotional significance because the reptomammalian mind marks such stereotypes as either enhancing or threatening our survival and reproduction. These stereotypes—which can generate positive or negative emotions such as hate, love, or fear—are then accessed by the preconscious alerting system in the early stages of neocortical processing. This early-stage primitive processing and identification of general and middle-level categories is consistent with the finding of neuroscientists that different categories of linguistic information are stored in different places in the brain, particularly nouns and other descriptive terms, with the more specific categories (unique entities or events) being stored further forward in the brain, where they are accessed in the later stages of neocortical processing. The neocortical processing of most sensory information begins in the rear of the brain and moves forward to the most advanced areas of the frontal and temporal lobes. Visual information, for example, is first routed to the primary visual areas of the occipital lobes, located in the very back of the brain.

The power of the human brain with its advanced neural system centered in the neocortex and the enormously enlarged prefrontal cortex can be partially tapped by the primitive neural system that embodies reptomammal awareness. The advanced neural system is

capable of creating elaborate meaning systems that are far beyond
the capacity of the primitive neural system. But these complex
meaning systems can be directly linked to stereotypes that our primitive mind creates. An intricate, paranoid meaning system can be
tied to primitive stereotypes embodied in general descriptive terms
such as *Latino*, *Jew*, or *black*. We see this over and over in all the hate
websites on the Internet. Obviously this was the case with the elaborate neo-Nazi rationalization for Aryan superiority that warped
the mind of Buford Furrow. These elaborate meaning systems are
not, however, governed by the complex mind but by the reptomammalian mind that contains the stereotypes they rationalize. You can
see this primitive control if you try to reason with people infected
by this kind of hate. They will continually spin out arguments,
excuses, and paranoid ideas in a determined effort to protect their
underlying prejudices and hostility. Their advanced neural system
has been enslaved by their primitive fear and hatred and is almost
powerless to serve as an objective check on these rationalizations,
which are constantly nourished by the reptomammalian view of the
world. The primitive neural system has concluded that the objects
of this stereotyped hate are a threat to survival and reproduction,
an assumption that it is loathe to give up, just as it is reluctant to give
up its phobias. Under the right circumstances, as with suicidal terrorists, such hate rationales can trigger savage aggression.

The purpose of complex thought is to identify and classify our
experience, both internal and external. The purpose of complex
emotion is to sort through these classifications and add a motivational layer to each experience, thought, and behavior. But hate dis-
torts this process. And the distortion is made worse because it is
difficult to change the primitive mind. The amygdala's judgments,
once made, are extremely difficult to alter. Our brains have evolved
so that whenever we perceive a serious threat, the older survival-
oriented areas tend to take precedence. The orbitofrontal cortex,
which is densely interconnected with both the prefrontal cortex and
limbic system, is a key area we activate when we try to alter these

primitive responses. One of the most important roles of the neocortex via the orbitofrontal cortex and other pathways is to inhibit the impulses of the primitive neural system. When a threat or opportunity is registered by the senses, the amygdala stamps a primitive emotional label, positive or negative, on the perception, which remains attached to the perception when it is stored in memory. The amygdala seems to store this information in a kind of database memory. The orbitofrontal cortex also makes emotional judgments but appears to store emotional information in a more abstract and flexible form. It is the orbitofrontal cortex that seems to contain specific rules such as "only poisonous snakes are dangerous." Because the orbitofrontal cortex does not appear to be involved in the preconscious alerting system, it can contain relatively specific categories that take longer to process. The hippocampus and orbitofrontal cortex are exceptions to the generally primitive architecture of the limbic system. And unlike the amygdala database, the rules stored in the orbitofrontal cortex can change rapidly depending on current information and context.

The information contained by the orbitofrontal cortex might be called one's general knowledge of the good and bad aspects of the world, and the rules and strategies for achieving the good and avoiding the bad. The orbitofrontal cortex's role is more consistent with sophisticated neocortical processing—not surprising given its intimate connection to the prefrontal association cortex. Its maps and models contain sophisticated categories of emotional learning capable of being quickly readjusted to changing circumstances, when the new circumstances indicate that the older emotional learning is obsolete. The orbitofrontal cortex takes the database built up by the amygdala and uses it to create cognitive maps of the world and expectations about the future. Using its own analysis—and its interconnections with the amygdala—it can, at times, modify the amygdala database. But the amygdala is so closely tied to primitive survival and reproduction that the architecture of the human brain does not make this an easy process.

Phobias about snakes, spiders, heights, and enclosed spaces are archaic remnants of an ancient world. As we have seen, psychologists call them prepared fears, and they seem to be genetically based tendencies that reflect the primitive living conditions of our ancient hominid ancestors. We treat phobias as a medical problem to be dealt with primarily through cognitive behavior therapy, which is remarkably effective. We must find ways to deal with hate in a similar fashion. The reptomammal inside our brain was formed in a world that existed millions of years ago. The last time its parameters were adjusted was more than one hundred thousand years ago, when the modern human brain evolved. At that time, when life was short and brutal, phobias and hate may still have served some useful purpose. But in a global civilization armed with lethal technologies, their utility has disappeared and their drawbacks have multiplied. They have been superseded by targeted fears and rational dislike, which are much more flexible, analytical, and specific. We no longer have to obsessively fear all snakes or all heights. We no longer have to obsessively hate all of "them"—all Serbs, all Croats, all whites, all blacks, all Muslims, all Christians. Both phobias and hate are relics of the distant past. Hate, in particular, is a dangerous anachronism. Through the primitive neural system, it can twist our very language and thoughts into prejudice, bigotry, and violence. Yet it is through our complex language and thoughts that we must address the perils of hate and, together, fashion solutions.

Primitive, violent hatred has its roots in the most ancient areas of the brain. It is a part of our reptomammalian nature that first evolved in the bleak kill-or-be-killed environment of millions of years ago. Our more advanced neural structures normally hold it in check, but in some mentally unstable individuals such as Buford Furrow, it is released with devastating effect. Yet it can also surface in seemingly average people in the presence of us-them divisions, a perception of danger, high levels of stress, and hate-filled meaning systems. Furrow's violent impulses were shaped and fueled by one of these meaning systems. But the family of Joseph Ileto and people of goodwill everywhere are fighting for different kinds of meaning systems: those that awaken our capacity for tolerance, empathy, and understanding.

In the aftermath of Buford Furrow's rampage, there were marches and rallies throughout Los Angeles and southern California condemning anti-Semitism and all hate crimes. Some of Joseph Ileto's grieving relatives became crusaders against anti-Asian bigotry. Strangely enough, the morning of Furrow's attack on the North Valley Jewish Community Center, the older students at the center were on a field trip to the Museum of Tolerance in West Los Angeles, which has extensive displays on the horrors that hate has brought to humanity, especially the Nazi Holocaust. Rabbi Marvin Hier, founder and dean of the museum and the associated Simon Wiesenthal Center, was shocked that such an attack could take place so close to home. "In one respect Buford Furrow was right when he said he was trying to register his crime as a 'wake-up call to America,'" Hier observed. "What these haters are doing in this country and all over the world is showing how much damage a single individual bent on destroying society can do."

The challenge of hate will take all our creativity and intelligence to overcome. One of the slain postal worker's cousins has turned the name Joseph Ileto into an acronym for understanding. On T-shirts and banners, J-o-s-e-p-h I-l-e-t-o now stands for Join Our Struggle, Educate to Prevent Hate. Instill Love, Equality, Tolerance for Others.

WAR AND GENOCIDE

Hate at its most atrocious annihilates mercy and feeds on the infliction of pain and death. One of the most graphic demonstrations of this terrible truth has been the Russian war to subdue Chechnya. Russian and Western human rights observers have gathered thousands of pages of documentation of torture, murder, looting, and rape committed by Russian soldiers in the most recent incarnation of this conflict in the rebellious North Caucasus province. Chechen fighters themselves have committed many atrocities as well as acts of terrorism. The Russian military uses a slang term to describe such fighting: *bespredel*. It literally means "no limits" and was coined by inmates in the Russian prison system. The latest war against the Chechens, which began in September 1999, at times reached such an intensity as to seem genocidal.

The motive for *bespredel* is simple: revenge, merciless and savage. "When you see your mates drop down on the ground, when you take your dead and wounded to the hospital, this is when hatred rises within you," said a twenty-three-year-old Russian officer. "And the hatred is against all Chechens, not just the individual enemies who killed your friends. This is when *bespredel* starts."

Many Russian soldiers have been surprisingly willing to talk about the terrible things they have done as long as their identities are concealed. They represent, according to one observer, "a Russian military culture that glorifies ardor in battle, portrays the enemy as inhuman, and has no effective system of accountability." Explains one twenty-one-year-old conscript: "Without *bespredel*, we'll get nowhere in Chechnya. We have to be cruel to them. Otherwise, we'll achieve nothing."

"Boris," an ex-soldier in his thirties, has had trouble sleeping since he returned from Chechnya. "I killed a lot," he said. "I wouldn't touch women or children, as long as they didn't fire at me. But I would kill all the men I met during mopping-up operations. I didn't feel sorry for them one bit. They deserved it. I wouldn't even listen to their pleas or see the tears of their women when they asked me to spare their men. I simply took them aside and killed them."

Although the soldiers were under orders to turn over any captured Chechen fighters to the proper authorities, they rarely did. "I remember a Chechen female sniper," said Boris. "She didn't have any chance of making it to the authorities. We just tore her apart with two armored personnel carriers, having tied her ankles with steel cables. There was a lot of blood, but the boys needed it. After this, a lot of the boys calmed down. Justice was done, and that was the most important thing for them." Boris sometimes wakes up at night "in a cold sweat, all enraged, and all I can see is dead bodies, blood, and screams."

Boris said he never killed civilians without being provoked, but others are not so scrupulous. A thirty-three-year-old Russian army officer said he drowned four women and a middle-aged man in a well. "You should not believe people who say Chechens are not being exterminated," he said. "In this Chechen war, it's done by everyone who can do it. There are situations when it's not possible. When an opportunity presents itself, few people miss it."[1]

The Chechens and the other mountain peoples of the North Caucasus have a long and violent history. They have been fighting the Russians since Ivan the Terrible tried to conquer them in the sixteenth century. Under dictator Joseph Stalin, Chechnya became part of one of the autonomous Soviet republics. The area was occupied by the Nazis during World War II. After the war, Stalin charged that the Chechens collaborated with the Germans and had the entire population shipped by train into exile in the deserts of Kazakhstan. When Stalin died in 1953, Chechens began migrating back to their native region. In 1994, following the collapse of the Soviet Union, the Chechens again revolted against Russian rule and during a two-year war fought the Russian army to a standstill. After the war, Chechnya was virtually independent. But Russia accused Chechen fighters of running gangs that kidnapped Russian civilians and engaged in torture, murder, and mutilation. The Russian media portrayed the Chechens as merciless bandits and terrorists. The Chechens were blamed for four bomb explosions in Moscow and other cities in the fall of 1999 that killed 305 people. Soon after, the Russian military attacked Chechnya with overwhelming firepower and laid waste to Chechen cities and towns, capturing the capital, Grozny, in February 2000. But many Chechen fighters refused to give up. The war shifted to a bloody guerilla conflict.

The 1999 attack on Chechnya was carried out with unbelievable ferocity and, according to many human rights groups, in violation of every rule of international law. Russia is a signatory of the Geneva Conventions and, according to the organization Human Rights Watch, "is obliged to respect human rights regardless of abuses committed by the other side." Russian soldiers, however, made it clear that their rules of engagement did not include the Geneva Conventions. They did, however, include *bespredel*.

"Andrei," a young soldier who turned twenty-one shortly after leaving the army, said captured Chechens knew they would receive no mercy. "You can see it in their eyes," he said. "They never tell us anything, but then again, we never ask. We do it out of spite, because if they can torture our soldiers, why shouldn't we torture them?" He coolly described his favorite method of killing prisoners: "The easiest way is to heat your bayonet over charcoal, and when it's red-hot, to put it on their bodies, or stab them slowly. You need to make sure they feel as much pain as possible. The main thing is to have them die slowly. You don't want them to die fast, because a fast death is an easy death. They should get the full treatment. They should get what they deserve. On one hand it looks like an atrocity, but on the other hand, it's easy to get used to. I killed about nine people this way. I remember all of them."

Russian authorities have promised a thorough investigation of possible war crimes in Chechnya, but Russian and international human rights groups say that little or nothing has been done. The Russian public, for the most part, has been indifferent to the fate of the Chechens. This attitude is reflected by the military. "We shouldn't have given them time to prepare for the war," said "Valery," a Russian lieutenant colonel. "We should have slaughtered all Chechens over five years old and sent all the children that could still be reeducated to reservations with barbed wire and guards at the corners. . . . But where would you find teachers willing to sacrifice their lives to reeducate these wolf cubs? There are no such people. Therefore, it's much easier to kill them all. It takes less time for them to die than to grow."

We see in this kind of reasoning the stark outlines of genocide. Hate and fear strongly activate the primitive neural system, which thrives on broad categories based on stereotypes, generalizations, and loose associations. The threat category "Chechen fighters" can easily enlarge to include all Chechens, because in a guerilla war the line between combatants and noncombatants is not always clear. Hate also promotes an emotional coldness toward enemy populations in which indifference to wanton killing and the desire for revenge can rapidly grow, unconstrained by any sense of proportionality. Thus, war can expand into holocaust, especially when the warriors are not operating under rational restraints but under the principles of *bespredel.*

RATIONALIZING GENOCIDE

There are a wide variety of rationales for genocide. But they all, in one way or another, involve making us-them distinctions between victims and aggressors. The motives for the systematic extermination of others are often a mix of primitive hatred, rational calculation, indifference, and impulsive violence. But the act itself is inevitably preceded by a methodical dehumanization of those who are to be exterminated—victims may actually be equated with vermin. Genocide is sometimes an act of revenge for real or imagined offenses. This is particularly true among warring groups when each considers the other group evil. A militarily stronger people may seek to exterminate a weaker people, which sometimes occurred when European colonists encountered aboriginal peoples. A minority group can become a scapegoat. Racial, religious, or ethnic groups may be viewed as inferior and subject to slaughter. All these rationales can be blended in various ways. But when they are infected by hate, the extermination can become linked to the primal goals of survival and reproduction. This kind of violence can go on for years, decades, or centuries until one side or another is defeated, exhausted, or destroyed.

The flawed logic of the primitive neural system makes transcending these cycles of violence immensely difficult. Primitive logic understands only generalized propositions such as "all Serbs are good" or "all Serbs are bad." Both of these propositions are incorrect, of course, because no large group of human beings is wholly good or bad. If the primitive neural system has decided that one of these propositions is correct ("all Serbs are bad"), then it will tend to selectively pay attention to individual cases that support this proposition. Post-Milosevic Yugoslavia is struggling with the consequences of years of primitive propaganda that smeared other ethnic groups, including Albanians. Though many Serbs now recognize that Milosevic's policy of ethnic cleansing directed against the Kosovar Albanians was wrong, continuing incidents of violence by ethnic Albanian rebels in southern Serbia, Kosovo, and nearby Macedonia have slowed the acceptance of this conclusion by Serbia as a whole. "It's an enormous problem," said Yugoslavian editor Veran Matic. "People in Serbia these days say, 'See, these Albanians are evil in general, and Milosevic was right.'" The only way to transcend this brand of primitive thinking is to shift control of thought and emotion to the advanced neural system and realize that Albanians—or any other group—cannot be stereotyped. Each group is a collection of unique individuals.

No species other than humans is capable of committing these kinds of horrors on the scale we see in Chechnya, or in a thousand other genocides and mass slaughters that have taken place over recorded history. And no nation is exempt. In the spring of 2001 it was revealed that Bob Kerrey, a former governor and U.S. senator who once ran for president, had led a seven-member squad of commandos during the Vietnam War that, during a night raid in February 1969, killed perhaps twenty civilians, including women and children as young as three years old. Kerrey received the Bronze Star after falsely reporting that his squad killed twenty-one Vietcong guerrillas in the attack. He received the Congressional Medal of Honor for his bravery in a later action in which he was seriously wounded. One of the former commandos said that most of the civilians that night were rounded up and shot at point-blank range on Kerrey's orders. Kerrey and the other members of the squad denied this account and said the killings took place after they were fired on in the Mekong Delta hamlet. "Though it could be justified militarily," said Kerrey in an April 2001 speech, "I could never make my own peace with what happened that night. I have been haunted by it for thirty-two years." The account of the raid set off a firestorm of controversy and a flood of accounts of atrocities that were committed by both sides during that long and ghastly war.[2]

HUMAN EVOLUTION: THE ARRIVAL OF THE MODERN HUMAN MIND

Other species are cruel as well, but their cruelty is almost insignificant compared with ours. In one famous case, primatologist Jane Goodall documented the extermination of one band of common chimpanzees by another at the Gombe Stream Reserve in Tanzania. But this only amounted to the killing of five mature males and at least one female by a rival band of eight mature males. And it took more than three years of intermittent attacks before the deed was completed and the victorious band took over the other band's territory. Humans, too, are territorial and this, scientists presume, is an important source of our innate tendency to divide the world into us versus them and fight over land. Yet for several million years, our hominid ancestors lived like chimpanzees in small bands using crude tools that could do relatively little damage. Around thirty-five thousand years ago, however, something mysterious happened that allowed our highest aspirations—and our darkest hates—to flower in ways the world had never known.

The Cro-Magnons lived in Europe during a portion of the last ice age. Archaeologists have a name for this period—Upper Paleolithic—and it covers the span of time from about forty thousand years ago to ten thousand years ago, when the ice age ended. An accumulation of discoveries of prehistoric artifacts and cave art, particularly the magnificent cave at Chauvet in France, which is both the most recently discovered of these Cro-Magnon caves and the oldest, has been dated to around thirty-two thousand years ago. Scholars see cave paintings and the artifacts that accompany them as critical but elusive clues to human nature itself. Although Upper Paleolithic art "is not relevant to the origin of modern humans, it is relevant to what it means to be modern humans," said anthropologist Margaret Conkey. Scholars do not use the term *revolution* lightly, yet many of them term the astonishing yet mysterious burst of creativity among the Cro-Magnons as the Upper Paleolithic revolution—a turning point in the history of life on Earth that marks the arrival on the world stage of the modern human mind. But with the modern mind emerged the beginnings of modern weapons— and the modern way of death.

Anatomically, Cro-Magnons were just like us. It seems, in fact, that our modern anatomy, including our exceptionally large brain, has been in place for at least a hundred thousand years. If you dressed Cro-Magnon women and men in modern attire, they would be indistinguishable from anyone else on the street. Nevertheless, we are confronted by a baffling riddle: although humans have looked like us for the past hundred thousand years or more, during much of that time they did not seem to act like us. The archaeological record, imperfect as it is, indicates that there were few signs of novelty among early human populations. Their tools remained basically the same—simple and uncomplicated—for tens of thousands of years. "If the origin of the human mind is to be understood, it is important to identify signals of distinctly nonhuman behavior," observed writer Roger Lewin. "Lack of innovation is surely one of them." Yet roughly thirty-five thousand years ago something remarkable happened among the previously stagnant Cro-Magnons—modern human behavior suddenly emerged. Within the buried remnants of Cro-Magnon villages and in their caves we find the first clear evidence of those quintessential human traits: originality, creativity, and invention.[3]

Although there are a few scattered signs of earlier experimentation, the Cro-Magnons displayed the first unmistakable burst of rapid innovation and modern human imagination. Simple stone weapons that had remained almost unchanged for well over a hun-

dred thousand years were swept away by new tools and other imple-
ments of exceptionally fine craftsmanship using materials that had
never before been employed: antler, bone, clay, and ivory from
mammoth tusks. There were tools constructed from several different pieces—a spear point set in a shaft, for example. In these compound tools we can see the early stirring of a trend that would
ultimately lead to the machine age (and the machine gun). Art
emerged for the first time not only in the cave paintings but also in
the tools themselves. Everyday items were decorated and carved.
From the cave of La Madeleine in France we find a spear-thrower
into which is carved the head of a bison licking its flank. From the
cave of Mas d'Azil comes another spear-thrower decorated with the
figure of an ibex giving birth to a calf. There are also mysterious
geometric features in many of the cave paintings: rectangles, curves,
grids, parallel lines of dots. Huge quantities of small carvings as well
as beads and jewelry used in the new art of body adornment have
been found at Upper Paleolithic sites. Flutes and other musical
instruments were carved from bone. There are graves in which the
dead are carefully laid out, covered with jewelry and flowers—a
poignant indication of spiritual awareness. Cro-Magnon settlements
grow in size, and there is evidence of long-distance trading in both
useful items and luxuries. More important, the style of art and art-
work varies, not only over time but from settlement to settlement
and region to region, a sure sign of original minds at work.

We can trace our obsession with novelty straight back to these
people. The Cro-Magnons, with their ever-changing art and artifacts, are the first to exemplify the peculiar human tendency to be
rapidly bored and perpetually curious. They were the first to produce different weapons and different cultures.

Why have humans evolved such a positive response to novelty
while other species have not? The answer seems to lie in the strange
twists of natural selection. Most animals are specialists. They are
born with some combination of keen senses, innate behaviors, and
specialized teeth, claws, and other physical attributes necessary to

make a living in the wild. At birth, a lion or bear has all the tools it needs to occupy its niche as a top predator. It must survive only to maturity. Not so a human being. We are generalists, a rarity in the natural world. We are born with the ability to walk upright, freeing our hands. Yet our hands alone are not adequate to keep us alive. When faced with a lion's teeth and claws, our hands are useless— neither strong enough nor menacing enough to protect us. But our hands are not meant to act alone. Unlike a lion's claws or an eagle's talons, and to a degree unmatched by other species, our hands have evolved as incomparable tools for making other tools. The human hand has developed a long, flexible, opposable thumb, allowing it to grasp and manipulate objects with extreme precision. Though by themselves our hands are virtually worthless against a large preda- tor, when holding a handmade ax, or spear, or gun, they can be deadly. This, then, is a crucial difference between humans and other animals. A lion cannot improve its teeth and claws through its own efforts. It is stuck with the tools it was born with. But human beings make their own tools. We produce whole technologies. And there is a powerful incentive to innovate. Improved tools mean a greater chance of survival.

Tools, of course, vastly amplified the negative effects of human anger and hate, but they also magnified the benefits of cooperative efforts mediated by positive emotions such as joy and love. With our tools, we can slaughter each other or travel to the moon.

To control and guide our toolmaking hands we have evolved a phenomenally large brain that contains relatively few instinctive behaviors yet has one astonishing innate talent: the ability to speak language so complex that it can express the most abstract and eso- teric thoughts and create elaborate mental models of the world around us. Tools plus language have produced culture, perhaps the most far-reaching human innovation. Through culture we organize ourselves into intricate societies and mighty civilizations that enable us to accumulate knowledge and wealth that can be passed from gen- eration to generation. This not only allows us to design the best tools possible given our sophisticated understanding of the environment, but also to flexibly design our behavior to take maximum advantage of our improving tools. Thus the versatile human brain, whose anatomy has remained unchanged for perhaps a hundred thousand years or more, is equally capable of wielding a stone ax with lethal efficiency, piloting a jet fighter in air-to-air combat, or using computer software to probe the secrets of our genetic code and design imaginative new medicines or horrific new weapons of bioterrorism. Which emotions prod us to take full advantage of the power of our hands and brain? Unquestionably, fear and hate are among the most important. We constantly seek better ways to defend ourselves and advance our interests. But we also experience the sheer pleasure of discovering what our minds, our hands, and our tools can do. Curiosity for its own sake is a recurring theme in human culture. Unfortunately, this curiosity has led us to create ever more novel and lethal technologies of war, death, and hate. This same curiosity, however, may spur us to find new ways to curb warfare and subdue hatred.

THE EMERGENCE OF LARGE-SCALE WARFARE

The entire area of research on human aggression is exceptionally controversial. Some scientists believe that large-scale warfare did not emerge until the appearance of more settled communities around ten thousand years ago. They believe that the Neanderthals died off over several millennia because they lost out in the economic competition with modern humans. And it is true that most of the existing hard evidence for violence among humans—in the form of skeletons showing severe injury probably inflicted by other humans—does not begin to appear in the archaeological record until around fifteen thousand years ago. But other scientists think warfare is much older. They point out that humans and common chimpanzees both engage in warfare. Each species may have inherited the practice from their common ancestors seven million years ago. These scientists account for the lack of archaeological evidence by pointing out how rare it is for such a record to exist, particularly because nomadic and seminomadic cultures would have had few cemeteries or other burial practices that might have preserved remains for thousands of years. Some point to suggestive evidence that around the time of the Upper Paleolithic revolution the efficiency of human hunting seems to have greatly improved. From this era onward, whenever human populations entered new territories—from Australia to North and South America—large game animals suddenly began disappearing in enormous numbers, often going extinct. During this same period the Neanderthals vanished. Wouldn't we expect Upper Paleolithic humans to have warred on each other as well?

Whatever the exact origin of warfare and the true fate of the Neanderthals, it seems clear that the Cro-Magnons developed some form of complex social organization that could be put to lethal use. The general importance of this innovation cannot be overestimated. For complex social organization gives humans a cultural form of unparalleled flexibility that can be shaped to accomplish a virtually infinite number of tasks—from hunting a herd of mastodons to landing on the moon. Individually, a naked human being is laughably weak compared to a lion or bear. But through complex social organization, human beings are almost infinitely powerful—powerful enough to wipe most other species, including ourselves, off the face of the Earth, whether by accident or design.

Before the Cro-Magnons, technology lagged far behind biology. The human brain was extremely advanced, but human tools were very simple. After the Upper Paleolithic revolution, however, biology began to lag behind technology, and it lags further and further behind with each passing century. Our emotional biology, in particular, has difficulty controlling technologies that are becoming ever more complex and powerful. The twentieth century was the bloodiest in history because we were unable to make the rational and emotional accommodations necessary to keep our tools of war in check. Constructive emotions such as joy and compassion were too often overwhelmed by fear, anger, and hate. Today the threat remains, and we continue to live under the cloud of weapons of mass destruction: nuclear, chemical, and biological.

6

THE PRIMITIVE MIND

EIGHT MONTHS AFTER SHE DISAPPEARED, they finally found fifteen-year-old Elyse Pahler. Her half-naked body was exhumed from a shallow grave. Over the grave, someone had drawn a pentagram. The police were led to the burial site, about half a mile from Elyse's home near San Luis Obispo, California, by a sixteen-year-old acquaintance of hers, Royce Casey. He told police that he and two friends—sixteen-year-old Jacob Delashmutt and fourteen-year-old Joseph Fiorella—had spent months planning to kill a young girl as a sacrifice to Satan, hoping to bring fame to the band they had formed. The band's name was Hatred.

The three boys pleaded guilty to killing Elyse, and each was sentenced to twenty-five years to life. Before entering his plea, Fiorella told authorities that prior to the murder the three had stayed up several nights in a row, taking drugs and listening over and over to their favorite music by a popular heavy metal group called Slayer, whose often violent, X-rated lyrics feature torture, rape, and the satanic sacrifice of women.

Casey said the boys lured Elyse to the eucalyptus grove, telling her that they would smoke marijuana. Instead, they attacked her, choked her with a belt, and then took turns stabbing her with a hunting knife. She reportedly fell to the ground, praying and calling for her mother. The boys then jumped on the back of her neck until she died. They left but returned later to have sex with the corpse.

"It gets inside your head," Fiorella was quoted as saying about the music of Slayer, which has written such songs as "Altar of Sacrifice," "Tormentor," "PostMortem," "Kill Again," "Serenity in Murder," and "Necrophiliac." "It's almost embarrassing that I was so influenced by the music," he said. "It started to influence the way I looked at things."

Elyse's parents have filed suit against Slayer and their recording company, which is affiliated with Sony Corporation. They argue that the band should be held at least partially liable for their daughter's death. They contend that Slayer's music exerts a dangerous influence over disturbed adolescents. The courts have consistently held that the right of artistic expression under the First Amendment protects recording artists from being liable for crimes committed by people who listen to their music. But the Pahlers argued that the real issue was marketing and that the band and its recording company violated California law by marketing harmful and obscene products to minors. "This isn't a case about art. It's about marketing," said David Pahler, the father of Elyse. "Slayer and others in the industry have developed sophisticated strategies to sell death metal music to adolescent boys. They don't care whether the violent, misogynistic message in these lyrics causes children to do harmful things. They couldn't care less what their fans did to our daughter. All they care about is money." The Pahlers argue that the warning stickers that record companies place on such albums actually serve as an advertisement to adolescents, because few record stores enforce age requirements for those who buy this kind of music.

The case finally came to trial in January 2001. Sony and Slayer were represented by some of the top First Amendment lawyers in the country. The judge expressed serious reservations about the merits of the lawsuit but gave the Pahlers more time to try to substantiate their argument that it was the marketing of the music to minors that prompted their daughter's slaying.[1]

This case is part of the larger controversy that has involved the Federal Trade Commission, the U.S. Surgeon General, and many politicians and parent groups. It involves the marketing of violent films and other forms of entertainment to minors and the possible role that such entertainment plays in provoking hatred and violence. We will explore the influence of the media more fully in Chapter 12. But for now it is important to realize that we are the only species that regularly uses art to influence our thoughts and feelings. The mystery of art and human behavior goes all the way back to the Cro-Magnons and the beginning of human culture. Art serves as a kind of dividing line between the primitive mind of early hominids and the modern mind of the past forty thousand years. And art continues to have the capacity to release the primitive power of the mind, for good or ill.

CRO-MAGNON ART

Anthropologist Richard Leakey has had a chance to inspect some of the most important Cro-Magnon cave sites, several of which have been closed to the general public to protect their fragile treasures. His visits included the celebrated cave of Lascaux in southwestern France. Lascaux, discovered in 1940, has been closed to the public since 1963, although its seventeen-thousand-year-old paintings have been marvelously duplicated in a nearby museum called Lascaux II. As a child, Leakey visited the original Lascaux with his parents, Mary and Louis Leakey, two giants of anthropology. When he returned as an adult, the "images of bulls, horses, and deer were as transfixing on this occasion as they were when I was a youth, as they seem to move before one's eyes."

He described a trip to another spectacular site: the cave of the Tuc d'Audoubert, one of three decorated caves on land owned by Count Robert Bégouën: "A narrow, winding passageway leads from bright sunlight several kilometers into the deepest gloom. The count's flashlight brings the walls to light with dancing shadows, and the clay floor glows orange. Eventually one reaches a small rotunda at the end of the passageway, and the count shines his light with appropriate drama on a spot at the center of the chamber, the ceiling sloping low to the floor beyond. There one sees the figures of two bison, superbly sculpted from clay, resting against rocks.

"I had seen pictures of these famous figures, of course, but nothing prepared me for reality. Measuring about one-sixth normal size, they are perfect in form, full of movement in their motionlessness; they encapsulate life. The skill of the artists who sculpted these figures 15,000 years ago is breathtaking, especially when one remembers the conditions under which they must have worked. Using simple lamps charged with animal fat, they carried clay from a neighboring chamber and created the animals' form with their fingers and some kind of flat implement; eyes, nostrils, mouth, and mane were created with a sharp stick or bone. . . . A third figure is crudely engraved in the floor of the cave near the other two, and there is another statuette, small and again in clay. Most intriguing, however, are heel prints, probably those of children, around the figures. Were the children playing while the artists worked? If so, why do we not see footprints of the artists? Were the heel prints made during a ritual, encapsulating some part of Upper Paleolithic mythology in which the bison figures were the central part?"

A team of archaeologists studied the acoustical qualities of three Cro-Magnon caves, including the cave of the Tuc d'Audoubert. They found that the areas of the cave with the highest resonance were most likely to have paintings, sculptures, or engravings. They commented in their report on the "stunning impact of cave resonance, an experience that would have surely been enhanced in the flickering light of simple lamps back in the Ice Age."

"It requires little imagination," wrote Leakey, "to think of Upper Paleolithic people chanting incantations in front of cave paintings. The unusual nature of the images, and the fact that they are often deep in the most inaccessible parts of caves, begs the question of a ritual. When one stands in front of an Ice Age creation now, as I did with the bison of Le Tuc d'Audoubert, the ancient voices force themselves on one's mind, with an accompaniment, perhaps, of drums, flutes, and whistles. . . . The language of art is powerful to those who understand it, and puzzling to those who do not. What we do know is that here was the modern human mind at work, spinning symbolism and abstraction in a way that only *Homo sapiens* is capable of doing. Although we cannot yet be sure of the process by which modern humans evolved, we do know that it involved the emergence of the kind of mental world each of us experiences today."[2]

Symbolism, abstraction, chanting, rituals—Leakey puts his finger on key elements that would differentiate the behavior of Cro-Magnons from any other species. If these were gods or spirits that the Cro-Magnons created, were they benign, or dark? Did they demand animal sacrifice? Human sacrifice? We don't know. Many cultures in the past ten thousand years featured religions that were quite bloody, including not only human sacrifice but cannibalism. What of these very earliest religions? Were they based on love? Or hate? Or some mixture? We are left to look at this art and wonder.

LANGUAGE

Yet the one human trait that underlies all these artistic elements is language, spoken and unspoken—the language of art and the language of ideas. Our complex language, which we learn automatically as children, is a singularly powerful tool not only for communication but also for abstract thought. Through it, we convey what we love and what we hate. And abstract thought underlies higher-level novelty. Although human beings speak many different languages, every language is generated by the same brain areas, and all languages have deep structural similarities. No other species has a complex language capacity like ours. Gorillas and chimpanzees have been taught human sign language, and there have been some amazing results. But even the best of them has developed a vocabulary of only a few hundred words with no evidence of complex syntax. The average human has a vocabulary of many thousands of words that can be combined into an infinite number of meaningful sentences.

Thus it may well have been complex spoken language that moved human culture into a new realm of innovation—from one dominated by new yet the same (copying the same tool types and behavior patterns over and over) to one that embodied the new and different. To devise a truly original tool, for example, you must first generate a model of it in your mind so that you can ponder and refine your ideas, perhaps talk about them with others, and plan exactly how you are going to fabricate it. "The role of language in communication first evolved as a side effect in the construction of reality," argued UCLA neurologist Harry Jerison. "We can think of language as being merely an expression of another neural contribution to the construction of mental imagery." Language frees the human imagination, giving us access to the past and the future. "Only language could have broken through the prison of immediate experience in which every other creature is locked, releasing us into infinite freedoms of space and time," said linguist Derrick Bickerton.

So was it language, not tools, that ignited the Upper Paleolithic revolution among the Cro-Magnons, producing the first recognizable modern human minds? Many scholars think so, but the issue is fiercely controversial. There is a wide divergence of opinion about how this might have happened. Some argue that spoken language is a trait that goes far back in the human lineage, perhaps all the way to the australopithecines. But others contend that complex spoken language is unique to modern humans and that earlier hominid species probably did not speak at all, except in the way that chimpanzees, gorillas, and other primates communicate. Yet one nagging question troubles everyone: if *Homo sapiens*, which appeared at least a hundred thousand years ago, had already mastered spoken language, what took humans so long to slough off the old stone technology and initiate the innovative, imaginative culture that has characterized human activity ever since?

Archaeologist Randall White, one of those who argues that complex spoken language emerged only about a hundred thousand years ago, believes that it took tens of thousands of years for the language capacity to mature. "This revolution was affected by neurally capable populations of *Homo sapiens* in an exceedingly long struggle," he said. "By 35,000 years ago, those populations . . . had mastered language and culture as we presently know them." He cites seven sudden Cro-Magnon breakthroughs that he attributes to the full maturing of spoken language: a rapid acceleration of technological and cultural innovation, a shift to bone and antler and away from total reliance on stone for the creation of tools, the inception of artistic expression, the beginning of regional differences in culture, evidence of long-distance trade, a substantial increase in population density, and the deliberate burial of the dead.

But the late Harvard archaeologist Glynn Isaac was one who argued that spoken language slowly developed for several million years and that innovations in stone technologies—particularly the introduction of the Acheulian technology about 1.6 million years ago and the Levalloisian tools roughly 250,000 years ago—were paralleled by advances in language and culture. "My intuition in this matter is that we see in the stone tools the reflection of changes that were affecting culture as a whole," he said. "Probably more and more of all behavior, often but not always including toolmaking behavior, involved complex rule systems. In the realm of communications, this presumably consisted more and more of elaborate syntax and extended vocabulary; in the realm of social relations, perhaps increasing numbers of defined categories, obligations, and prescriptions; in the realm of subsistence, increasing bodies of communicable know-how." Although White and Isaac strongly disagree about how long hominids have had complex language, their overall conclusion is similar: the gradual increase in language capacity finally reached a critical mass among the Cro-Magnons around thirty-five thousand years ago, which triggered the Upper Paleolithic revolution.

The issue of when humans began to speak is unresolved and may be unresolvable. Both sides have searched the fossil record, looking for the presence or absence in early hominids of the physical traits needed to produce spoken language. But the evidence is subject to contradictory interpretations, in part because of the incompleteness of many skeletons and in part because language relies on the brain and other soft body parts that don't fossilize. "What it is going to take to *settle* the debate about when language originated in humans is a time machine," paleoneurologist Dean Falk ruefully observed. But there is indirect evidence that by fifty or sixty thousand years ago all humans were speaking complex language exactly the same way we do today. There had, by then, been a great geographic dispersal of *Homo sapiens* into relatively isolated populations, all of whom spoke languages with the same underlying structure. The archaeological and genetic evidence indicate, for example, that Australia was populated around fifty thousand years ago. Because it is highly unlikely that an identically structured capacity for complex language would have developed independently in these different populations, it seems safe to assume that this language ability had already evolved in the ancestral population of all these human groups. Thus it is probable that Cro-Magnons had been using complex language many thousands of years before the Upper Paleolithic revolution.[3]

Whatever the actual mechanisms and time line, the hypothesis that humanity's first modern burst of creativity somehow involved complex spoken language is seductive. For this kind of language does many things. Just naming objects is an act of creativity. If we can name things, we can organize them. And if we can organize them, perhaps we can control them. Language is a supple and powerful tool for making dynamic mental models and imagining how things might be transformed in new and different ways. Language gives us a simple, efficient way to share our dreams. It unleashes one of the most formidable human forces: persuasion. A visionary energized by love or hate might be able to use the power of persuasion to overcome even the most determined resistance. Both love and hate are contagious; they spread through our words. But when joy is reinforced by the concrete results of originality and imagination—better tools, spellbinding art, richer adornments, greater prosperity, happier lives—the momentum for liberating the human mind and human culture from their static shackles may be irresistible.

THE RISE OF CIVILIZATION

Yet there is one final avenue of analysis that might yield insights into the mysterious origin and timing of Cro-Magnon innovation. The Upper Paleolithic revolution has certain parallels to another revolution that occurred little more than five thousand years ago: the sudden rise of civilization in the great river valleys of the Old World. Civilization represents an immensely significant shift away from the nomadic hunter-gatherer or scavenger-gatherer way of life, which dominated most of human history, to a more settled life in cities and towns. The hallmark of civilization is elaborate social differentiation and specialization; and because cities have the wealth to support large classes of artists, craftspeople, and intellectuals, they became—and remain—the most potent centers of novelty in human culture. Within a few centuries after the first cities arose in the Near East, Egypt, India, and China, civilization produced such far-reaching innovations as writing, wheeled vehicles, bronze tools, monumental architecture, sailing ships, and the plow.

Because it happened relatively recently, we have a much better understanding of the reasons for the origin of civilization. Its roots go back about ten thousand years to the end of the last ice age, when a drier climate and the spread of deserts seems to have led populations of hunter-gatherers in the Near East to establish more permanent settlements near reliable sources of water. These people began experimenting with the cultivation of certain types of wild grasses, which led to the domestication of wheat and barley. At around the same time, animals began to be domesticated for meat and milk. With these momentous innovations came one of the most significant inventions in human history: agriculture. It was agriculture that became the foundation for civilization because, unlike the average hunter-gatherer, farmers can produce much more food than they need to feed their families. The surplus can be used to feed city dwellers. But even after agriculture was perfected in the Near East around 6500 B.C., it would be roughly three thousand years before the first civilizations began to emerge. As with the Upper Paleolithic revolution, there was a significant delay in making the final breakthrough. But in this case, we have a pretty good idea why.

Although early agriculture was highly productive, it was not at first a particularly stable way of life. It tended to exhaust the soil after a few years, forcing farmers to move on. Several thousand years were needed to master agriculture in the large river valleys, where a constant supply of river water allowed the construction of intricate irrigation networks and, especially in Egypt, annual floods renewed the fertility of the soil. Along the Tigris and Euphrates Rivers in what is now Iraq, the first stable agricultural communities slowly began to form, and population densities increased. More people meant more complex social arrangements. A priestly class arose that also served an administrative function. Priests supervised the construction and maintenance of irrigation systems and mediated disputes among the farmers. Supported by the large surpluses of food generated by this new style of agriculture, settlements increased in size until the lower Tigris-Euphrates valley was dotted with small cities. These were the cities of the Sumerians of Mesopotamia, and they seem to have constituted humanity's first civilization. Recent excavations have indicated, however, that small cities may have been spread across a larger area than was originally assumed—beyond the boundaries of the Tigris-Euphrates valley. And some archaeologists now believe that civilization appeared somewhat earlier than we once thought. Nevertheless, within a few centuries of the emergence of the Sumerians, civilizations also arose along the Nile in Egypt and in India along the Indus River. It took several more centuries before civilization emerged in the Yellow River valley of China. From that time to this, human cultural evolution has disproportionately centered on the rise and fall of civilizations. And with civilizations we have moved into the realm of warfare—and hate—on a grand scale.[4]

CONSCIOUSNESS: SOURCE OF SELF-AWARENESS AND SELF-HATRED

The process that began ten thousand years ago provides us with a suggestive pattern. An important initial innovation (agriculture) fails to flower into a new cultural form (civilization) until it finds the right environment (large river valleys). But once river valleys were successfully farmed, their food surpluses allowed populations to increase, requiring a more sophisticated form of social structure that culminated in cities and civilization. Can we compare this pattern of change to the Upper Paleolithic revolution? There are points of similarity. What was the fundamental innovation that was waiting for the right conditions to evolve into a more creative form of social organization? The obvious answer is complex spoken language. But there is more to it than that. Besides complex language, the modern human mind has another ingredient that we have not yet considered: consciousness. This is the source of both self-awareness and self-hatred.

Consciousness is even more controversial than language. Just defining it is difficult, but certainly it includes being able to generate a mental model of the environment that includes the self. In other words, as conscious beings we are self-aware. We are aware of our own shifting thoughts, feelings, and motivations, and this allows us to imaginatively infer what is going on in other people's minds—a valuable ability in a social species if we are trying to anticipate and influence what others are going to do. But the mental models we create and manipulate contain more than the facts, as we perceive them, about the world and ourselves. They contain our values: what we want and don't want, like and dislike. As we communicate with others and interact with the environment, these values can change. Innovation in tools and artistic expression, for example, can become more highly prized.

Just as we are not sure when complex spoken language emerged in human populations, we are unsure when consciousness first appeared. Unlike agriculture, however, which was a human invention, language and consciousness appear to be innate biological traits under genetic control, not cultural inventions. Healthy children automatically and without instruction pick up the language spoken around them. At birth, infants are sensitive to the full range of sounds used in every human language. All five thousand or so existing human languages bear fundamental similarities, and any child can become fluent in any language if he or she is immersed in it at an early enough age. Similarly, children become self-aware as a normal part of development, though our understanding of this process remains extremely limited. Most children begin to recognize themselves in a mirror between eighteen and twenty-four months of age. Some experts believe that neither fully complex language nor consciousness existed until the time of the Cro-Magnons. Some even argue that the Cro-Magnons themselves were not self-aware in the same way that we are, although this view is in the distinct minority. Actually, there are a number of signs that Cro-Magnons were quite self-aware and that their art was a reflection of their consciousness.

Many of the cave paintings contain meticulously rendered hand-prints in which the artists placed their hands against the wall and carefully spattered paint around them to leave a clear impression of the outline. Although the cave artists generally portrayed animals rather than human beings, there are several examples of chimeras—animals with human features. And a number of examples survive of human figures carved in ivory and other materials. The elaborate burial of the dead by the Cro-Magnons is also persuasive evidence of self-awareness.

In fact, consciousness may be extremely old. Many studies suggest that of all animal species only humans and the great apes—chimpanzees, gorillas, and orangutans—are able to recognize themselves in a mirror and pass other tests indicating self-awareness. If provided with a mirror, wild chimpanzees, for example, will usually learn within a day or two to use it just as humans do—to assiduously groom themselves. In contrast, monkeys and smaller apes either ignore their own reflection or treat it is as another animal. They do not seem to be self-aware. Genetic and fossil studies indicate that apelike primates evolved from monkeys around thirty million years ago. This ancestral population would ultimately give rise to all apes, large and small, as well as hominids. Around twenty million years ago, the first ape group—the ancestors of the gibbons—split off as a separate species. Gibbons are small, tree-dwelling apes found in Southeast Asia. They show no sign of self-awareness and do not recognize themselves in a mirror. After the gibbons branched off, the remaining apelike population contained the common ancestors of humans and all large apes. The first kind of great ape to emerge from this ancient population was the ancestor of the modern orangutan, which split off around fifteen million years ago. Like the other great apes, orangutans recognize themselves in a mirror. Gorillas diverged around ten million years ago. The remaining primate population eventually split in two, with upright-walking hominids diverging from our closest ape relatives, the knuckle-walking chimpanzees, around seven million years ago.

It seems unlikely that consciousness evolved independently in humans, orangutans, gorillas, and chimpanzees, but rather that hominids and the great apes inherited self-awareness from a common ancestor. This suggests that consciousness arose in the ancestral apelike primate population between the time that non-self-aware gibbons and self-aware orangutans branched off. In other words, basic consciousness may have evolved between about twenty million and fifteen million years ago.[5]

HUMAN SOCIAL ORGANIZATION

What may have been missing from human culture prior to the Upper Paleolithic revolution was a form of social organization large enough and sophisticated enough to allow the complex specialization necessary for innovative human culture to begin. Upper Paleolithic Europe toward the end of the last ice age may have provided the hospitable circumstances necessary for this increase in social complexity, including a more moderate climate and large migrating herds of animals. Linguistically related semipermanent settlements may have rapidly increased in population, allowing the development of trade over short and long distances. Thus, there may have been two general stages of human cultural breakthrough over the past forty thousand years. The first was a protocivilization that emerged most dramatically in the Upper Paleolithic based on loosely connected groups of cyclically stable settlements with relatively large populations. Some of these settlements seem to have been arrayed around spiritually oriented cave sites such as Altamira. This protocivilization was probably built on advanced hunting techniques and possibly the management of game animals such as reindeer, which may have been an early precursor of full-blown animal domestication. This economic base would have provided the surplus resources necessary to create a complex social organization. The second stage of cultural breakthrough began around thirty thousand years later in the Near East with the gradual emergence of true civilization based on the invention of agriculture, the domestication of animals, and the development of the city-based culture we call civilization— an advanced form of complex social organization that remains dominant today.

Both these cultural innovations represented a quantum leap in human social organization and innovation. In the case of civilization, farmers in the great river valleys of the Old World went from simple villages and tools to the wheel, the plow, and the great pyramids in only a few generations. In the case of protocivilization, Cro-Magnons went from the primitive, stereotyped social organization and technology, which *Homo sapiens* inherited from their ancestors when they first emerged more than a hundred thousand years ago, to an innovative culture and technology. The key to both protocivilization and civilization, it seems, was to have a large enough population and a settled enough way of life to allow complex specialization, the hallmark of all forms of civilization. A protocivilization would allow humans to begin to fulfill the virtually unlimited potential of their big brains, complex language, self-awareness, symbolic thought, and capacity for culture and technology, which could not fully flower within a primitive social organization operating at a subsistence level of existence.

Given the primitive social organization (small bands of nomadic hunters) in which the overwhelming majority of *Homo sapiens* probably lived for the sixty thousand years or so before the Upper Paleolithic revolution, it is not surprising that specialization would have been rudimentary: the men hunted and scavenged while the women gathered plant foods and cared for the children. Survival was constantly threatened, and leisure was at a premium, enjoyed sporadically at best. Yet think of the enormous time it must have taken to decorate Altamira and the other Cro-Magnon caves. The Cro-Magnon culture was clearly vigorous enough to spare these artists for long periods from the daily grind of accumulating food and protecting the group. Only a protocivilization of the kind that must have existed during the Upper Paleolithic revolution could produce the relative wealth, leisure, and safety that would permit the emergence of complex specialization. In this setting, skills could evolve and be perfected through concentrated effort, including specialized artists (who decorated the caves and created musical instruments and new forms of body adornment), shamans (who created the rituals in the caves, including the music), toolmakers (who developed compound tools), traders (who traveled great distances seeking valuable goods), hunters (who developed complex, highly organized, and highly productive methods of hunting), and, perhaps, killers motivated by primitive fear and hatred. This last group would probably have been a subset of hunters or a new dimension of the hunting culture that was devoted to efficiently bringing down the most dangerous game of all: human beings. These specialized killers are still with us today. We call them soldiers. The first victims of this new culture may have been the Neanderthals. The latest victims are still being tallied in places such as the Middle East, the Balkans, and Rwanda.[6]

Specialized killers within a complex social organization can be frighteningly effective. Advanced technology is not necessary. It took only one hundred days of interethnic savagery in 1994 to kill eight hundred thousand people in Rwanda (some estimate the toll to be closer to a million), mostly with machetes and clubs and only a relatively small number of firearms. Compare this to the killing that Jane Goodall documented in Tanzania of one small band of chimpanzees by another beginning in 1970. The victorious chimpanzees, operating within a primitive social organization that may resemble that of early hominids, took more than three years to accomplish the task through a series of skirmishes in which victims were beaten, kicked, and bitten.

THE DRIVE FOR MEANING

The Upper Paleolithic revolution seems to mark the era when humans shifted fully from stereotyped behaviors to self-created, innovative meaning as a guide for their culture. "The drive for meaning," said psychologist Uta Frith, "appears to be a general organizing principle of the mind. . . ." Without our sense of meaning, we are lost and dysfunctional even though we may be entirely conscious. The survival and reproduction of human beings is guided by flexible structures of cognitive and emotional meaning, not detailed instinctive behaviors. We are a generalist species, individually frail compared to other predators. We survived and ultimately thrived using tools, complex language, and culture. Genes prescribe the regularities of perception and mental development that shape our acquisition of culture. But our genetic programming endows us, in large part, with general capacities rather than specific instincts. Language is a perfect example. We are born with the capacity to learn any natural language. We are not, however, programmed to speak one single language, although there are certain structural similarities among all human languages. Most important, we are not born knowing what to say. We are free to use the power of language in novel and infinitely varied ways.[7]

Genes look to the past. They preserve adaptations that have functioned successfully to adapt a species to its niche. Through instincts, which are hardwired into the brain, genes determine the meaning and purpose of most animals' lives, innately fixing what is important and unimportant. They shape not only the most basic urges such as feeding, mating, and survival but also more elaborate behaviors such as nest building and the rearing of young. Within eighteen hours of hatching, for example, a duckling will imprint on its mother. The duckling does not know that this is its mother or even understand the concept of mother. It is simply programmed by its genes to follow anything that exhibits certain visual and auditory cues. Konrad Lorenz, the Nobel Prize–winning ethologist who first described parental imprinting in the scientific literature, showed that in the absence of their mother, ducklings permanently imprint on almost anything that is presented to them in the right way: a red ball, a box, even him. It was not unusual to see Lorenz walking around the farm where he conducted his research followed by a group of ducklings that had imprinted on him.

For humans, however, meaning is learned, not innate. It is the product of an ever-shifting scheme of categories and values created by individuals, groups (such as the family), and the culture as a whole. The categorization of the world by the advanced neural system through learning and memory is an essential function of the complex human brain, which creates representations or models of the inner and outer environment and the interaction of the self with the world—a process we call consciousness. Human meaning looks to the present and the future as well as the past. It is open to novelty, not just tradition. Meaning shapes our values, which in turn shape our purposes and goals. Our core motivation consists of our primitive emotions. Joy, for example, is an extremely useful and flexible emotion because it allows us to value almost anything we choose—from general relativity to baseball cards—and receive an emotional reward whenever we accomplish one of our goals, whether it is finding a new solution to the general relativity equations or acquiring a baseball card signed by a famous slugger such as Mark McGwire or Barry Bonds. But hatred is also flexible; we are free to hate whatever or whomever we choose.

Our sense of time, space, and possibility separates us from all other species, even our closest relative, the chimpanzee, with whom we share roughly 99 percent of our genes. The 1 percent genetic difference, which shapes a brain that is larger and more complex than the chimpanzee's, gives us the intellectual power to transform ourselves—and the world—through pure thought. "Although chimps are much closer to us than some people would like to admit," said zoologist Desmond Morris, "we are somehow over a whole new threshold, even a whole new world. The human mind has become just that little bit more complicated than the chimpanzee's mind. And that was enough to take us not ten degrees but a million degrees further. We can sit down and close our eyes and think for two hours, and when we open our eyes at the end of that time, apparently having done nothing, we are different people."[8]

Because human beings have so little instinctive guidance, each of us is on a quest for meaning—meaning that provides values, purpose, and goals for us, both as individuals and as social beings. Although we may simply choose to accept the meaning supplied to us by our family or our culture, we have the capacity to define and redefine ourselves, our lives, and even the larger social order in light of our own values and experience. Love and hate can be powerful forces in shaping this process. Conflict among meaning systems is the source of some of our most profound hatreds, including the strife rooted at least partly in religion that roils the Middle East, Northern Ireland, the Balkans, and the Indian subcontinent.

The human brain has evolved the neural mechanisms necessary to construct our own purpose and goals by generating dynamic models of ourselves and the world that are pregnant with meaning. Language allows us to create meaning through stories and other complex sequences of ideas, both factual and imaginative. We search for meaning not only using natural language but also using culturally devised symbol systems such as written language and mathematics. Language is a potent force in establishing culture by enabling us to collectively define and share our meanings and purposes. It allows us to vicariously participate in the thoughts and feelings of others and create the elaborate behaviors and tools on which culture depends. Meaning depends on context, and context is often cultural, though it can also be individual or a manifestation of groups smaller than an entire culture. Art, including ice age art, and the other products of the human mind are full of meaning and symbolism within the context of a particular culture. When the culture is lost, however, the original context and meaning may be lost, too, unless there is some way to reconstruct it. The process of discerning meaning involves two steps: categorization and valuation. We are immersed in an infinite amount of stimuli, both internal and external. Our brain must divide this stimuli into useful categories, judge the relative importance of these categories, and use its judgments to guide our behavior. In other species, instinct through the genes both categorizes reality and assesses the importance of these categories to survival and reproduction. Because we have escaped much, but not all, of the instinctively preordained meaning that guides other species, we are comparatively free to apply whatever valuation standards we choose. We can choose complex categories and interconnect them in complex ways. Or we can follow our primitive tendency and choose the simple, binary categories that hate thrives on: us or them, friend or enemy, superior or inferior. We can even choose self-destructive values if we wish.

Researchers have found that the drive for meaning in human beings is part of our basic memory process. In one study, each member of a group of research subjects was told several stories. All the stories were fairly involved. Later, each individual was asked to recall the stories. According to neuroscientist Irving Kupfermann, "The versions that the subjects recalled were shorter and more coherent than the stories as originally told, containing reconstructions and syntheses of the original. The subjects were unaware that they were substituting, and they often felt most certain about reconstructed parts." The individuals were not consciously trying to fill in the gaps in their memory, concluded Kupfermann, "they were merely recalling in a way that interpreted the original material so it made sense." One of the fundamental findings of memory research is that the brain's multiple memory systems do not record what happens to us precisely as it occurs but actively shape and reshape experience into coherent frameworks of meaning. This is one reason eyewitness accounts sometimes prove shockingly inaccurate. Memory is not a mechanism of passive storage but an active process of reconstruction and reformulation that is part of the search for meaning. But this automatic drive for meaning can introduce distortions into our interpretation of reality that we must be alert to.[9]

An animal guided by instinct is designed to stay in the rut created by instinct. To such an animal, a novelty may spark fear—because it is something the animal is not instinctively prepared for—or no reaction at all—because the novelty is literally meaningless within the context of the animal's genetic program. In contrast, a species like ours with relatively little instinctive knowledge has evolved to be attentive to and curious about novelty, because novelty represents things we don't know about ourselves and our world. We create structures of meaning and behavior to explain what we don't innately know. We then use these structures to shape our culture and control our environment. We are designed to learn, and in order to learn effectively about our environment we must explore. Every novelty represents a challenge, an unknown. This is why we are innately curious. This is why we want to know about the stars, about our brain, our genes, our consciousness, about each other.

Though every normal human being is curious, the meaning systems we create also shape the application of that curiosity and the velocity of innovation. Western high-technology culture tends to encourage novelty and change at an almost breathtaking pace. Traditional cultures may prefer a more stately tempo.

Because we have the maximum behavioral flexibility of any species, we have the maximum propensity to be bored. Boredom not only tends to keep us from being stuck in a rut, it kicks us out of our ruts. Boredom (in the active, human sense) is an instrument of curiosity because it tends to keep us searching for new kinds of novelty in the environment and in ourselves. The exploration of novelty, no matter how esoteric it may seem, can lead to powerful new tools. Albert Einstein's purely mathematical insight that energy and matter are equivalent ($E = mc^2$) was later used to create not only nuclear energy but also nuclear weapons, the ultimate nightmare of hate.

For human beings, the brain must perform the primary function of conferring meaning and purpose on our existence. We are the exception. In virtually every other species, genes play a far greater role. Most animals deemphasize intelligence and rely almost completely on instinct, with learning and innovation playing only a subsidiary part. This is true even of the great apes. If we drive ourselves to extinction with our wildly dynamic culture, then this evolutionary experiment will have failed.

The enormous brain that fills our domed heads generates a vast variety of emotions. Not surprisingly, our motives for exploring our environment and ourselves are a mixed bag and include fear, hate, anxiety, greed, and pain. But boredom, joy, and love play a uniquely prominent role in the human emotional system as well, giving us a restless tendency to satisfy our curiosity for its own sake that can lead to spectacular breakthroughs. What any given individual finds boring or interesting is a product not only of cultural conditioning but of his or her unique tastes and experience. In exploring novelty, no one is interested in everything or is capable of exploring everything. Everyone is different. What you hate may fascinate me. Whom you hate may be my closest friend. The exceptional power of love and hate in human motivation flows from these emotions' fantastic flexibility. As a population of individuals with different tastes and interests, we collectively explore many different aspects of the environment and communicate our discoveries to each other using complex language. In this way we learn about things that personally interest us and may, perhaps, have great significance for our lives. Yet some of what we learn will be dark, even dangerous, and will have a negative influence. Some argue that the art that influenced the boys who killed Elyse Pahler had the capacity to release the primitive power of the mind for evil purposes. This was the tragedy for Elyse Pahler, for her family, and for the boys who killed her.

7

SELF-HATRED, SELF-ESTEEM, AND SUICIDE

ERIC HARRIS AND DYLAN KLEBOLD possessed the most dangerous emotional mix possible: angry, filled with hate, yet suicidal. The two teenagers made five secret videotapes documenting their motives for committing the most deadly high school attack in the nation's history. On one of the tapes the two spew out their hatred for "n———rs, spics, Jews, gays, f———ing whites." Says Klebold, "I hope we kill two hundred and fifty of you." Harris reportedly stopped taking his antidepressant medication to allow his anger to grow. "More rage. More rage," he says on one of the tapes. "Keep building it on." They made their last tape on the morning of April 20, 1999, just before leaving for Columbine High School, where they would kill thirteen people and wound twenty-three before killing themselves. "It's a half hour before our judgment day," Klebold says into the camera. "I didn't like life very much. Just know I'm going to a better place than here." Klebold then takes the camera and points it at Harris. "I know my mom and dad will be in shock and disbelief. I can't help it," Harris says. "It's what we had to do," Klebold adds. Harris finishes quickly: "That's it. Sorry. Good-bye."

In their seriously disturbed mental state, the frustration and powerlessness they felt about being bullied and teased boiled over. Harris complained that people continually made fun of him, "my face, my hair, my shirts." Klebold said, "If you could see all the anger I've stored over the past four f——ing years."[1]

REACTING TO HELPLESSNESS

Klebold and Harris took common adolescent frustrations and carried them to insane extremes. Teenagers, like all human beings, abhor helplessness. We fight for meaning, control, power, and authority over our own lives, and often over the lives of others. Helplessness is the source of much of our greatest misery and our worst fears. It extinguishes joy and breeds hate. It destroys our self-esteem and fuels self-hatred. Our dread of helplessness percolates into our dreams. One common nightmare is that we are trying to escape from some awful thing or are trying to move toward something we want but are barely able to budge. Somehow, we are stuck in a sort of maddening slow motion.

The more ancient areas of the brain tend to equate everything we experience with enhancing or detracting from the prime evolutionary directives of survival and reproduction. This is the primitive subtext of our lives and powerfully influences our emotions. For example, the intense joy that scientists such as Einstein feel when they make some apparently esoteric discovery flows from the limbic system, which has evolved in humans to assume that advances in meaning will somehow enhance our survival and reproduction. The limbic system has enormous difficulty grasping the detailed complexities of the modern world. Its primitive architecture evolved hundreds of thousands of years ago in the life-or-death environment inhabited by early hominids. It continues to react as if we were living in that ancient environment. Thus, seemingly trivial annoyances or frustrations may produce irrationally strong negative emotions because our primitive neural system wrongly interprets them as significant threats to our survival or reproduction. The limbic system, for instance, tends to view helplessness in the face of authority—seeing the lights of a police car flashing in our rearview mirror—as signaling a serious threat, and thus we may emotionally overreact to an irritating traffic stop. Minor mishaps on the highway may escalate into road rage. Bullying and teasing can also be misinterpreted as a life-or-death threat, generating a potent fight-or-flight response. As with Klebold and Harris, this primitive overreaction can be grotesque if not modulated by the advanced neural system.

A sense of helplessness can skew our judgment. Most of us fear flying far more than we fear driving, though driving is much more dangerous than flying on a scheduled airline. This is because with driving, we are in control. But if something goes terribly wrong in a plane at thirty-five thousand feet, we are completely helpless. Intense, helpless fear is the definition of human terror. And terror is what we loathe the most. This is one reason there was such an acute identification with the horror of the passengers of the four hijacked airliners on September 11, 2001. It also helps explain why we felt such admiration for those on United Airlines Flight 93 who overcame their sense of helplessness and fought their hijackers for control of the aircraft. There is only one group of people that consistently shows very little fear of flying: pilots. They have a sense of control. But September 11 shook the confidence of even the most experienced commercial airline pilots because, like the passengers, the pilots of the hijacked planes became helpless victims.

Helplessness is an affront to our very nature. With so little aid from instincts in orienting us in the world, we must learn all we can and use this knowledge to plan our actions accordingly. We admire confidence, which reflects a sense of being in control. And we tend to equate meaning with control. After the September 11 attacks, there was a general frenzy to find out as much as possible about such topics as Islamic fundamentalism, airline safety, and anthrax. Our collective desire for control (via meaning) is insatiable. Civilization itself is a massive defensive structure designed to give us far greater control over our environment than we would have in the wild. We begin as helpless, dependent infants eagerly trying to understand and manipulate everything that is going on around us. As we mature, our minds become masses of plans and dreams, loves and hates, hopes and fears. We obsess about the future and suffer the pain of anxiety. Whenever circumstances force us into a situation in which we feel helpless, our basic survival strategy—planning and control—is no longer available. But if we gain or regain a significant measure of control, we are rewarded with a delicious sense of pleasure. This helps explain the ecstatic reaction of so many winners of lottery jackpots. The huge amount of money gives them a perception of vastly greater control over how they will live their lives.

Surveys have shown that the happiest people are generally those who feel in control. This tends to translate into high self-esteem. Given the architecture of our nervous system, if we succeed in finding meaning and control in our lives, we are usually rewarded with an enhanced sense of self-worth, which is a primitive signal that we are fulfilling important evolutionary goals. But people who feel frustrated, helpless, or trapped have little sense of control and often have low self-esteem. Those who are bullied, as Klebold and Harris felt they were, fit this description, and surveys have shown that the self-esteem of the bullied is normally very low.[2]

If hate and self-hate as a result of feelings of helplessness mutate into suicidal violence, there is a special danger. This can lead, as it did with Klebold and Harris and other perpetrators of school shootings, to a kind of conscious, suicidal terrorism. When suicide is acceptable to people seething with hate, they may decide to take others with them.

CONSCIOUSNESS OF HUMAN MORTALITY: "THE ULTIMATE CONCERN"

Humans have an unusual relationship with death. It seems that we alone among all species on Earth are aware of our own mortality. We must seek meaning in our lives—or assume our essential meaninglessness—within the context of our mortality. This unique awareness of death profoundly shapes each one of us and the cultures we live in. Prior to about eighteen months old, children do not recognize themselves in a mirror. But as the neocortex matures, consciousness emerges. By around two years old, children become aware of themselves and begin to use the words *I, me,* and *mine.* Not long after becoming self-aware—usually by age four—a child begins asking the seminal question: am I going to die? This early recognition by human beings of their mortality, and the mortality of every living thing, tends to generate an underlying sense of anxiety and doubt that we grapple with the rest of our lives. What is the point of a life that appears to end in nonexistence? What, if anything, comes after death? Biologist Theodosius Dobzhansky called the awareness of death that accompanies the awareness of self "the ultimate concern." It underpins the pervasive spiritual quest of human beings. The paramount human question is the meaning of our brief existence. All known cultures feature spiritual beliefs of some kind that seek to answer this question.

The recognition of our mortality, however, makes us vulnerable to a sense of hopelessness and depression, which are the primary warning signs of suicide. We, in fact, are the only species in which large numbers of individuals commit violent suicide.

MOOD DISORDERS

A sense of helplessness, meaninglessness, and despair is closely connected to clinical depression—the prolonged state of sadness and hopelessness that is one of the most devastating mental illnesses. Some studies indicate that the incidence of depression has risen ten-fold among Americans born since World War II. The reasons for this increase are not completely clear. The rising rate of depression has been accompanied by an increase in suicides, especially among younger Americans, whose suicide rate has tripled in the post–World War II period. Yet this same period has seen an unprecedented increase in prosperity and opportunity. Why this surge in suicides even among those in the upper socioeconomic strata? University of Pennsylvania psychologist Martin Seligman points to the rampant individualism and frantic lifestyle of the postwar years and suggests that these have had the effect of isolating the individual. If anything goes wrong in one's life there is no one to blame but oneself. In sus-ceptible people, this can foster self-hate and depression. This sense of isolation, according to Seligman, is often accompanied by a grow-ing sense of meaninglessness because of an overall postwar decline in the influence of meaning systems that encompass something larger than the self—spirituality, patriotism, and community spirit, for example, as indicated by surveys of such things as regular church or synagogue attendance and voter participation. The focus on some larger purpose can shift an individual's attention away from his or her personal difficulties and inevitable mortality. Isolation and meaninglessness are a particular problem for teenagers, who tend to have a hormonally heightened emotional sensitivity that makes them vulnerable to despair and depression as they struggle to find their identity in the adult world. A pathological, self-reinforcing feedback loop can kick in: meaninglessness leads to depression and depression leads to an even greater sense of meaninglessness as coherence disintegrates in the face of the illness.[3]

The link between larger purpose and suicide rates was strikingly illustrated by what happened in the 1930s and 1940s. During the Great Depression of the 1930s, when the U.S. economy collapsed and millions were out of work, the suicide rate soared. But after the Japanese attack on Pearl Harbor in 1941, which plunged America into World War II, the rate of depression and suicide suddenly and dramatically dropped. There was an overwhelming sense of national meaning and purpose as Americans united to defeat fascism. A similar drop had been recorded during World War I. It remains to be seen whether this phenomenon reappeared after the September 11 attacks.

Studies have found a complex connection between clinical depression, hate, and aggression. Depression can lead to both self-hatred and aggression against the self in the form of suicide. But in some instances, hatred and violence can turn outward—depression can provoke hostility and aggression toward others. Many researchers have noted that anger, violence, and revenge seem to be primitive antidotes for depression. Hatred and revenge can give an individual a sense of meaning and purpose that counters the hopelessness of depression and grief. This was undoubtedly at work among the Russian soldiers in Chechnya who vowed to revenge their dead and wounded comrades. Vengeful behavior has been noted in cultures around the world. "Why such violence might be a cure for depression or grief is another question," observed Harvard biologist Melvin Konner, "and the answer involves presently unknown mechanisms." One possibility is that violence can be exciting as well as energizing and may serve as a compelling distraction from the anguish of depression. If this is true, then it raises the chilling possibility that the counterpart to the rising rate of depression and suicide among young people is a rise in hatred and violence toward others, which may be an effort by some young aggressors to self-medicate for the depression they feel in a seemingly meaningless and pointless world. Remember that prior to the attack in Littleton, Colorado, Eric Harris was being treated with an antidepressant. In fact, there has been an explosion in the prescription of antidepressant medications for troubled young people. Kip Kinkel—who murdered his parents and classmates in Springfield, Oregon—had been prescribed an antidepressant: Prozac. Having a serious psychological disorder such as depression generates powerful feelings of being trapped, helpless, and frustrated that are strongly correlated with low self-esteem. And psychologists have found that both low self-esteem and threatened self-esteem have a significant correlation with hostility toward others and anger at oneself. Low self-esteem appears to be interpreted by the primitive neural system as signaling an ongoing threat to survival and reproduction. And like all such threats, this tends to shift control of thought, feeling, and behavior from the advanced to the primitive neural system.

Despite the growing number of young people treated for depression, U.S. Surgeon General David Satcher reported in 2001 that undertreatment is a major problem for both adults and children with all kinds of mental illnesses, including depression. Satcher estimated that fewer than half of children with major mental disorders receive any treatment at all. A survey of one juvenile detention center revealed that two-thirds of those detained had significant psychiatric disorders. The inadequacy of mental health services for children and adults is compounded by the reluctance of many to seek treatment. People suffering from a serious mental illness often struggle not only with self-hatred but also with the stigma placed on such illnesses—a stigma that itself is based on primitive stereotypes.

Maniac is the classic pejorative term for someone suffering from severe mental illness. The word epitomizes our fear of insanity and our caricature of it: the disheveled madman with wild eyes and a crazy laugh. As Klebold and Harris went about their deadly work at Columbine High School, everyone noticed their deranged laughter. "They were, like, orgasmic," said nineteen-year-old Nicholas Schumann. The word *maniac* is derived from *mania*, which is one-half of a hideously painful and destructive illness that afflicts tens of millions of people worldwide: manic depression. This is an illness in which extreme euphoria alternates with extreme hopelessness. These shifts in mood can take place over a few weeks, a few hours, even a few minutes. Manic depression—which psychiatrists refer to as bipolar disorder—is perhaps the deadliest psychiatric disease. It combines the pain of depression with the energy of mania, giving its victims the vigor they need to take desperate action. Untreated, up to 20 percent of manic-depressives will take their own lives. But advances in understanding manic depression have provided important clues to the fundamental neural mechanisms underlying aggression, self-hatred, self-esteem, and meaning.

One of the nation's leading authorities on manic depression—which affects an estimated five million people in the United States—is Kay Redfield Jamison, a professor of psychiatry at the Johns Hopkins University School of Medicine. In a textbook that she coauthored on the illness, the disease is described this way: "Manic-depressive illness magnifies common human experiences to larger-than-life proportions. Among its symptoms are exaggerations of normal sadness and fatigue, joy and exuberance, sensuality and sexuality, irritability and rage, energy and creativity." But Jamison has also provided a more personal description of the disorder in her brilliant book *An Unquiet Mind*. For she herself suffers from manic depression. "The ideas and feelings are fast and frequent like shooting stars, and you follow them until you find better and brighter ones," she wrote. "But, somewhere, this changes. The fast ideas are too fast, and there are far too many; overwhelming confusion replaces clarity. Memory goes. Humor and absorption on friends' faces are replaced by fear and concern. Everything previously moving with the grain is now against—you are irritable, angry, frightened, uncontrollable, and enmeshed totally in the blackest caves of the mind."[4]

Depression alone that is not interspersed with manic episodes is called unipolar disorder—an illness first described by the Greek physician Hippocrates in the fifth century B.C. Unipolar depression is more common than manic depression and is estimated to affect about fifteen million people in the United States. Both depression and manic depression can run in families, but researchers are concluding that the genetic component is quite complex. Inherited depression sometimes begins as a child. One victim, whose three sons and daughter also show signs of unipolar disorder, remembered his first experience with the illness on a trip to an uncle's farm when he was seven years old: "I should have been excited when I got there. And I wasn't. The animals were there; the barns and granaries were there. Just joyous things to do. There was no joy in it at all. It was absolutely bleak. I felt hopeless. I couldn't understand what was going on." This utter despair exacts a terrible price. Every year, around thirty thousand Americans commit suicide. Suicides outnumber murders three to two, and 60 to 80 percent of those who commit suicide are estimated to have some form of depressive illness. Clinical depression is the number one risk factor for suicide. Although the largest number of suicides occur among older Americans, suicide is now the third leading cause of death among adolescents and young adults.

Within the context of suicide, hate can take three general forms: self-hatred, hatred of life, or some combination of the two. A suicide can be prompted by self-hatred alone as an individual turns his aggression against his despised self. But in many suicides there is no self-hatred, only hate for a life that has been made unbearable by suffering, including the indescribable mental torture of depression itself. Here, the individual may decide that the kindest thing to do is to put himself out of his misery.

The full range of emotional experience can be divided into general categories according to the nature and duration of the experience, though these categories are far from absolutely precise. At the most basic level are the daily fluctuations we experience in our emotional lives, involving relatively transitory episodes of anger, fear, joy, sadness, hostility, and the other emotions. Strong emotions usually pass fairly quickly. Psychiatrists generally prefer the term *affects* to *emotions*, because they believe it is a more objective measure of emotional response. *Affect* refers to the outward signs that a person displays of his or her emotional state, rather than simply the subjective perception of the emotion he or she may report. When an emotion or affect is sustained over a relatively long period of time, it becomes a mood. Newlyweds, for example, may remain in a loving mood throughout their honeymoon and beyond. In most cases, however, moods are not as intense as the strongest emotions. After a bitter argument, you may stay in an angry mood for days, yet your anger is usually not as intense as it was at the height of the argument.

If intense, crippling emotions are sustained over long periods of time, however, or if they periodically reoccur, they may be the manifestation of a mood disorder. Disorders of mood are often contrasted with thought disorders such as schizophrenia, which are characterized by inappropriate and disordered thinking. In general terms, intense, sustained euphoria constitutes the particular mood disorder mania. Intense, sustained sadness or anguish constitutes clinical depression. But not always. The context is important. Extended periods of sadness are sometimes normal. A husband who loses his wife to cancer will probably be depressed for a long time. This is a normal part of the grieving process. Eventually, the depression will lift. But if it doesn't, or if the depression returns over and over, then it has become a mood disorder. Intense, sustained, obsessive hostility constitutes hatred. Although hate has not traditionally been classified as a mood disorder, it has all the characteristics of one. Like mania and depression, intense hatred or self-hatred can cripple and distort one's life and damage the lives of others. I would argue that in the modern world all forms of hate are obsolete and, like depression, should be treated as a mental health problem. Suicidal self-hatred is already classified as a psychiatric disorder, as are certain types of neurotic self-hate.

Terms such as *emotion*, *affect*, and *mood* do not completely capture the total spectrum of emotion-like states that we experience. The pain of an arthritic knee or the pleasure of a back rub are not usually considered emotions. But they contribute significantly to our moods and the emotional tone of our lives. To encompass both emotions and raw states of pain or pleasure, we might simply employ the concept of feelings. In everyday conversation, this is the term we normally use ("that feels good").

There is one other category of emotional experience to consider, and it is the longest lasting of all: temperament. Although this is a more controversial area, many neuroscientists believe that a combination of genetic factors, upbringing, and life experience creates a general emotional tendency in most people. Temperament is related to mood and establishes a kind of emotional baseline that may last for years, even a lifetime. Triumphs and tragedies come and go, and so do the strong emotions that go with them, but temperament is the emotional state that a person always tends to return to. We all know people (including ourselves) who generally tend to be cheerful, anxious, angry, sad, sullen, or some other complex but characteristic blend of emotions.

The study of manic depression, in particular, is providing us important clues about how specific structures and neurochemicals in the human brain generate aggression, hate, and meaning. A revolution has taken place at the intersection of psychology and neuroscience in the rapidly maturing discipline of neuropsychology. There are dozens of different kinds of chemicals in the brain and body that play a part in our thoughts, feelings, and behavior. These include neurotransmitters—which operate in the brain's information processing cells, or neurons—and hormones. The effect of any given neurochemical depends on many factors, including its concentration, the functional area of the brain that it is affecting, the type of receptors it activates, and its interaction with other chemicals. Neurons are studded with many different kinds of microscopic switches called receptors. As we have noted, one well-known neurotransmitter—serotonin—activates a minimum of fifteen separate types of receptors, each of which seems to have a different effect on brain function. In all this complexity, certain patterns are beginning to emerge, especially in the family of neurotransmitters known as monoamines, which includes serotonin, dopamine, and noradrenaline. All three of these neurotransmitters seem to be involved in depression, both unipolar and bipolar.

Manic depression is associated with dramatic swings in the amount of dopamine in the frontal lobes, which include a large area of neocortex as well as the underlying orbitofrontal cortex. In mania, an increase in dopamine helps produce a condition that clinicians sometimes refer to as exaggerated meaningfulness. To someone in the manic stage, every thought may seem profoundly meaningful. Dopamine in the frontal lobes appears to mediate the assembly of thoughts and feelings into systems of meaning. The manic individual may believe that his insights are so important that he becomes intolerant and angry at those who even hesitate to agree with him. These meaning systems may take the form of elaborate conspiracy theories that push the patient into paranoia. As the mania proceeds, this sense of meaning often becomes completely divorced from rationality, and the patient may begin hallucinating and become delusional. Depression, however, is associated with abnormally low levels of dopamine in the frontal lobes. In this case, the patient suffers from the opposite condition: exaggerated meaninglessness. Meaning disintegrates and the severely depressed individual often feels that his or her life is utterly worthless and hopeless. This is often accompanied by feelings of self-hatred and low self-esteem.

Serotonin also plays a critical role in both depression and manic depression. Many of the newest antidepressant medications, such as Prozac, regulate serotonin. Like dopamine, serotonin is active in the frontal areas of the brain. One important function of the frontal lobes is to inhibit aggressive impulses that originate in the primitive neural system. Patients with clinical depression normally have abnormally low levels of serotonin. Researchers have found that the lower the level of serotonin, the more likely a person is to commit suicide. And those with the lowest levels of serotonin tend to use the most violent methods of suicide. Low levels of serotonin are also associated with impulsive aggression toward others. You will remember that a high concentration in one particular kind of serotonin receptor in the orbitofrontal cortex—the serotonin-2 receptor—is associated with well-tuned social behavior among primates, including humans. A deficiency in this type of receptor has been linked with noncooperation and hostility toward others.[5]

Noradrenaline is a central component in the preconscious alerting system. It tends to sensitize and energize the brain. Mania has been linked with abnormally high levels of noradrenaline, and the manic patient tends to display enormous mental energy and extreme sensitivity. In the depressive stage, however, which is associated with low levels of noradrenaline, the patient is usually listless and desensitized to normal emotions, especially positive emotions.

There are many hypotheses about what triggers mood disorders such as depression and manic depression, but there is as yet no clear scientific conclusion. One idea that has emerged in recent years is that manic depression may be a form of epilepsy, involving seizures deep in the limbic system. Certain anticonvulsant drugs that have the effect of damping down these electrochemical seizures have also shown promise in treating bipolar disorder.

The pattern of manic and depressive episodes can vary. Some manic-depressives have more bouts of depression than mania. With others, this pattern is reversed. And still others simply alternate between mania and depression. In both depression and manic depression, certain rhythmic elements have been noted in some patients. Episodes of mania and depression may consistently last only a specific number of days. Or they may regularly occur at certain times of the year. Research into these patterns suggests that there are links between mood disorders and disruptions in the body's natural rhythms, including sleeping and waking cycles. These cycles include rhythmic changes in the balance of neurochemicals such as dopamine, serotonin, and noradrenaline.

For millions of years, hominids evolved within and lived by the rhythms of sunrise and sunset set against the backdrop of the changing seasons. Some researchers argue that the unnatural rhythms of industrial civilization, which are measured by the clock, can have a disruptive effect on brain chemistry. Internal rhythms affect many biological states, including moods. Some people, for example, are more cheerful and alert in the morning, while others don't experience this state until much later in the day. Depression and manic depression seem to involve pathological changes in these internal rhythms. Waking a patient in the middle of the night and keeping him awake can sometimes temporarily restore a healthier overall rhythm and bring short-term relief of symptoms. In the most severe cases of depression, where suicide is an imminent risk and standard antidepressants either have not worked or will take too long to work, patients sometimes undergo electroconvulsive therapy. While the patient is under a short-acting general anesthesia, a brief, powerful electrical current is passed through electrodes attached to his or her scalp. This induces a generalized motor seizure that usually lasts no more than two minutes. A series of treatments is normally administered over several days, and in almost two-thirds of cases the depression fades away shortly thereafter. Scientists are not certain why electroconvulsive therapy works, but it, too, may somehow restore normal biological rhythms.

Because this devastating illness often emerges in people in their teens and twenties, there is now a search through the human genome to find genetic markers for those who might have a tendency to develop bipolar disorder. There is a feeling among a number of experts that if we could genetically identify the vulnerable population, there might be ways—through medication and lifestyle changes—to get these people through this time in their lives without ever developing the illness and its accompanying risk of suicide. Avoiding stimulants such as cocaine and amphetamines would, of course, be essential. Some experts also believe that erratic sleep schedules, jet lag, and other conditions that disrupt the body's rhythms are especially risky for those with a tendency to develop manic depression. Once this critical period has passed, however, it is thought that a person is much less vulnerable to the illness, so he or she might then be able to lead a perfectly normal life.

Mood disorders seem to be more prevalent in exceptionally creative individuals. Jamison and others have studied large groups of artists and intellectuals and found an unusually high incidence of depression and manic depression. As the manic state progresses, however, productive activity disintegrates, usually replaced by self-destructive and delusional behavior. The manic-depressive may become quick to anger and quick to hate. Nevertheless, as many as 50 percent of people being treated for bipolar disorder do not stay on their medication. Some miss the high of mania. Others object to the side effects of medication. Some simply habituate to feeling better and forget how chaotic their lives were before they began treatment. But always in the background is the huge risk of suicide that this disease poses if not treated properly. Many who suffer from depression and manic depression abuse alcohol, which can provide a temporary relief of symptoms. But alcohol significantly increases the risk of suicide. It tends to spur impulsive behavior by releasing the more primitive limbic system from the inhibiting influence of the frontal lobes.

Psychiatrists often advise the friends and family of those who may be suffering from manic depression not to be afraid to ask affected individuals if they are having thoughts of suicide. Sometimes manic-depressives are willing, even relieved, to discuss their feelings. If they have been having suicidal thoughts, the next step is to find out if they have a plan. Having a specific plan is the most serious indicator of an impending suicide. If there is a plan, psychiatrists recommend using common sense to try to keep them from carrying it out. If they have a gun, for example, a family member or friend might ask them to give it up, at least temporarily. At that point, everything possible should be done to get the person into immediate treatment. Some manic-depressives are in such deep denial that an aggressive intervention is called for, with family and friends confronting them directly about their symptoms and the destructive effects of the illness.

There are excellent medications for bipolar disorder. The most effective is the metal lithium in the form of lithium salts, which works in 50 to 80 percent of patients to stop manic-depressive episodes completely, often with relatively few side effects, and controls certain forms of unipolar disorder as well. Studies have shown that lithium reduces the suicide rate for manic depression almost ninefold, making it one of the most—if not *the* most—lifesaving treatments in psychiatry. Unlike well-known drugs such as Prozac (the brand name for fluoxetine), lithium is a common metallic element that cannot be patented. Any pharmaceutical company can manufacture and sell it, and thus it will never make the profits of a drug such as Prozac. Because no large drug company is behind lithium, it has tended to be a low-profile medication. But it is probably responsible for saving the lives of hundreds of thousands of people around the world.

Though the use of lithium to treat manic depression spread throughout Europe in the mid-1950s, today lithium remains a mystery in neuroscience. No one has yet determined exactly how it works. Somehow lithium seems to prevent the abnormal fluctuation of neurochemicals such as dopamine, serotonin, and noradrenaline. But the discovery of lithium as a treatment for bipolar disorder did solve one other mystery. Since at least the second century A.D., physicians have recommended that patients suffering from mania and melancholia—the older term for depression—drink the water from mineral springs. Many fashionable resorts grew up around mineral springs, which the wealthy would visit to "take the waters." The treatment at these spas frequently worked, and the reason, we now know, is that the mineral water often contained traces of lithium.

Scientists have begun exploring the possibility that lithium and certain other drugs that control manic depression may also be able to control destructive outbursts of anger and hate in certain groups of violent men. In one study conducted by Michael Sheard, a psychiatrist at the Yale University School of Medicine, half of a group of men with a history of violent outbursts and antisocial behavior were given lithium. The other half received an inert placebo. None of the men knew whether they were receiving lithium or the placebo. Over a three-month period, the men taking lithium exhibited substantially fewer incidents of impulsive violence. But if they were taken off the drug, the violence returned. It may be that certain kinds of outbursts of anger and hate are linked to disorders in natural biological rhythms that lithium is sometimes able to correct. Antisocial aggression and hatred come in many different forms, so it is unlikely that science will ever be able to develop a pill to control them all. But if we move into an era in which hatred, like depression and phobias, is treated as a medical problem, then researchers may be able to develop medications that are helpful in specific kinds of cases.

SELF-HATE AND EATING DISORDERS

Given the complexity of our self-aware brains and the many manifestations of self-hate, having a love-hate relationship with oneself is quite common, especially among adolescents. This often involves one's sense of identity and self-esteem. Self-love can combine with self-hate as our capacity for self-criticism is activated as the brain develops. With consciousness, we gain the ability to know the self, to objectify the self, and to hate the self. Consciousness creates a model of the self that we can make judgments about, including primitive emotional judgments. We use this model to value ourselves, producing a sense of self-esteem that ranges from high to low. These judgments about the self can take the form of hatred—intense, persistent dislike that involves self-stereotypes: "I'm stupid," "I'm a failure," "I'm fat." The evolutionary goal of self-hate is to mark characteristics that threaten our survival and reproduction and eliminate them. Just as in the hatred of others, however, the primitive neural system in self-hate tends to reason in terms of simplistic binary categories such as good-bad. Such binary values can be applied to other generalized binary categories such as fat-thin and attractive-ugly. Many kinds of self-dislike and self-criticism can be completely reasonable and healthy. We may be rationally dissatisfied with our physical condition, our job performance, our speaking ability, or our social skills. This kind of self-criticism can motivate us to do something about our shortcomings, which can actually improve our success in life, including our chances of finding a compatible mate. Being sexually desirable is so important to the primitive neural system, humans are capable of obsessively pursuing almost any kind of behavior to achieve it. When rational self-dislike slips into obsessive self-hatred, the primitive neural system's tendency to create negative, binary stereotypes takes over. Perhaps you know people who are attractive and successful by any reasonable standard yet insist that they are unattractive or second-rate in some way. They see flaws in themselves that no one else can see because they have irrationally stereotyped themselves. As with other forms of hate, it is almost impossible to talk them out of this attitude. Their self-esteem is often very low. These people can be terribly unhappy and feel hopelessly trapped in their inadequate self, which can lead to a constant sense of frustration and, in the most extreme cases, depression and suicide.

Eating disorders represent a troubling love-hate relationship with oneself and with food. In the Western world, this is largely a problem for females, though the rate of eating disorders among males is increasing. Surveys show that up to 80 percent of women are dissatisfied with their bodies. Some experts go even further and say that virtually all women in Western society are dissatisfied with their bodies at some time in their lives. The problem seems to be spreading through almost all age groups. Many nine-year-olds and ten-year-olds are now dieting, though they are often within their normal weight range. Excessive dieting this young can deprive the body of nutrients needed for healthy development. The multibillion-dollar diet industry often plays on the fears of women—and men—in this image-conscious culture. They contribute to the estimated seven million women and girls with eating disorders in the United States, along with about one million men. The major eating disorders—anorexia nervosa and bulimia nervosa—have become well known.

Anorexics obsessively starve themselves. Although anorexia has traditionally affected mostly white women, in recent years it has been spreading to all racial and ethnic groups, perhaps a sign of the penetration of popular, image-conscious culture. It is a particular problem among college women. Bulimia nervosa has been known for millennia (the ancient Romans suffered from it) but was officially labeled a psychiatric disorder only in 1979. Bulimia involves bingeing and purging, usually through vomiting or the use of laxatives. Bulimia usually develops around age eighteen and is often accompanied by depression and self-loathing.

Few women escape the battle with their bodies. One recent study showed that many five-year-old girls now fret about their weight. The study found that girls whose weight was above average not only felt worse about their bodies, but also worse about their intelligence than girls with lower body weight. Girls whose parents worried that they were overweight also tended to feel inferior. "It was startling," said Kristen Krahnst-ver Davison, a specialist in human development at Pennsylvania State University who helped conduct the study. "If girls are showing these issues at age five, it doesn't look hopeful for what is going to happen to them as teenagers or as young women."[6]

Western society has developed an extreme emphasis on a slim body image for women. And increasingly the ideal man is being stereotyped as slim and muscular, with a rippling abdomen. The cultural influence of these kinds of images is suggested by studies showing that female immigrants from non-Western societies almost never develop eating disorders in the first or second generation—second-generation women tend to be strongly influenced by the culture of their mothers. But those in the third generation and beyond develop eating disorders at the same rate as the rest of society because they have been completely immersed in their new culture. There is a paradox: modern culture holds up the ideal of physical attractiveness based on slimness yet encourages obesity with heavy promotion (especially to the impressionable young) of both junk food consumption and sedentary activities such as television viewing. An estimated 15 percent of American children are obese, with at least another 10 percent significantly overweight. One in five Americans has a serious weight problem, and there is now an epidemic of obesity-related diabetes.

Being overweight often leads to an obsession with weight and dieting. Yet excessive dieting and exercise in vulnerable individuals are major risk factors for eating disorders. Concern with body image is a result of shame, guilt, and fear of social rejection or discrimination ("people hate me"), which is a product of judging ourselves by standards set by others rather than standards that might be personally meaningful. Experts say the focus should be on health, not body image. The overemphasis on body image leads to the irrational glorification of anorexic-looking women whose health may be put at risk by their efforts to attain the preferred appearance. Anorexia is a deadly psychiatric condition. It kills one-half of 1 percent of sufferers each year, often through depression-induced suicide. Besides a rise in eating disorders, another warning sign of serious problems with body image among many women, particularly younger women, is the growing number of women undergoing plastic surgery at an early age.

Some women see dieting as a form of control over their lives, but those who suffer from eating disorders are tormented by an irrational fear of fat. They often feel ugly, unloved, alone, full of self-hatred, and a disappointment to their loved ones. In addition, the price of long-term eating disorders is physically devastating. Excessive dieting can shut down the production of estrogen, which stops menstruation and causes loss of bone mass. Young anorexic women can have bones so brittle they easily fracture. Extreme, long-term starvation can damage or destroy fertility. People with eating disorders may suffer from malnutrition that can cause severe osteoporosis, low blood pressure, and damage to the kidneys, liver, and heart. Singer Karen Carpenter, who suffered from anorexia, died in 1983 of heart failure at age thirty-two.

A study by the Mayo Clinic found that eating disorders have been increasing by about a third every five years since the 1950s. They affect mostly women, with those between the ages of fifteen and twenty-six the most vulnerable. Certain female occupations that demand slimness, such as ballerinas and models, have especially high rates of eating disorders. The problem has become so severe that many ballet companies and some modeling agencies now offer counseling on eating disorders and free bone scans. And with a growing emphasis on a trim and muscular male body image, the incidence among men is rising. Eating disorders have always been a problem among jockeys, amateur wrestlers, and other weight-conscious males. For a jockey, weight is a rational concern. But the limbic system understands only survival and reproduction and is not rational in a neocortical sense. Anxiety about weight can easily cause us to slip into irrational behaviors. A jockey might limbically link his weight to survival, because his livelihood depends on it. Our image-conscious culture compounds this problem. The limbic system is tuned by culture and experience. Equating excessive slimness with sexiness can forge a limbic link between the primal evolutionary goal of reproduction and a slim body. The emergence of meaning systems that worship appearance over health is dangerous when combined with the irrational tendencies of our primitive neural system. As we have seen, meaning systems can be decoupled from the objective requirements of survival and reproduction if they form a primal emotional link with the limbic system. As stated previously, because being sexually desirable is so important to the primitive neural system, it is capable of obsessively pursuing almost any kind of behavior to achieve it: dieting, purging, excessive exercising, even starvation. The primitive neural system can forge a similar limbic link between excessive slimness, social acceptance, and social status. Status within the group in the harsh world of our hominid ancestors meant enhanced opportunity for survival and reproduction through preferred access to food and mates. Cultural images make it all too easy for women—and increasingly men—to develop a love-hate relationship with their bodies. Given this primitive sensitivity to body image, offhand comments such as "you look a little heavy" or "your thighs are too big" can have devastating long-term consequences, particularly to hypersensitive young people. A vulnerable individual's sensitivity may vary depending on internal and external factors, and the same person may shrug off such a comment at one moment yet be profoundly hurt by it at another. Repetition is important. If these kinds of comments are repeated frequently, it is more likely that at some point they will be perceived at a moment of maximum sensitivity. Complimenting someone who uses excessive dieting or exercise to control his or her appearance can be just as dangerous.

Eating disorders have been reported for centuries, but the motives for these disorders have changed, depending on the prevailing cultural meaning systems. In the past, there were often spiritual motivations for starving. It was a form of asceticism that demonstrated religious fervor. Today, an estimated three out of every hundred girls will develop some form of eating disorder, mainly because of the exaggerated cultural emphasis on slim appearance. In the vulnerable population, various stresses can trigger eating disorders, including the identity problems of going through puberty, sexual abuse, breakups with boyfriends, and teasing. Those under stress may feel helpless; controlling food intake may be one way to feel a sense of control. Researchers have found that those most vulnerable to eating disorders include perfectionists who are more disturbed than average about their perceived flaws. Those who are suffering sexual abuse may starve themselves to become less attractive. And some people use starvation as a slow form of suicide to punish parents or others with whom they don't get along.[7]

Anorexia requires intensive treatment by a team of specialists including a physician, psychotherapist, family therapist, and nutritionist using both individual therapy and group therapy. Of the anorexics who seek treatment, nearly 50 percent relapse in the first year. But the relapse rate is lower if the patient reaches a normal weight before leaving the hospital. Reaching a normal weight may be the most important indication that in-patient treatment can be ended because it seems to restore a more normal brain chemistry, which reduces the addictive quality of the anorexia. As with depression, serotonin seems to be involved in eating disorders but in a complex way that is not well understood. Somehow eating disorders seem to disrupt brain chemistry. Although antidepressants such as Prozac and Paxil, which regulate serotonin, generally don't work on underweight anorexic patients, they can be effective when a patient has reached a normal weight, thus helping to prevent relapses.

Bulimia seems to provide a kind of high or at least a numbness to stress and anxiety. It can also have an addictive quality. Antidepressants and cognitive behavior therapy can be useful in controlling mood and changing the eating patterns of bulimics. Treatment can take several years to complete both for anorexia and bulimia. Research has shown that when allowed to eat all they want, bulimics don't seem to feel full until they have consumed about twice as much food as the normal person. The process of bingeing and purging seems to change the body's metabolism so that food is held in the stomach longer than normal. As we eat, small amounts of food go from the stomach to the small intestine. This triggers the release of hormones that travel to the brain and create the sense of being full. Because a bulimic's stomach appears to empty more slowly, a bulimic often doesn't feel full until an abnormally large amount of food has been consumed. Just as with anorexics, the cure rate with bulimics is around 50 percent. But a sizeable proportion of others who undergo treatment improve significantly.[8]

Like many college freshmen, Anna Eidson coped with the stresses of a new environment by eating. She had put an extra fifteen pounds on her five-foot, six-inch frame by the time she returned to her suburban Kansas City, Kansas, home for Christmas. She was upset when she found that she couldn't fit into the black pants and vest that she had chosen to wear to a Christmas formal. "I said to myself, 'I am going to eat only salad, bagels, and water,'" she recalled. "No meat, no protein, no dessert." She lost ten pounds in two weeks and was flattered by the compliments from her friends. She continued to diet, cutting back to water and two bagels a day. "I thought life would be perfect at 110 pounds," she said. "I was starving myself so I could go home—back to my parents, to the comfortable, controlled life I knew. I wanted to be small again."

Eidson kept losing weight. "I was exhausted all the time," she said. "My period stopped for four months; my hair was thinning. But I never connected it with not eating." Finally, some friends confronted her and urged her to seek help. A counselor told her she had anorexia but she was not alone and there was treatment available. Eidson began seeing a psychiatrist. But her weight loss continued. Her parents checked her into an in-patient eating disorder unit at a local hospital. As part of their therapy, Eidson and the other patients were forbidden to talk about dieting, calories, fat content, and other weight-related subjects that obsessively concern most anorexics. She received extensive individual and group therapy. Eidson said she was relieved to get help. "I had lost all sense of taste," she said. "Hunger pains were nothing to me. There were two people inside me. The irrational side took over and wouldn't let me eat. Finally the split personality decided that what I was doing was wrong, and I began to eat." Eidson returned to school and graduated with her class in the spring of 1999. Yet she still struggles with anorexia. "Unfortunately, if I get upset and stressed or there's change, the first thing that goes is my eating," she said. "But now I'm able to notice the warning signs and can ask for help. I have the tools to handle it."

ADDRESSING THE PROBLEM OF SELF-HATE

The case of Anna Eidson and thousands of others like her makes plain that linking slimness to desirability and acceptance is playing with fire in an evolutionary sense because, for the vulnerable, it tends to engage the powerful, primitive neural system that can operate outside of rational control. We naturally love ourselves and strive to succeed, but if cultural standards are too exacting or unrealistic, the self-hate mechanism can be activated in a desperate attempt to correct perceived flaws. Thus begins a cascade of irrational, self-reinforcing behaviors in which the primitive mind may drive an individual to destruction.

Self-hate incorporates the same four core elements as hate—obsessive, intense dislike; negative, binary stereotyping and generalization; lack of empathy; and a basic sense of hostility—in slightly different ways. The purpose of self-hatred, as we have discovered, is to mark and eliminate qualities of the self that are perceived to threaten survival or reproduction. But as self-criticism becomes self-hate, our response to these negative qualities becomes a form of obsessive dislike. This dislike becomes a negative stereotype ("I'm ugly") that lowers self-esteem. With self-hate, lack of empathy and hostility tend to fuse into a sense of anger and frustration directed at the self. Self-hate and the accompanying low self-esteem can be particularly tenacious. They create a risk of depression and suicide. In a small number of people, perhaps 1 to 2 percent of the population, irrational self-hate takes the form of a condition called body dysmorphic disorder, which is characterized by disabling obsessions with minor or imagined physical imperfections. These individuals may suffer from eating disorders, as they compulsively try to alter their appearance. They also make up a significant percentage—estimates range from between 7 and 15 percent—of those who seek plastic surgery, often repeatedly. But they are rarely happy with the results. "These people imagine themselves to be ugly, and no matter what you do to help them they are dissatisfied," said Barry Weintraub, a Beverly Hills plastic surgeon. The limbic system can create perceptual filters that distort our view of the world and of ourselves. These filters, which are a kind of stereotype, are preconsciously superimposed on our perception so that, in this case, when people with a body dysmorphic disorder look in the mirror they actually see themselves as ugly. Similarly, an eighty-pound anorexic can look in the mirror and see herself as fat. These filters operate with hate as well and can, for example, create an irrationally paranoid view of the world.

The problem of self-hate must first be addressed by shifting control of behavior to the advanced neural system. Those treated for eating disorders, for example, go through therapy sessions that teach them the psychological and neuroscientific basis of their disorders. The advanced neural system provides a way to control primitive impulses and develop a more realistic self-appraisal. But this must be accompanied by the kind of intensive behavior therapy required to slowly reeducate the primitive neural system and rationally realign its image of the self. One psychologist suggests that to avoid developing a negative attitude and negative self-image we should be specific about our faults and failings but optimistic about our prospects. One should always avoid generalizing from negative experiences. If you do poorly on a test, for instance, you might conclude that you didn't study enough for that particular exam and determine that you'll do better next time rather than make a negative generalization: "I'm stupid" or "I can't do math." Another important task is to overcome a sense of being trapped by a negative self-image. This might involve various forms of disciplined personal growth, such as acquiring a new skill or making positive connections with other people—focusing on something other than yourself. The overall goal is to find a rewarding sense of meaning that transcends primitive self-obsessions. We must learn to treat ourselves with for-giveness, empathy, and understanding rather than guilt, shame, regret, and anger.[9]

8

SEXISM, RACISM, AND OTHER CULTURAL PHOBIAS

A CULTURE GIVES MEANING to sexual behavior: in some cultures this meaning is death. Thus it is with "honor killing" in certain Arab countries. A woman suspected of sexual impropriety, even when there is no proof, instantly shifts her emotional position in the family. Instead of being a loved member (*us*), she becomes a hated *them* whom her own relatives must kill to restore the family honor. This killing of girls and women by their relatives has been going on for centuries in certain parts of Jordan, Egypt, Syria, Lebanon, and other nations—though a growing number of reformers in the Arab world are seeking to abolish the practice. Honor killing is often punished lightly, if at all, and is sometimes not even considered murder. "Women are largely looked upon as bodies owned and protected by the husband, by the father, by the brother or even other relatives," said Salwa Bakr, a prominent Egyptian feminist writer. "And these crimes are committed under the pretext that these men are defending not only their honor, but society's morality."

Many Arabs bristle at criticism from the West. "When a Western man kills his lover or wife, the crime is called a crime of passion," said one Arab sociologist. "But when it happens in Arab societies, it is called a family honor killing, and we are viewed as barbarous." Without question, the analysis of any practice in any culture must be quite specific in order to avoid the primitive tendency to negatively stereotype all members of a group (Arabs, in this case) because of the behavior of a minority. The same stereotyping problem emerged much more forcefully after the September 11 terrorist attacks. As we shall see in subsequent chapters, the problem of violence against women afflicts developed countries as well as the developing world. In the United States, a woman is far more likely than a man to be injured or killed by someone with whom she has had an intimate relationship. Racism, sexism, and other forms of bigotry plague almost every society. And primitive stereotypes have been an obstacle around the world in the ongoing campaign to secure equal rights for women.

Honor killing is far from universal in the Arab world. Yet where it has taken root, the practice is so ingrained that even victims of the attacks sometimes say the violence is justified. "He shouldn't have let me live," said seventeen-year-old Roweida, whose father shot her three times after she confessed to an affair. Like dozens of other young women with similar tales, she is being held in a Jordanian prison for her own protection. "A girl who commits a sin deserves to die," she said. But Dr. Hani Jahshan, deputy medical examiner of Jordan, reported that in performing autopsies on the victims of these killings, he often finds they are still virgins. In one case, a seventeen-year-old girl was arrested as a runaway. Her father learned that the girl and her sixteen-year-old sister had been in a restaurant at which men were present. Dr. Jahshan examined the seventeen-year-old and found that she was a virgin. The family assured him that nothing would be done to her. But two weeks later she was back—in the morgue, along with her sister. Her father and two brothers had killed both girls because they could not believe they were innocent of sexual misconduct.[1]

Social psychologists have long observed that binary superior-inferior distinctions—which are at the heart of most forms of bigotry, including racial and gender prejudice—have a wide range of consequences. The primitive neural system of those designated as inferior can easily absorb this characterization and build it into their subconscious self-image. Honor killing not only ranks the males of a family as superior to the younger females but gives them life-or-death responsibility over the women's perceived sexual behavior. A young woman such as Roweida seems to have accepted this inferior position and to have adopted the value system that deems her behavior worthy of death. Thus, a prejudiced environment can alter the attitudes of those labeled inferior and drastically affect the behaviors of those deemed superior. In another cultural setting, the fathers and brothers who brutally kill these young women might never dream of engaging in this kind of intrafamily savagery. But the cultural meaning system that justifies honor killing so powerfully activates the primitive hate response that any reservations are swept away and empathy shuts down. Nevertheless, women and men are capable of creating their own systems of meaning that reject and subvert prevailing cultural practices. This makes change possible, though often in the face of enormous obstacles. As these cultures evolve and this practice eventually disappears, future generations will undoubtedly look back on such murders with incomprehension.

WHEN HATE BLENDS WITH FEAR

Honor killing tragically illustrates the obsessive quality of hate and how intense hatred can blend with phobic fear. The foundation of honor killing is a kind of cultural phobia: an obsessive fear of sexual contamination of females so great that young women are rigorously excluded from even casual contact with unknown men. If there is such contact—even if it is perfectly innocent—the phobic fear can switch to murderous hate. Thus, a phobic reaction that represents the defensive or flight response is transformed into a phobic reaction that represents the aggressive or fight response. We often see a similar pattern in racial and ethnic prejudice. There is an obsessive fear of contamination of one race or ethnicity by another "inferior" race or ethnicity. Such contamination is avoided through a system of segregation such as the apartheid scheme of South Africa or the Jim Crow laws in the United States. If segregation is breached or even threatened, however, fear undergoes a terrible transformation into hatred and violence, as we saw during the civil rights movement of the 1960s.

Our us-them divisions are often built on meaning rather than strict kinship or territoriality, making humans unique among all species. This allows us to be extremely dynamic and flexible in forming us-groups. We can define ourselves through religion, ideology, culture, ethnicity, profession, or a thousand other forms of shared meaning. But this also tends to make us unstable, even violent, when meaning systems clash or are transgressed. Honor killing involves a primitive cultural meaning system linking groups of blood relatives together into clans. Transgressors are almost instantly transformed into objects of revulsion, hatred, and violence within the clan—them—even though they might be a daughter or a sister. The meaning system requires that the chastity and fidelity of women, both in reality and appearance, must be maintained at all costs to preserve the purity of the clan lineage.

In Pakistan and other Muslim countries, the fundamentalist Islamic schools known as *madrasas* that have proliferated in recent years take thousands of boys away from their families for at least eight years, usually from the ages of sixteen to twenty-four. The boys live in sparsely furnished dormitories and have no contact with women. They spend long hours memorizing the Koran but also are taught a curriculum that preaches hatred of the West in general, and America in particular. These schools educated virtually all the Taliban leadership and many members of the Al Qaeda terrorist network.

The lessons of these *madrasas* were enshrined as social policy in Afghanistan, including policies that governed women. The Taliban and their Al Qaeda allies adopted a primitive us-them attitude toward women, who were subject to beatings—even death—for violating Taliban rules. The extreme oppression of women by the Taliban underscores a problem in many Muslim countries and throughout the developing world. Under the Taliban, women were virtual prisoners. They could not work outside the home, were deprived of an education, and could not leave their house unless accompanied by a male, even if they were wearing the required head-to-toe covering, or *burka*. Aside from being a violation of basic human rights, neuroscience is learning exactly why this kind of social organization creates fertile ground for hatred and violence.

THE STATUS OF WOMEN

Violence is overwhelmingly a problem of male behavior. In every culture ever studied, men commit the overwhelming majority of violent acts. The precise reasons for men's susceptibility to violent behavior have not yet been worked out. It is much more complicated than just the male hormone testosterone and appears to involve the interaction of many hormones and neurochemicals as well as the sex-specific structure of the hypothalamus. But one fact has emerged from a number of scientific studies: the more densely wired the orbitofrontal cortex, the more that hate and violence in males is suppressed. The orbitofrontal cortex—part of the massive human prefrontal cortex—is the area that gives us our capacity for empathy-advanced impulse control. When men and women live together and raise their children in an equal setting, the men tend to activate this empathy center much more frequently as they interact with their wives and children. And this empathetic attitude toward others by men tends to strongly influence their sons.

If a culture treats women and children as greatly inferior, however, then men in their roles as husbands and fathers are more likely to act dictatorially and are less likely to engage their sense of empathy in an effort to understand the feelings of others. In many ways, the brain is like a muscle, strengthening or weakening with use and disuse. The frequent activation of the orbitofrontal cortex increases its mass and the density of its synaptic connections with other areas of the brain. The orbitofrontal cortex is a major bridge by which the advanced centers of the neocortex suppress unwanted limbic impulses, including the aggressive impulses that lead to hatred and violence. Dozens of studies of violent criminals in prisons throughout the world have shown that poor prefrontal cortex functioning is one of these men's most common neural characteristics.

There are many pressing needs in the world, including greater democracy and tolerance as well as dramatic upgrades in education and basic infrastructure. But none is more urgent in developing nations than rapidly improving the status of women—though this, of course, is related to these other issues. Progress on the status of women will help address another major problem: soaring population growth. A recent United Nations report estimated that the current world population of six billion will balloon to almost eleven billion by 2050. Practically all this growth will come in developing nations, which are the least equipped to handle it. The majority of Muslim countries, for example, have very high birth rates with more than half the population under twenty years old. This places a great strain on these societies' resources and creates a large population of undereducated, unemployed young men in whom frustration, hopelessness, and anger can fester into hate. The U.N. report went on to find that if the status of women in the developing world could swiftly be improved, this rate of growth might be cut in half. Women with more choices and better education tend to have fewer children.

The outlook for women's rights in the Islamic world includes some positive trends. In 2001, for example, the parliament of Turkey—a largely Muslim country—passed sweeping changes in its civil code formally recognizing women and men as equals. The revised code replaces provisions that, among other things, gave only husbands the legal right to make decisions related to home and children, required wives to seek their husbands' permission to work outside the home, and gave women who divorced only the property legally registered in their names. Property and assets are now to be divided equally.[2]

THE CORE ELEMENTS OF HATE

Hatred, when directed at individuals or groups, is a product of a perceived threat or pain-producing circumstance that causes us to stereotype the source as the enemy—the rejected other. The damage, defeat, or destruction of our enemy tends to reduce or eliminate the threat along with accompanying negative emotions. This can give us a profound sense of relief, even pleasure, as well as a perception of greater control over our lives, in part through the release of our obsession with the hated enemy. Thus, an honor killing is sometimes followed by a macabre celebration by the family of the dead woman. We see something similar in the relief frequently expressed by family members of a murder victim when the murderer is executed. When we are at war, we often cheer at reports that the enemy has suffered a bloody defeat. Our limbic system has evolved to allow us to be indifferent to—or even take pleasure in—the suffering of "them."

Hate has four core elements: obsessive, intense dislike; negative, binary stereotyping and generalization; a lack of empathy for the object of the hatred; and a basic sense of hostility that can trigger aggression—the fight response. Through stereotyping, hate involves prejudice, but prejudice doesn't necessarily involve hate. Some European colonists, for example, felt paternalistic rather than antagonistic toward indigenous peoples. But these kinds of us-them distinctions always have the potential to blossom into hatred. Hate is more complex than instinctive emotions such as fear or surprise. It has no characteristic form of physical expression. The physical manifestation of hate can range from instant, violent rage to cruel laughter and perverse joy. But the underlying theme of all these forms of expression is hostility. A wide variety of emotions and feelings can be the source of hatred: frustration, envy, grief, pain, fear, anger, disgust. Intense dislike in the context of hate means that the primitive neural system has marked a phenomenon as a significant threat to survival and/or reproduction.

Studies of human behavior have identified at least eight major sources of prejudice and hatred: group fitness, identity, competition for scarce resources, control and dominance, powerlessness, fear and pain, status, and social roles. Almost all involve elements of the us-them distinction. The basic us-them dynamic is often described as group fitness. This is the tendency of members of an in-group (or us-group) to value themselves more highly than they value non-members—a primitive tendency to promote group cohesion, which can be crucial in coping with threats. One's sense of identity can also promote unfavorable contrasts with others. The Nazis defined the Aryan master race by belittling other "races." Sometimes, the sense of identity of longtime adversaries begins to derive solely from their opposition to each other. David Grossman, an Israeli novelist, has argued that this is a major problem in the Middle East conflict: "All of us, Israelis and Palestinians, were born into this conflict. Our identity is formulated, to no small extent, in terms of hostility and fear, survival and death. Sometimes it seems as if Israelis and Palestinians have no clear identities without the conflict, without the 'enemy' whose existence is necessary, perhaps vital, to their senses of self and community." The competition for scarce resources is another potent source of us-them divisions. In the case of Israel and the Palestinians, there is a bitter struggle over a relatively small amount of land that has great political and emotional meaning. The primitive neural system tends to see the world as a zero-sum game—your gain is my loss—making it much more difficult to resolve these conflicts unless there is a pronounced shift to the advanced neural system, which has a far better chance of putting such disputes in perspective and reaching an intelligent compromise. Seeking control and dominance is another basic human tendency that often leads to conflict, especially when an in-group seeks to dominate an out-group ("them"). A sense of powerlessness and vulnerability can also lead to prejudice and hate, as the primitive neural system perceives itself as being trapped by a threat. Palestinians regularly express their sense of powerlessness, helplessness, and frustration in the face of Israeli military might. Fear and pain are related feelings that tend to push the primitive neural system into overdrive and may create hatred of whoever or whatever produces these feelings. One's social status can also lead to primitive prejudice and us-them divisions. We tend to positively stereotype those of higher status (celebrities, for example, in Western culture) and negatively stereotype those of lower status. And, finally, social roles can cause us to prejudge others and ourselves with stereotyped expectations. Employer-employee, doctor-patient, husband-wife, and a slew of other social roles come with preconceptions that may or may not fit our individual abilities and needs. Soldiers, teachers, or police officers may behave quite differently—and treat other people quite differently—in their social roles than they do when they are off-duty, as it were. The problem with social roles often comes when there is a presumed superior-inferior relationship with other people.

THE ROLE OF GENETICS AND THE FICTION OF RACE

Culture plays a vital role in defining our racial and ethnic attitudes. These attitudes evolve, and science is challenging many traditional us-them assumptions. At a White House ceremony on June 26, 2000, President Clinton, Francis S. Collins (director of the National

Human Genome Research Institute), and J. Craig Venter announced to the world that a rough draft of the human genome—the genetic recipe that creates human beings—had been completed. At the ceremony, which British Prime Minister Tony Blair joined by satellite, Venter described how illusory racial differences are at the level of genes. Venter, head of the private biotechnology company Celera Genomics, one of two competing groups mapping the genome, explained how his company had sequenced the DNA of three women and two men of diverse racial categories including African-American, Hispanic, Asian, and Caucasian. "We did the sampling not in an exclusionary way," said Venter, "but out of respect for the diversity that is America and to help illustrate that the concept of race has no genetic or scientific basis. In the five Celera genomes, there's no way to tell one ethnicity from another . . . as individuals we are all unique and population statistics do not apply. . . ."

Human races, science is concluding, are fictions created by cultural meaning systems. The reason is that our species, from an evolutionary standpoint, is brand-new. There has not been enough time for significant genetic differences to accumulate among different human populations. Species such as chimpanzees and gorillas, which are several million years old, have far more genetic variation among regional groups than we do. The genetic differences between two different populations of gorillas—mountain gorillas and lowland gorillas—are fairly substantial. In contrast, modern humans seem to have evolved from a group of a few thousand individuals little more than a hundred thousand years ago. Scientists are learning that many of the differences in physical appearance among different human populations may boil down to the tiniest of genetic divergences—perhaps variations in only a single gene that affects the skin.[3]

That traditional human racial classifications have a primitive us-them origin is evident from the categorical way they are applied. Recall that the general architecture of the primitive neural system, with some exceptions, creates binary categories into which phenomena are placed using either-or logic. Someone is either one of us or one of them, a friend or an enemy, good or bad. To the primitive components of the brain, one cannot be both. This mutually exclusive categorization promotes rapid processing of sensory data and quick reactions to threats. A preconscious alerting system scans all the data flowing through our senses before we are even consciously aware of what we are seeing. Traditionally, this kind of simplistic pigeonholing is how racial categories have functioned. One is either white or black, not both, regardless of any multiracial background. Or, more generally, white or nonwhite. Even if a person had one "white" parent, he or she is generally classified in the nonwhite category. Where racial mixtures have been acknowledged, it is often with a new limbic category that has a negative connotation: "half-breed" or "mulatto," for example. Clearly, these racial categories functioned to make not only us-them but also superior-inferior distinctions. Nineteenth century ethnologists in Europe and America even classified whites into different races. One popular scheme identified three white races: blond, blue-eyed Teutonics (deemed the superior race); brown-haired Alpines; and slender, dark-haired Mediterraneans. This sort of racial classification was later incorporated by the Nazis. The immigration laws of many countries, including those of the United States, reflected pronounced racial preferences, even among different groups of "whites." In early nineteenth-century America, for example, Irish immigrants were often classified as blacks.

Thoughtful people have always recognized the absurdity of these kinds of racial schemes. Frederick Douglass, the passionate abolitionist and friend of Abraham Lincoln, called such arbitrary and prejudiced racial thinking "diseased imagination." One of the most brilliant orators America has ever produced, Douglass was born a slave in Maryland in 1818 to an African-American mother and a white father, whom he never knew. He escaped to the North when he was twenty and, though self-taught, quickly became one of the leading political and social figures of his day. Douglass once told an audience how an artist, who had been commissioned to paint his portrait, requested that "[I show] my full face, for that is Ethiopian. Take my side face, said I, for that is Caucasian. But should you try my quarter face you would find it Indian. I don't know that any race can claim me, but being identified with slaves as I am, I think I know the meaning of the inquiry."

Nazi ideology decried racial impurity. White supremacists continue to echo this. But modern science has shown that human races are an illusion, genetically speaking, and racism is just a particularly venomous form of us-them stereotyping. Most of the genetic variation among humans—90 percent or more, according to some estimates—occurs within human racial groups, not between them. That means there are likely to be far greater genetic differences between two randomly selected "Caucasians" than between a randomly selected Caucasian and an African-American. The differences among human population groups are not genetic but overwhelmingly cultural: different languages, different customs. Reflecting the wisdom of Frederick Douglass for the first time, the census in 2000 allowed Americans to place themselves in multiracial categories, consisting of from two to six different racial combinations. Although only a relatively small number chose to do so, the percentage is expected to grow in future years. Nevertheless, the binary bias remains. According to guidelines from the federal Office of Management and Budget, those who classify themselves as white and something else will generally be "allocated to the minority race." Although some groups argue that multiracial categories will weaken the enforcement of civil rights laws, and it is true that racial classifications can make it easier to track the prevalence of, say, diabetes in the African-American community, the untold damage that primitive racial categorizing has done to the social fabric of humanity makes one long for a more benign form of classifying ourselves that recognizes each of us, first and foremost, as unique individuals rather than members of any category, whether based on race, ethnicity, gender, religion, nationality, class, sexual orientation, or any other grouping. Frederick Douglass was a pioneer in fighting for what Nelson Mandela calls a nonracial democracy. A friend and supporter of Susan B. Anthony and other leading feminists of his day, Douglass edited a crusading newspaper, the *North Star*, whose masthead proclaimed: "Right is of no sex, truth is of no color."

Francis S. Collins, who directs the federal government's National Human Genome Research Institute—a leader in the publicly funded effort competing with Venter's group to complete the sequencing of the human genome—points out that the small amount of genetic variation among the earliest *Homo sapiens* (a population of perhaps ten thousand individuals) seems to be the same genetic variation present today. The genes of any particular human being are 99.9 percent identical with the genes of any other human being. More than virtually any other species, we all belong to the same immediate genetic family. This is the scientific basis of our common humanity. But science is also discovering the foundation of our unique individuality. Although human beings seem to have fewer genes than once thought, geneticists are finding that each human gene has many more variants than expected. A gene variant is called an allele. Different alleles for the human eye color gene, for example, can produce eyes that are brown, blue, gray, or green. The complexity and variability of each human gene means that there are an astronomical number of possible combinations of human alleles. Each one of us represents a unique amalgam of alleles that will never reoccur naturally—without some artificial process such as cloning.[4]

The racial, ethnic, and other distinctions we make among ourselves and often use to hate, oppress, and kill each other are biologically superficial. Genetically, there are no significant differences among human groups. Each group is made up of genetically unique individuals who are closely related to the individuals in all other groups and to the population of human beings that began our species little more than a hundred thousand years ago. But the architecture of our primitive neural system has nevertheless evolved to seize on just these kinds of generalized and often irrational group distinctions as it ceaselessly and fearfully surveys its surroundings for any signs of a threat. Tolerance is not innate; it must be learned. We must consciously design and rigorously apply strategies that neutralize the primitive tendency to make these distinctions.

Science is one important cultural institution that employs the advanced neural system to bridge these kinds of primitive differences in a peaceful global effort to increase human knowledge. The genome project is a dazzling example of the human drive for meaning as expressed through an international scientific undertaking involving thousands of men and women from many cultural backgrounds. The detailed map of the human genome is an achievement that represents "a pinnacle of human self-knowledge," observed the *New York Times*, with staggering implications that "will in time redefine knowledge of ourselves, our history, our innate capacities and our relationship to the rest of creation. The conditions of human existence, the reach of human abilities, the purpose of life—at least in a biological sense—have boundaries that are engraved in the genome's gnomic text."[5]

Science seeks to rigorously order the natural world in ways that make sense, that have meaning. This is a process that is both analytical and intensely emotional. With few specific instincts to guide us, we humans organize ourselves to understand nature and control it, often through the creation of new technologies such as genomics. Scientists can barely conceal their excitement at having such a powerful new tool. "I truly feel this is going to revolutionize medicine because we are going to understand not only what causes disease but what prevents disease," said geneticist Stephen T. Warren, editor of *The American Journal of Human Genetics*. "We will understand the mechanism of disease sufficiently to do rational therapy. We will be able to predict who is at higher risk for particular disease and provide advice to individuals as to how best to maintain their health."

Novelty breeds novelty; discovery breeds discovery. "The beauty of science is that all important discoveries are made by building on the discoveries of others," said Venter. Nearly fifty years ago, when James Watson and Francis Crick wrote the paper announcing their discovery of the double helix design of DNA, they made one of the most famous understatements in the history of science: "This structure has novel features which are of considerable biological interest." What Collins, Venter, and their colleagues set out to do was unravel the giant helical DNA molecules coiled within the twenty-three pairs of human chromosomes—one set is contributed by each parent—and figure out the exact sequence of three billion or so chemical units that are contained within the DNA. These chemical units are a language that consists of four letters: the bases adenine (A), cytosine (C), guanine (G), and thymine (T). The double helix of DNA is like a winding staircase, and the bases are the steps. Human DNA contains about the same number of letters as would fill a thousand books of a thousand pages each. All the genes that make up a human being are spelled out in this language. Almost every gene contains a formula for making a specific protein, and these proteins give us physical form and govern the chemical processes that keep us alive and well. By understanding how all these genetically orchestrated proteins interact—a daunting project that is just beginning—we will understand exactly how our bodies and brains are created, how they operate, and how they protect and repair themselves. This will provide us with the innermost secrets of all our biological processes, including our emotions—specifically, for our purposes, the emotion of hate. Geneticists have been surprised by how few human genes there seem to be: only about thirty thousand. But many human genes appear more complex and versatile than, say, the genes of a fruit fly. Now that the genome has been largely mapped, geneticists can identify every human gene and study how these genes function, individually and collectively. "We've got another century of work ahead of us to figure out how all these things relate to each other," said molecular biologist David Baltimore, a Nobel laureate.[6]

Already, scientists are probing the genetic basis of disease. Researchers, for example, have found that in certain breast cancer patients a gene they have named HER2 is overactive, producing so much of a growth-inducing protein that their cancer is able to survive all medical efforts to destroy it. By locating and studying this gene, however, a new drug called Herceptin was developed that suppresses this growth protein and gives those with the HER2 gene a much better chance of survival. In the future, doctors may find ways to turn on genes inside cancer cells that order the cells to self-destruct. And this strategy—turning genes on and off at will—could potentially affect the treatment of mental illness as well as physical illness.

Almost every cell in the body has a complete set of the twenty-three human chromosomes. But in each cell only a certain number of genes are turned on. This depends on the type of cell and what it happens to be doing at the time. Many diseases may be cured or controlled by finding ways to order certain genes—such as those orchestrating the immune system—to work harder or other genes to stop working at all. Collins has speculated on the effects of this new knowledge over the next forty years. He believes that within ten years genetic tests will be developed that can tell each of us our predisposition for developing the twenty-five major causes of illness and death, including cancer, heart disease, diabetes, and osteoporosis. Such tests could be a source of dread. In essence, science will be able to peer into the future and predict your major illnesses, perhaps even what you are likely to die of. "I think young people are the ones who are afraid to see the future," said James Watson, a guiding force behind the human genome project. "Old people see the future and would like to reverse it." There will be cures available for some of these major illnesses. But for others, doctors will be able to advise patients about medications as well as changes in diet, exercise, and other health habits that will minimize the chance of becoming ill. By the year 2020, doctors will tailor the prescription and dosage of medications to each individual's genetic susceptibilities and sensitivities. This should substantially increase the effectiveness of drugs and cut down on unwanted side effects. In the following twenty years, not only will gene-based drugs, therapies, and outright cures be developed for most diseases, but science will make huge strides in understanding how genes affect longevity as well. By 2040, Collins believes, people in the industrialized world will be living on average to ninety years of age in robust health.

The swiftly growing understanding of the human genome should have a major impact on mental health as well. "One of the greatest benefits of genomic medicine will be to unravel some biological contributions to major mental illnesses like schizophrenia and manic-depressive disease" and allow us to design new therapies, Collins said. But this is an area in which complexity seems to be the order of the day. Our behavioral tendencies often involve the interaction of multiple genes and the environment. Scientists had hoped that this would not be the case for mental illnesses and that they would be more like Huntington's disease and cystic fibrosis, whose causes have been traced to mutations in single genes. But after a number of false starts in which researchers claimed that a major mental illness such as manic depression had been linked to a single gene—claims that were later retracted—the medical community is reluctantly concluding that most serious mental illnesses seem to be produced by the effects of a number of genes. As Collins and other geneticists constantly point out, genes are not destiny. In mental illness as well as in all other complex behaviors, the environment plays a massive role and interacts with genetic tendencies in complicated and poorly understood ways. This interplay of genes and environment has been shown in studies of identical twins, who have identical sets of genes and thus are nature's clones. If, for example, one identical twin is diagnosed with schizophrenia—a mental illness in which heredity seems to play a major part—the other twin has just a 30 to 50 percent chance of developing the disease. Thus far, only with Alzheimer's disease is there hope that a severe mental disorder can be traced to mutations in one or two genes. The complexity of mental illness is not surprising, however, given the complexity of the human brain.[7]

The weight of the human brain at birth is about three-quarters of a pound. By about a year old, brain weight has doubled. But it is not until around seven years old that the brain is almost the adult weight of three pounds. The reason for this massive growth is not a significant increase in the number of neurons—the hundred billion or so information-processing cells that make up the brain. An infant is born with virtually all the neurons he or she will ever have. Most cells in the body are replaced periodically. It was once thought that neurons were not replaced at all. New research, however, indicates that we may grow new neurons in key brain areas such as the hippocampus. But the number seems to be comparatively small. Unlike most other cells, your neurons are capable of living as long as you do. The vast majority of neurons in your brain at this moment were there when you were born. Because it is the pattern of connections among neurons that stores learning and memory, if neurons were steadily dying and being replaced the way skin cells are, we would constantly lose a portion of our stored knowledge.

What multiplies the weight of an infant's brain is not an increase in the gray matter—the cell bodies of the neurons—but a vast increase in the white matter, which represents the branching of projections from the neuron cell bodies that form an astonishingly complex wiring network as literally trillions of connections are made among neurons. A single neuron may have thousands of different connections. Most of these are insulated by a sheath of a fatty, whitish-looking substance called myelin. The point of connection between two neurons is called a synapse, so these are synaptic connections, which use both electrical impulses and neurochemicals to communicate. The process of wiring the infant brain is quite elaborate, often involving a huge overproduction of synaptic connections that are later pruned back as circuits are optimized. If all the neuron wires in an adult human brain were laid end to end, they would stretch nearly to the moon. This colossal increase in wiring and insulation is due not only to automatic developmental processes as the various parts of the brain are wired together, but also to the

immense amount of cultural learning that must take place before a
young human being is ready to function within a specific society.
Making and breaking synaptic connections continues throughout
our lives. Learning involves wiring and rewiring the neurons of the
brain and this, in turn, involves switching genes on and off within
the nucleus of the neuron.[8]

The mapping of the human genome leads us down new and
unexpected paths that are fraught with fantastic opportunities—and
booby traps. All these advances in genetics assume in the long run
that each one of us will have our entire genome sequenced, and perhaps carry this sequence around with us on a computer chip embed-
ded in something like a credit card. This is not some prospect for the
distant future. The speed of genome sequencing is increasing rapidly while the cost of sequencing is dropping sharply—from ten dollars per unit of DNA in 1988 to less than four cents per unit as the
new century began. Because gene sequencing depends on computers, which are themselves increasing in power while decreasing in
relative cost, these trends are expected to accelerate. But this raises
immensely important issues of privacy and discrimination. Both the
public genome sequencing effort, headed by Collins, and the private
sequencing effort, headed by Venter, have kept the identities of those
whose DNA they are sequencing a closely guarded secret (the public program, which involves sixteen centers in six countries, is using
fragments of DNA from a dozen individuals). Other than reading
your thoughts, there is no more complete violation of privacy than
sequencing your DNA without your permission. "In terms of public exposure," noted one observer, "being stripped naked in Times
Square would be only mildly revealing compared to having one's
genome accessible on an open database. That is because all people
probably carry some gene variants that could predispose them or
their children to disease."

Bioethicists see many kinds of potential dangers in DNA
sequencing, from discrimination in hiring and insurance coverage
to more informal sorts of bias—a person might be shunned by

potential marriage partners because he or she carries a strong genetic tendency to develop Alzheimer's disease. In our darkest vision of the future, knowledge of the human genome might be hideously misused. Genetically engineered humans might become the basis of hate-producing us-them distinctions. Horrific new diseases could be created as superweapons of biological warfare.

Though the genetic differences among human groups are exceptionally small, some fear that what differences there are will nevertheless be used to intensify parochial divisions and hatred. "Most geneticists wax euphoric that so many of our genes are in common, that the genome map will show us to be a happy band of brothers and sisters," said Arthur L. Caplan, director of the University of Pennsylvania's bioethics center. "I doubt it. . . . People don't realize how important that drive is to understand ourselves. In most parts of the world we define ourselves by blood and kin, and those are just surrogates for genes."[9]

Despite the biologically homogeneous nature of human beings, there is one genetic difference that separates us into two groups: the Y chromosome. At conception, the female always contributes an X chromosome to the embryo, while the male contributes either an X or Y chromosome—an X chromosome will mean the embryo will develop into a female, and a Y chromosome will mean a male. Men are XY and women are XX. There is a furious debate about how much this distinct genetic endowment shapes innate differences between men and women. Do their genes make women inherently vulnerable to the kinds of oppression that honor killing represents, for example? In past few decades, there has been a tendency to highlight innate differences between men and women. But this "men are from Mars" approach has recently fallen into disfavor with many researchers because it tends to oversimplify and promote unwarranted stereotypes, especially in popular culture. According to social psychologist Carol Tavris, "Sex differences that show up in any study tend to be artifacts of education, power, and immediate social context and the historical moment, which is why they wax and wane with the times." Yet sex chromosomes do have certain consequences in sex-specific aspects of brain development and cultural differences, though these are far from clear-cut and are still being worked out. Unquestionably, however, the fact that men are, on average, the larger and more physically aggressive gender can have important consequences for the status of women.

Stanford University psychologist Eleanor E. Maccoby points out that there appears to be a universal tendency of boys and girls to self-segregate and develop separate cultures with different play styles and ways of interacting. Boys' groups, said Maccoby, are generally "more cohesive than girls' groups: more sexist, more exclusionary, more vigilant about gender-boundary violations by their members, and more separate from adult culture." As the gender-based cultures that Maccoby identifies develop among children, said Tavris, "as with any two nations, schools or ethnic groups, boys and girls identify with their own in-group, they stereotype and disparage members of the out-group, and they misunderstand or feel uncomfortable with the other group's ways of doing things." Maccoby believes that childhood gender self-segregation has some lingering affects on adults, influencing men's and women's habits and preferences. Yet what is true of children is not always true of adults. Cultural and personal meaning systems can play a major role in neutralizing adult gender differences. Maccoby concludes that in modern industrialized societies there tends to be great individuality and less pronounced gender differences among adults. If given the opportunity, both men and women engage in a vastly wider range of activities than are permitted by tradition-bound cultures. In the developed world, a random group of fifty-year-olds of both genders is far more diverse in their interests and pursuits than a group of five-year-olds.[10]

With the mapping of the human genome, we are now in a position to manipulate the precious message of human life that our sexual bonds have so carefully preserved for a hundred thousand years. There will be a temptation to begin genetically designing our offspring, particularly if certain sets of gene variants or alleles turn out to be linked to traits such as high intelligence. Already, couples undergoing in vitro fertilization have the ability to select the sex of their child. One day, they may be able to select much more. "Many people would be repulsed by the idea of optimizing embryos to have tall, handsome, thin, athletic, intelligent babies who will be able to predict the stock market," said Mildred Cho, a senior research scholar at Stanford University's Center for Biomedical Ethics. "But it's a private matter. And that would be hard to regulate." It is impossible to know whether selecting detailed traits for our children will ever be feasible. The human genome is extremely complex, and researchers have run into major difficulties in trying to develop techniques such as gene therapy, which seeks to introduce healthy genes into the body to compensate for a known genetic defect. But the human taste for novelty invariably entices at least a few people to try something new. Already there have been efforts on the Internet to market the sperm and eggs of individuals considered to have desirable traits—a low-tech attempt at genetic engineering. And there is a major controversy about whether human beings should be artificially cloned. "There is no doubt that knowledge about different alleles will create the temptation to optimize one's offspring in terms of their genetic endowment," said Robert Weinberg, a geneticist at the Whitehead Institute of Cambridge, Massachusetts, one of the major scientific centers involved in the public effort to sequence the genome. Identifying genetic aspects of intelligence, Weinberg said, would open "a whole Pandora's box of possibilities, where someone like myself is no more qualified than someone with a minimal understanding of genetics to make ethical and moral choices. This has to be a society-wide debate, not one involving just geneticists or bioethicists."

Obviously, all these advances raise exceptionally difficult social questions. The culture of innovation in the biological sciences—a descendant of the culture of innovation that began with the Upper Paleolithic revolution—is accelerating so rapidly that there are concerns about society's ability to keep up—to create systems of meaning within which these powerful technologies can be used wisely. Not only is the human brain proportionately larger than that of any other species, our limbic system, too, is the largest. This means that our emotional lives can be almost infinitely complex and unpredictable, compounding our difficulties in trying to shape a rational strategy.[11]

Enormously critical issues are rapidly being pushed into the public arena. We have already genetically engineered certain animals, crops, and other organisms. Human genes have been spliced into bacteria so that these bacteria can more cheaply produce human hormones such as insulin. All this has generated a backlash in some quarters, with fears being raised about the eventual effects on our health and the environment. But we have witnessed only the first glimmer of a social upheaval. Within this new century we will in all likelihood have a complete understanding of not only our own genome, but also of the genomes of every other species. This will make us masters of the evolution of all life on Earth, including the very form of human nature. Our drive for meaning will be stretched to the limit as we are forced to answer the most profound questions of all. Who are we? Whom do we want to be? What is life? What do we want it to be? Hovering over all these issues is the challenge of controlling our hatred and selfishness so that this knowledge can become a benefit rather than a danger to humanity.

9

HOW HATE MESSAGES ARE SPREAD THROUGHOUT THE MODERN WORLD

OFIR MEANS MERCIFUL IN HEBREW. But sixteen-year-old Ofir Rahum was shown no mercy on the road from the West Bank city of Ramallah to the Jewish settlement of Psagot. The bullet-riddled body of the Israeli boy was discovered in a shallow grave. He was buried on January 19, 2001, another victim of the back-and-forth attacks that claimed so many lives after the second Palestinian *intifada* began in September 2000. But Israel found this crime especially shocking because Rahum was apparently lured to his death through the Internet, a victim of the growing worldwide problem of cyberhate, or using the Internet to spread hate messages and to recruit those who would band together to commit hate crimes.

HATE ON THE INTERNET

The Internet mirrors human nature with all its strengths and flaws, including hatred. It has its share of predators, and Rahum was

apparently one of the victims. Web surfing is popular in Israel, and
Rahum was an Internet buff who told friends that he had begun a
romantic relationship in cyberspace with a woman in her twenties.
He described her to friends as a dark-haired, English-speaking tour-
ist. Israeli authorities believe she may have been Palestinian. Rahum
said the two had met once in Jerusalem and, afterward, had continued their relationship on the Internet. They arranged to meet again.
He never returned from that meeting. Palestinian gunmen are
believed to have ambushed the couple as they traveled to Ramallah.
Rahum was slain and his body secretly buried. The Palestinian
Authority denied any responsibility, formally condemning the
killing—an unusual step in the bitter conflict. It was Palestinian
investigators who discovered Rahum's remains after being notified
by the Israelis that the boy was missing.

Like many young Israelis, Rahum had his own website that wel-
comed cybersurfers and promised daily updates on his doings and
interests. It had links to his favorite songs and to other friends on
the Web. After his death the site was flooded with messages of con-
dolence from around the world. "I wish you would have remained
anonymous and a stranger to us all," said one. The Internet served
as a battlefield of the *intifada*. Hackers sympathetic to each side sab-
otaged the websites of the other side, including sites belonging to the
Israeli government and the militant Islamic Hezbollah movement.

The unusual nature of Rahum's murder received massive coverage in the Israeli press. "Death Trap on the Internet!" a headline
proclaimed. Rabbi Michael Melchior spoke at Rahum's funeral. "We
have all come to know you in the last twenty-four hours," he said.
"How terrible it is that we raise our children to be merciful and com-
passionate, not to fear others, to approach them and support them,
only to have them approach others and have the worst of all happen." Rahum's parents were inconsolable. "Keep your children away
from the Internet," they said in a statement. "It is what dragged him
away, and it is what killed him."[1]

But the Internet itself is simply a communications system. Only its millions of users can imbue it with meaning. Unlike the telephone network, the Internet gives everyone a chance to communicate in the open and at virtually the same time through Web pages, E-mail, and chat rooms. It is as if you could listen in on telephone conversations going on around the world. Some people compare the Internet to a town where the blinds are always up so you can observe everyone living their lives. You can see what they love. You can also see what they hate. And much of this hatred is extremely ugly. The Southern Poverty Law Center in Montgomery, Alabama—one of the leading organizations that tracks hate on the Internet—reports that there has been an explosive growth in hate-oriented websites. For the first time, naked hate designed for maximum appeal is easily available to the mainstream on a worldwide basis at several thousand websites, many of which have elements designed to attract children.

Like the Internet itself, hate websites were initially developed in the United States. Perhaps the first such site—Stormfront.org—appeared in 1995. It was created by former Ku Klux Klan member Don Black, who is sometimes called the godfather of hate on the Net. Black bubbles over with enthusiasm about his website, which represents a quantum leap over an old-fashioned hate newsletter. "We suddenly have a mass audience rather than a small clique of subscribers," he said. Black's site preaches racial and ethnic hatred. His son, Derek, has his own section on the site, called Stormfront for Kids, featuring an unauthorized version of the popular computer game Doom, which has been modified so that players shoot and kill blacks. These kinds of hate sites often feature graphics of lynchings and other racist images. They espouse a whole range of vicious and often paranoid meaning systems and a long list of grievances. White supremacism is especially popular. One strategy used by some hate groups is to set up their websites so that a child searching for information to do a paper for school—on Martin Luther King Jr., for example—will turn up a racist website such as the one entitled, "Martin Luther King: The Beast as Saint."

HOW PURVEYORS OF HATE REACH THE MASSES

Empathy is one of the mind's most advanced capacities, but it can be a double-edged sword. Adolf Hitler and the Nazi movement are a textbook example. Empathy can be used to minimize or dissipate hate, but selective empathy can also be used to create hatred, as when people empathize with a purveyor of hate such as Hitler or the many hatemongers and demagogues on and off the Internet. Hatemongers seek empathy for themselves but not for their victims. Hitler, in particular, yearned for sympathetic identification in his testament to racism and megalomania, *Mein Kampf* ("My Struggle"). Those who identify with a charismatic, divisive leader are more likely to buy into to his us-versus-them mentality. A relentless campaign to make emotional connection with the masses was a central part of Hitler's strategy. It was characteristic of his demagogic speaking style, which often began at almost a whisper, with reasonable tones, and then built to a volcanic shriek of emotions. To those who identified with him, he was expressing their frustrations, anger, and hopes in an overwhelmingly powerful way. To those who did not, Hitler's speeches seemed like the ravings of a lunatic. Hitler and Nazism continue to have a magnetic effect on some extremist elements, including skinheads and groups such as the Ku Klux Klan and the Aryan Nation.

One religious variation on these sorts of hate groups and neo-Nazi ideas is called the Christian Identity Movement. It preaches that Christian whites are superior to all other groups, particularly Jews, gays, and blacks. Like Osama bin Laden's distorted vision of Islamic jihad, the Christian Identity Movement weaves paranoid ravings and selective quotations from the Bible into a bizarre meaning system. Such white supremacists say that Christ will not return until the Earth is purged of nonwhites. They predict bloody race wars in the near future. Generally, however, they are careful not to cross the line between free speech and criminal conspiracy. Because of law enforcement's success in penetrating and prosecuting groups such as the Ku Klux Klan, the currently preferred strategy is to use hate websites to encourage lone wolf attacks. A lone wolf is someone, such as Timothy McVeigh, who decides—apparently on his own—to carry out an act of violence like the bombing of the federal building in Oklahoma City. It costs very little to set up a hate website that may be seen by thousands of people, some of whom could be dangerous sociopaths. The idea is to focus these lone wolves' violent impulses on the particular groups that are the objects of hatred. Purveyors of hate can thus encourage terrorist activities without being held directly responsible.

LONE WOLVES AND MILITIA ORGANIZATIONS

Lone wolves are angry, hate-filled, often mentally disturbed individuals who generally have few, if any, formal connections with hate groups. They are unusually vulnerable to messages of hate because this worldview gives them an enemy to blame for their own frustrations. Because they are not taking orders from anyone, lone wolves are difficult to identify until after they have struck. Many of the hate sites on the Web treat them as heroes. There are more than a dozen websites dedicated to glorifying the Columbine killers, Dylan Klebold and Eric Harris, who had spouted racial and ethnic slurs on their own hate-drenched website.

McVeigh, a veteran of the Gulf War, was loosely connected to the antigovernment militia movement. This was a paramilitary culture that arose in the mid-1970s in the wake of disillusionment with the government's conduct of the Vietnam War. Members of the movement were generally working-class whites disturbed by the social turmoil of the time. They were attracted by the militia's conspiracy theories accusing the government, along with liberal activists and racial and ethnic minorities, of plotting to take away their freedoms.[2]

It is no coincidence that paranoia and hate are so often found together. Paranoia tends to create a sense of being trapped, which may generate a powerful fight response by the primitive neural system. But the relationship is two-way. Not only can paranoia produce hate but hate also can produce paranoia, as the hater's sensitized limbic system begins to see threats and conspiracies everywhere.

Militia members sometimes refer to the American government as ZOG—the Zionist Occupation Government—which indicates their mixture of antigovernment hate, paranoia, and anti-Semitism. Militia members are especially angry about gun control, which many militias believe is a government plot to disarm the citizenry in preparation for a military takeover of the United States by the antiwhite United Nations. The militia movement experienced rapid growth after Congress passed the Brady Bill in 1993, which imposed a waiting period for handgun purchases and banned outright certain kinds of assault rifles. The Brady Bill was named for James Brady, who was serving as President Reagan's press secretary when he was severely wounded during the attack on Reagan by John Hinckley at the Washington Hilton. McVeigh said that it was the passage of this gun control legislation that convinced him to begin actively plotting the bombing in Oklahoma City. One of the leading proponents of militia-style paranoia is author William L. Pearce. His novels, notably *The Turner Diaries* and *Hunter*, glamorize characters who kill minorities and stage violent attacks on the federal government. On his website, Pearce delivers a weekly address that gives his own special twist to current events. McVeigh had a copy of *The Turner Diaries* with him when he was captured.

Ironically, the militias have gone into decline in the years since McVeigh's 1995 bombing. The deaths of nineteen children among the 168 people killed in Oklahoma City helped discredit the movement. It also brought a crackdown by the federal government on many militia members for a variety of crimes, including illegal weapons violations. True to their extreme paranoia, some militia members argued that McVeigh was a dupe of the government which, they say, orchestrated the bombing of the Murrah Federal Building so that "ZOG" could come down hard on the militias. The Southern Poverty Law Center reported in May 2001 that the number of identifiable militia organizations had dropped from a high of 858 in 1996 to 194. The last major flurry of militia activity was in 1999, when some militia leaders predicted the violent collapse of civilization with the dawn of the new millennium and the Y2K computer bug. When that failed to materialize, the decline resumed. But the center also reported that many militia members have drifted into even more militant racist, bigoted, and anti-Semitic hate groups, whose numbers are growing and whose messages are being spread at a terrifying rate across the Internet.

In scanning the websites of these groups, one is struck by how venomous and brutish they are. Hate is an obsolete and reconstructed remnant of an ancient past. It threatens the continued existence of our species in this era of weapons of mass destruction. There is something not quite human about the hate-inspired slaughter advocated by many of these groups, something primeval and terrifying, the nature of which can be found deep within the folds of our brain.

A dramatic shift forward in human brain architecture with our relatively small occipital lobes and oversized frontal lobes signifies a momentous evolutionary shift to meaning and away from instinct in our behavior. We have moved from the ape pattern of primarily visual dominance to a kind of inner eye that relies on planning, scenario spinning, imagination, and consciousness. It is this kind of imaginative vision that has allowed us to comprehend the billions of microscopic chemical units that code for the human genome and to create such things as computers, the Internet, and new technologies—knowledge that is vastly beyond the reach of any other species. But this kind of sweeping vision also allows us to classify humanity into superior and inferior groups, marking some for oppression and extermination. We have created the technologies that we use for good or ill, for love or hate, including the Internet—which helped take the life of sixteen-year-old Ofir Rahum.

10

THE TOXIC WORKPLACE

WORK IS LIKE PLAY for very few people. Too many come to hate their jobs. Burnout ranks as one of the top problems in today's workplace. Usually, through some mixture of overwork, difficulties with coworkers, personal problems, lack of success, or declining interest, the burned-out worker begins to withdraw emotionally from the workplace. Sometimes the burnout flows from lack of challenge— the boredom reflex. As a worker disconnects, any pleasure in work vanishes, replaced by a slew of negative feelings. "Without work, all life goes rotten, but when work is soulless, life stifles and dies," wrote Albert Camus. Whereas happiness boosts energy and attention, frustration and hate sap both, leading to physical and mental exhaustion and other potential health problems as well.

Today's frenetic, competitive, stressful workplace adds to this problem. The Internet is creating huge opportunities, but also huge uncertainties and huge disappointments. In addition, the new international corporate environment, in which downsizing and restructuring are common, makes it more difficult for an employee to forge a deep, long-lasting connection with an employer. For victims of burnout, the result is declining performance and increasing illness. In some cases, this can be accompanied by a severe mental breakdown that leads to uncontrolled hatred, anger, even bloodshed. The growth in workplace violence is alarming. It costs businesses more than four billion dollars a year. But the human cost is infinitely greater. Over the past decade, the rate of workplace homicide doubled. Murder has become the number one cause of death for women in the workplace, and it is the number three cause of death for men. The importance of coming to grips with burnout and stress cannot be overestimated.

Nearly a thousand workers are murdered on the job every year. It is the fastest-growing category of homicide. Studies indicate that about one in twenty workers is physically assaulted annually. One in six workers reports being sexually harassed, and one-third report being verbally harassed. All this breeds anger and hatred, which can develop when one feels he or she is trapped, unappreciated, or the object of prejudice or threat. Surveys find that more and more workers feel a lack of respect from their employers and a lack of voice in matters that affect them. These kinds of issues were present in an unusual walkout that occurred at the giant aircraft manufacturing company Boeing. After a forty-day strike—their longest previous strike lasted one day—Boeing engineers went back to work in March 2000. The major issue in the strike was not money but respect. For many years, Boeing thought of itself as a family. But in the 1990s, the company faced difficult economic challenges and placed a greater emphasis on profits and competitiveness. Top company officials made statements that many Boeing engineers interpreted to mean that engineers could be replaced if need be. Some longtime Boeing engineers reported incidents in which they were treated disrespectfully by managers. As part of their new contract, the engineers have a larger say in the company.

When workers talk about respect, they are expressing in part their desire to have an emotionally rewarding connection with their employer, something that appears to be disappearing in many sectors of the economy. In one study by Donald Gibson, a professor at the Yale School of Management, 25 percent of workers surveyed by the Gallup organization described themselves as "at least somewhat angry" on a continuing basis at work. These employees were more likely to report being bored, having low energy, and feeling trapped in their jobs. "A turbulent economic environment that has produced, on the one hand, productivity and growth and, on the other, wrenching change and uncertainty has buffeted the workplace," Gibson concluded. "While a majority of employees are responding to these conditions with reports of workplace satisfaction, there remains a substantial portion who are dissatisfied, even angry, at work. Most visibly, anger is linked to workplace aggression, which appears to be increasing. We are weekly confronted with stories of workers taking aggressive, even violent, action particularly against supervisors."[1]

Widespread worker dissatisfaction and anger have prompted the study of a phenomenon called desk rage, which joins road rage, air rage, parent rage, and a slew of other forms of rage as a feature of postmodern society. In one national survey of more than a thousand workers, nearly a third admitted to yelling at someone at the office; 65 percent said workplace stress was at least occasionally a problem, 23 percent reported that stress had driven them to tears, and 34 percent blamed their jobs for causing them loss of sleep. Other surveys have found a rising rate of incivility in the workplace that has significant consequences for those on the receiving end. It is a prime source of fuel for on-the-job hatred. One study of workers who had been treated rudely reported that half said they lost work time as a result of worrying about the rude treatment. A third said they intentionally reduced their commitment to their employer. Nearly a quarter said they no longer were doing their best work. And 12 percent said they quit their jobs. A typical case involved a San Francisco–area woman in her twenties who said she resigned after a senior member of her department threw a tantrum. "He stormed into my office and started screaming and yelling every swearword in the book," she said. "Then he went back to his office and started throwing things and slamming doors. I felt physically scared and threatened." She was right to be concerned. Sometimes such explosions can have far more serious consequences.

WORKPLACE SHOOTINGS

He called himself "Mucko" because it was a version of his last name that his young nieces and nephews could pronounce. Michael McDermott was a big man—more than six feet tall, weighing almost three hundred pounds—with a full beard, glasses, and a quiet, friendly demeanor. His colleagues knew him as a self-taught computer whiz and something of a loner. He worked as a software tester at an Internet consulting firm in Wakefield, Massachusetts, a small town along the high-tech corridor near Boston. But as Christmas 2000 approached, the forty-two-year-old McDermott was having financial problems. The IRS notified his employer, Edgewater Technology, that he owed back taxes. In a meeting with the accounting department, McDermott was told that the IRS was asking that his wages be garnished, which meant that a portion of his paycheck would automatically be deducted to pay off his back tax bill. Colleagues reported that McDermott, who was divorced and lived by himself, became extremely angry. The accountants said that they would wait until the first of the year to begin the garnishment, so as not to spoil his holidays. For the next several weeks, everything seemed to return to normal. But then, according to police, at 11:14 A.M. on the day after Christmas, McDermott—who had no previous criminal record—walked into the reception area of Edgewater Technology and, witnesses reported, "seemed to go crazy."

He was carrying a shotgun, a semiautomatic rifle, and a semiautomatic pistol. Immediately, he sprayed the reception area with bullets, killing receptionist Janice Hagerty and another woman. He proceeded down a corridor to the accounting department and shot to death two men and one woman.[2]

The gunfire and screams alerted other workers in the area who tried to flee or hide. One woman crouched behind a coat slung over a chair in one of the offices. McDermott sprayed the office with bullets but, miraculously, she was not hit. Other workers barricaded themselves behind a closed door. McDermott blew the door open with his shotgun and killed a man and a woman. He then returned to the reception area and sat down in a chair. The whole attack had lasted no more than eight minutes. When the police entered the building, they found McDermott still sitting in the chair, an AK-47 assault rifle and shotgun within easy reach, and the revolver in his pocket. But he made no effort to resist being taken into custody. Four women and three men lay dead, including a company vice president. One of the slain employees, twenty-nine-year-old Jennifer Bragg-Capobianco, had given birth to her first child ten weeks before. Another, Rose Manfredy, would have celebrated her fiftieth birthday the next day. All the victims were riddled with bullets. Two days later, as McDermott was escorted into the Middlesex County courtroom to be charged with the seven deaths, one observer said he scanned the packed courtroom "with reptilian eyes devoid of emotion."

This was another in a long string of highly publicized workplace shootings that mirror the school shootings that have periodically shocked the nation. In February 2001, an ex-employee of a truck-making company entered the suburban Chicago plant where he had worked and shot four employees to death before taking his own life. He had worked as a forklift operator at the plant for thirty-nine years but was fired when he was accused of being part of an internal theft ring. In March 2000, a fired employee killed five people at a Dallas-area car wash. In November 1999, a copier repairman in Honolulu who was afraid he was about to be laid off fatally shot seven people at the Honolulu offices of Xerox Corporation. And in July 1999, a day trader who suffered heavy losses in the stock market killed nine people at two Atlanta brokerage offices and then himself. When police entered his suburban Atlanta apartment, they found he had also killed his wife, five-year-old son, and three-year-old daughter. These workplace killings are often sparked by financial problems, job-related difficulties, or other kinds of bad news that ignite feelings of anger and hatred. The rampage that Michael McDermott is accused of carrying out bears some resemblance to Buford Furrow's attack on the North Valley Jewish Community Center and in nearby Chatsworth. But the hated "them" in the McDermott case were his fellow employees rather than Asians or Jews.

What pushes someone such as McDermott over the edge? We still don't understand the brain well enough to know for sure. Even if someone has trouble with violent impulses, he or she usually knows these impulses are wrong and may try to seek help, as Furrow did a number of times. But McDermott didn't, and neither do most other workplace killers. One thing we do know is that these shootings are almost always committed by males. "Men are nine times more lethal than women," according to neuroscientist Debra Niehoff. Researchers are still arguing about the reason for this, sorting through the various contributions of brain structure, hormones, neurochemicals, and environment. As with all forms of human aggression and violence, there is no simple answer. Hormones such as testosterone, for example, have been found to have extremely complex effects and seem to interact with many other hormones and neurochemicals. And the violent crime rate for women is increasing.

PREDICTING VIOLENT BEHAVIOR

There are no foolproof ways to predict violent behavior among adults or young people. For some, history can be a good indication.

But the penchant for violence depends on the relative balance between the primitive neural system and advanced neural system (which changes dynamically with time and context), the array of chemicals in the brain (there can be imbalances), any structural abnormalities (brain damage or brain tumors), and the particular meaning system that motivates an individual. There is also evidence that childhood abuse and neglect as well as other forms of intense, long-lasting stress at any time of life can damage the nervous system and derange the threat-detection apparatus of the primitive neural system, making it either far too sensitive or far too insensitive. "The process begins," said Niehoff, "with a nervous system biased toward survival and social responsiveness, equipped to respond aggressively or fearfully when the threat to survival is extreme. The constitutional boundaries of such a nervous system are not constant but vary from individual to individual, reflected in differences in perceptual acuity, interactive style, attentiveness, and social orientation. . . . As stress wears away at the nervous system, risk assessment grows less and less accurate. Minor insults are seen as major threats. Benign details take on a new emotional urgency. Empathy takes a back seat to relief from the numbing discomfort of a stress-deadened nervous system. Surrounded on all sides by real and imagined threats, the individual resorts to the time-honored survival strategies: fight, flight, or freeze." If the nervous system is sensitized, emotional reactions can balloon out of proportion. But if stress desensitizes the nervous system, then individuals move beyond the reach of emotion. "No warning bell of anxiety or disgust sounds when they're about to commit an atrocity," said Niehoff. "Conflict is no longer stressful, so they can fight and not feel a thing."[3]

If the primitive neural system slips out of the control of the advanced neural system, we enter the simplistic reptomammalian world of general and middle-level categories. To the limbic system, one's job is lumped into a category that might be called "getting food and other necessities," and a threat to one's job—though one may easily find another better one—is often accompanied by disproportionately strong emotions, even hatred, because the limbic system interprets this threat as a threat to survival, which it might have been a hundred thousand years ago. The limbic system also tends to equate feeling helpless or frustrated at work with being trapped and threatened. Fear and frustration are important sources of hate. If, for example, we fear our boss, we may also grow to hate him. Even after we quit our job we may still hate him—though he has no further power over us—because hatred creates long-term hostility that does not easily disappear. The limbic system identifies not only threats to survival and reproduction but also opportunities to enhance our survival and reproduction. A primitive sense of frustration can follow our thwarted attempts to take advantage of these perceived opportunities—failure to obtain a coveted promotion, for example. This, too, can lead to anger and hatred.

A threat can elicit stereotyped reactions of fight or flight. In humans, however, stereotyped defensive or flight reactions also extend to gestures of appeasement: averting the eyes, shrugging the shoulders—which indicate, as Darwin said in his book on emotions, "the absence of any intention to resist." Let's say your boss called you in and said you're doing a poor job. You could react with one of the primitive neural system's prepackaged responses: flight (try to get out of there as soon as possible), fight (angrily argue with him or her), or appeasement (try to soothe him or her and adopt the body language of acquiescence: averted eyes, shrugging, drooping shoulders). Appeasement might be followed by fear and avoidance once you leave your boss's presence. All these are relatively primitive responses, though they could be mixed with advanced neural elements that might involve deferentially discussing the problem with him or her using complex language and categories—unless you completely panicked, froze, or collapsed. There are strategies, however, that more fully involve the advanced neural system. You could go over your boss's head, try to outwit your boss, or organize your colleagues against him or her. But any of these strategies might also lead to mutual animosity, even hate. Ideally, if you and your boss were able to empathize with each other, the two of you could intelligently explore the problem and negotiate a mutually agreeable compromise. In the process, by understanding each other's problems, the two of you might discover a creative option that could improve not only your performance but the company's as well. What is especially important is that you perceive yourself to have some control over the situation. It's not surprising that many surveys show that a primary factor in job satisfaction—even more than money—is having a good relationship with the boss.

STRESS AND CONTROL

Stress, in and of itself, is not necessarily harmful. Improving mental and physical skills requires undergoing a certain amount of stress. But stress is damaging when it is intense, long-lasting, and accompanied by a sense of being trapped and helpless. Having a good relationship with the boss provides a sense of control over one's destiny at work. A boss who is indifferent, even antagonistic, can instill a sense of helplessness and frustration, which the primitive neural system tends to interpret as a threat to survival. A perception of control can have a powerful effect on one's health. One study of top executives at Fortune 500 companies found that their mortality rate was almost 40 percent less than comparable individuals in lower-ranking positions. Other studies have found that top managers often report a fulfilling sense of purpose and believe they are in control of their lives. This is mirrored by surveys that show an overwhelming number of workers prefer jobs that give them a sense of meaning and purpose. The effects of controlled versus uncontrolled stress have been measured in the laboratory. If two groups of laboratory rats regularly receive identical amounts of stress (in the form of mild electrical shocks, for example), but the first group has some element of control over the stress, it is the second group that generally has many more health problems. The first group of rats may simply see a flash of light prior to the shock, while the second group receives no warning. Just the ability to use the light flash to predict when the stress will occur tends to keep the first group healthier. The level of stress hormones in the helpless second group generally remains higher, suppressing the immune system and damaging the body.

Many of these findings were called into question in the 1960s when some researchers concluded that competitive workaholics—labeled "Type A personalities"—were more vulnerable to heart disease. This suggested that hard-charging executives, though they had more control over their lives, might nevertheless be risking their health. But on closer examination, scientists found that it was the subjective perception of control that appeared to matter most. Executives who behaved as if they were constantly under siege and reacted with primitive hostility—what we now call desk rage—were at the highest risk of dying. "Ambition and workaholism were not the culprits," said Niehoff. "Of all the Type A traits originally described by cardiovascular researchers, hostility turned out to be the best predictor of future heart disease. Corporate executives could breathe a little easier. Only hard-driven, intense people who also yelled at secretaries, fumed at the line in the copy room, and raged over trivial mistakes of coworkers—individuals some researchers labeled 'Type H'—faced a greater chance of developing clogged arteries and dying of heart attacks."[4]

Uncontrolled stress damages the body by affecting the amygdala, the hippocampus, the hypothalamus, the pituitary gland, the adrenal glands, and the brain stem's locus ceruleus. These are all central components of the primitive neural system's preconscious alerting system. The amygdala, hippocampus, and locus ceruleus are densely interconnected, and all respond to threats. When these areas detect a threat they signal the hypothalamus, which secretes an emergency hormone, corticotropin-releasing factor (CRF). CRF is detected by the pituitary, which releases an emergency-response hormone of its own—adrenocorticotrophic hormone (ACTH). It is ACTH that stimulates the secretion of adrenaline, noradrenaline, and other stress hormones into the bloodstream. In the meantime, other pathways from the brain to the body are accelerating heart rate and respiration, shutting down nonessential functions, and affecting a wide array of other biological responses that are coordinated by a major branch of the autonomic nervous system called the sympathetic nervous system. The preconscious alerting system of the primitive neural system may become overly sensitized or desensitized by excessive stress—too jumpy or too unresponsive. Its complex feedback relationships are desynchronized. Key components can be damaged. Constant surges of blood pressure damage the interior walls of arteries. Plaques formed of scar tissue can eventually impede blood flow or stop it completely. Hormones such as cortisol, associated with long-term stress, degrade the hippocampus. It is the hippocampus that helps couple memory with emotion through its intimate ties to the amygdala. During a threat, the locus ceruleus sprays noradrenaline into the hippocampus, sensitizing it and tending to make memories sharper and more long-lasting. One of the symptoms of excessive, long-term stress is abnormal forgetfulness. Damage to the hippocampus can be reversed if the stress response is reduced in time.

Job burnout is a condition caused by too much stress and too little control. Its warning signs include increased irritability, hypersensitivity to perceived slights or injustices, excessive emotional outbursts at work, problems sleeping, physical symptoms such as indigestion, lower productivity, frequent absences from work, and changes in eating or drinking patterns, including the increased use of drugs or alcohol. Other symptoms include increased forgetfulness, a growing sense of meaninglessness at work, and a rising level of general hostility, which may affect personal and family relationships. The outcome of burnout can be a sense that "I hate my job"— hatred that can easily spread to coworkers. It can also spread to one's self in the form of self-hate.

Many of the suggestions for coping with burnout fall under the strategies advocated in this book for curbing and eliminating

hate: be specific, empathize, communicate, negotiate, educate, cooperate, put things into perspective, avoid feeling trapped, immerse
yourself, and seek justice not revenge. Experts recommend communicating with your coworkers or supervisors in specific, nonthreat-
ening terms about what is causing you this kind of stress. Try to
negotiate a reasonable solution. And try to keep things in perspective. Don't let work completely dominate your life and occupy your
mind. This has become more of a problem with cell phones, pagers,
E-mail, and the Internet. Take breaks from work and do other things
with family and friends. Avoid feeling trapped in your job. Consider
your options, even if they include seeking employment elsewhere.

Stress and sleeplessness form a vicious circle, one contributing
to the other. An important effect of sleep deprivation is to impair
the functioning of the frontal lobes, which are a key center of the
advanced neural system deeply involved in impulse control. The
frontal lobes are also the source of our mental agility—the ability
to easily shift our attention from one thing to another. Mental agility
is essential in an era of what is often called multitasking, in which
people are juggling multiple tasks at the same time. But sleeplessness reduces mental agility, and this can make work life and daily
life much more stressful, reducing one's capacity to manage and control. One obvious strategy is to break this cycle by getting more
sleep. Although individuals vary in their sleep requirements, experts
recommend eight hours of sleep per night for the average adult. But
one survey found that almost two-thirds of adults indicated that they
sleep seven hours per night or less. Many said they watched television late into the evening rather than sleeping. In addition, the average couple in 2001 worked the equivalent of seven weeks more per
year than in 1990. Long hours, a hectic schedule, and too little sleep
impair the functioning of the advanced neural system and make it
more likely that we will shift control to the primitive neural system
with its primitive responses. This increases irritability and impul-
siveness, which contribute to the incivility, desk rage, road rage, and
other kinds of anger and hate that appear to be growing in fre-

quency. Sleeping an additional hour or two a night, or taking a nap during the day, can make an amazing difference in attitude and performance over the long run.[5]

If burnout persists, however, it may be wise to seek professional help. Many of the symptoms of burnout are also symptoms of depression. Long-term burnout can sometimes lead to clinical depression. The American Psychiatric Association considers individuals to be suffering from clinical depression if they have five or more of the following symptoms nearly every day during a two-week period: a depressed mood most of the time (in children or adolescents this may be indicated by irritability), a markedly diminished interest or pleasure in most activities, a large increase or decrease in appetite, insomnia or excessive sleeping, restlessness or slowness of movement, fatigue, feelings of worthlessness or inappropriate guilt, indecisiveness or diminished ability to think or concentrate, and recurrent thoughts of death or suicide. Someone who is truly suffering from depression must have one or both of the first two symptoms, and his or her condition must not be caused by a medication, another medical condition, or normal grieving. Immediate treatment with either psychotherapy, antidepressant medication, or both is a matter of urgency because, as you will remember, depression is the number one risk factor for suicide.

The novelist William Styron, who suffered bouts of depression, graphically described the allure of suicide for the depressed: "[My psychiatrist] asked me if I was suicidal, and I reluctantly told him yes. I did not particularize—since there seemed no need to—did not tell him that in truth many of the artifacts of my house had become potential devices for my own destruction: the attic rafters (and an outside maple or two) a means to hang myself, the garage a place to inhale carbon monoxide, the bathtub a vessel to receive the flow from my opened arteries. The kitchen knives in their drawer had but one purpose for me. Death by heart attack seemed particularly inviting, absolving me as it would of active responsibility, and I had toyed with the idea of self-induced pneumonia—a long, frigid, shirt-sleeved hike through the rainy woods. Nor had I overlooked an ostensible accident . . . by walking in front of a truck on the highway nearby. . . . Such hideous fantasies, which cause well people to shudder, are to the deeply depressed mind what lascivious daydreams are to persons of robust sexuality." Estimates are that from 5 to 12 percent of men and 10 to 20 percent of women in the United States will suffer at least one major depressive episode sometime in their lives.[6]

As we have seen, depression and suicide have been linked to abnormally low levels of serotonin. Some of the most popular and effective antidepressants in recent years—drugs such as Prozac, Paxil, Zoloft, and Luvox—increase the availability of serotonin in the brain. Such powerful medications should, however, be used with great care, given serotonin's association with aggression. No two people's brain chemistry is exactly the same and, in rare cases, drugs of this kind appear to be associated with violence toward the self and others—though whether such effects have an actual, causal relationship with these medications is a matter of debate in the scientific community. Drugs in this class have been the subject of lawsuits in certain cases of murder and suicide that occurred following their use. The package insert for Prozac, for example, mentions reports of "suicidal ideation" and "violent behaviors." But, again, there is no definitive scientific consensus as to whether there is a causal connection. The best advice for those using these drugs is to immediately report any abnormal thoughts, impulses, or behaviors to one's physician.

Brain-imaging studies of long-term victims of depression often show the size of key brain structures such as the hippocampus to be significantly smaller than those of people without depression. This indicates that depression may somehow activate the stress response, generating hormones such as cortisol that damage the hippocampus. There are a number of experts who believe that the causes of depression may center on the core of the preconscious alerting system: what neuroscientists call the hypothalamic-pituitary-adrenal

(HPA) axis. This is the system linking the hypothalamus, pituitary gland, and adrenal glands that is crucial for initiating the fight-or-flight response. The hypothalamus, when signaled of a threat by the amygdala and locus ceruleus, uses the emergency-response hormone CRF to control the output of hormones from the pituitary gland, which hangs from a slender stalk at the bottom of the hypothalamus. When signaled by the hypothalamus, the pituitary gland releases its emergency-response hormone, ACTH, causing the adrenals to secrete stress hormones that galvanize the body. There are feedback relationships in this system that reduce the production of CRF and ACTH if it becomes excessive. But with depressed patients, this feedback relationship seems to break down. The hypothalamus continues to produce large amounts of CRF, even when the threat has disappeared. Many studies have shown that CRF concentrations in the cerebrospinal fluid of depressed patients are significantly higher than in the spinal fluid of people who don't suffer from depression. The purpose of CRF is to heighten mental and physical alertness to prepare you to meet a threat while shutting down unnecessary functions that drain the body's energy, including the digestive system and reproductive system. When you experience a sudden surge of fear, anger, or hate, you immediately tend to lose your appetite for food and sex and become wide awake. Laboratory animals exposed to excessive levels of CRF exhibit symptoms that include loss of appetite, decreased sleep, decreased sexual activity, increased restlessness, and fearful and withdrawn behavior in unfamiliar environments. All these are symptoms of depression in humans. Antidepressants and electroconvulsive therapy, when successful in lifting a patient's depression, appear to reduce the CRF level to normal.

This hypothesis is undergoing extensive study, but it offers at least a partial explanation for desk rage, burnout, certain kinds of hatred, and the sometimes violent behavior that can accompany these states of mind. Not everyone reacts to extreme stress by developing depression. Some people are much more resilient to stress than others, and we don't yet know why. But there is evidence that certain kinds of depression may run in families. This inherited susceptibility to depression may be linked to a CRF feedback mechanism that is genetically less robust than normal. Levels of stress that most people would handle without difficulty might be enough to damage a weakened feedback mechanism and lead to the overproduction of CRF. Anyone, however, whose normal threshold for stress is exceeded for long enough—as in job burnout situations—may suffer from excessive CRF production and slip into depression.[7]

Depression doesn't instantly occur when CRF is overproduced; rather, it appears to be the result of a long exposure to this emergency-response hormone. At an intermediate stage—prior to the onset of clinical depression—this overactivity of the primitive neural system tends to make us hypersensitive to our environment, easily triggering primitive emotions and feelings such as fear, anger, hatred, jealousy, resentment, and frustration, all of which are common in stressful environments. At the same time, the hyperactivity of the primitive neural system makes it harder for the advanced neural system to exert control, leading to more impulsive outbursts of the kind we see in desk rage or road rage. This condition is not irreversible, and if the strain diminishes, our feedback mechanism and CRF production can recover and return to normal. But if a high level of stress continues, we may begin to feel not only restless and irritable, but exhausted as well. This is burnout. The CRF continues to keep us alert, at the cost of normal sleep, and the constant overactivity of the HPA axis soaks up all our energy—we are like a soldier trying to maintain wide-eyed vigilance for months on end, waiting for the enemy to attack. Within the reptomammalian mind, the overactivity of the HPA axis signals that our life is in imminent danger. Eventually, the brain collapses into depression under the weight of this hyperactive stress response and energy drain. Depression is characterized by abnormally low activity in many areas of the brain. But the CRF overproduction has not gone away. The hypersensitized primitive neural system spasmodically tries to arouse us from our lethargy to either fight or flee. Some imaging studies suggest that depression can be accompanied by aberrant activation patterns of the limbic system, particularly the amygdala. If the amygdala and other limbic structures are, at times, being abnormally stimulated by CRF exposure, this may stimulate aggressive impulses that are directed toward the self (suicidal self-hatred) and, in rare instances, aimed at others (homicidal hatred and rage). Before the North Valley Jewish Community Center shooting, Buford Furrow sought treatment for both suicidal and homicidal impulses. And a substantial number of workplace and school shootings are followed by the suicide or attempted suicide of the attacker, as was the case at Columbine High School with Eric Harris and Dylan Klebold.

Imaging studies indicate that one other key area of the brain seems to be atrophied in long-term depressives. It is called the subgenual prefrontal cortex and is an area of the orbitofrontal cortex that is about the size of a thimble located approximately two-and-a-half inches behind the bridge of the nose. Researchers have long considered this area to be important for emotional control. In patients with inherited depression, they found that the subgenual prefrontal cortex is significantly less active than normal. "Most of the time the differences we find in the brain are very subtle," said Dr. Wayne Drevets, who led a team of neuroscientists from Washington University in St. Louis. "To see something stand out to this degree is remarkable." When the team used advanced imaging techniques to examine the area more closely, they discovered that it contained from 39 to 48 percent less brain tissue than normal in those patients with long-term, hereditary depression. Drevets and others believe that the subgenual prefrontal cortex may be an important trigger for both depression and mania. When the subgenual prefrontal cortex does not function properly, said Drevets, "abnormal swings in mood may occur." If the site is underactive, depression sets in. But when it is overactive, the wild euphoria of mania begins.

Imaging research has shown that another area of the limbic cortex tends to be overactive during depression. This is the anterior cin-

gulate cortex, farther back and higher up on the inner face of the
hemisphere than the subgenual prefrontal cortex. Whereas the subgenual prefrontal cortex lies in the frontal lobes and is part of the
newest and most advanced region of the limbic association cortex,
the anterior cingulate cortex is one of the most ancient areas of the
limbic cortex. The anterior cingulate cortex enables us to focus
attention on our inner thoughts and feelings. It plays an important
role in the conscious perception of pain—both physical and mental. The underactivity of the subgenual prefrontal cortex and the
overactivity of the anterior cingulate cortex may help explain the
subjective perception of so many severely depressed patients. They
describe a general emotional deadening combined with the sensation of a searing but indescribable kind of mental pain. It may well
be that the inactivity of the subgenual emotional control center produces this deadening of emotion. At the same time, the high activity of the anterior cingulate cortex forces an obsessive focus on the
resulting internally generated mental pain and all the negative
thoughts that go with it. In an intermediate case, such as high stress
or burnout, where full-blown depression has not yet developed, the
underactivity of the subgenual emotional control center might
diminish the capacity to empathize with others while stanching the
normal flow of emotions that tends to wash away the sting of emotional upsets. The simultaneous overactivity of the anterior cingulate cortex would obsessively focus one's attention on the pain of
such upsets and one's fantasies of revenge. This might lead to hatred
and rage, which could explode in a violent outburst.

Something like this may have happened with Michael "Mucko"
McDermott. He had apparently been under long-term financial
strain that could have left him feeling trapped. It was reported that
several months prior to the shootings, McDermott secretly moved
out of an apartment at night, owing several thousand dollars in back
rent. If his primitive neural system were already sensitized by stress,
the IRS garnishment might have created a violent obsession. People who knew McDermott were at a loss to explain the extreme sav-

agery of his attack. Less than twenty-four hours after he was arrested, his quirky humor was still on display in the form of the message he liked to use on his home answering machine. It featured McDermott imitating the voice of a perpetually bemused character from the radio drama and science fiction novel *The Hitchhiker's Guide to the Galaxy*: "Here I am, brain the size of a planet, and what does he have me doing? Reduced to answering the phones. Phones. Oh, how I hate the phones. They're so depressing."

11

LOVE-HATE RELATIONSHIPS

SOME YEARS AGO I received a frantic phone call from a journalist friend of mine with news that I still find hard to believe. He told me about a mutual acquaintance of ours—a newspaper reporter—whom he and I had met about a year before. Both of us had thought of the man as a friendly, hard-working person with a quiet sense of humor. What we didn't know was that he and his wife were having marital difficulties. The two finally separated after several attempts at reconciliation. Distraught, the man quit his job and prepared to move to another city. Apparently he decided to telephone his wife before he left. An unfamiliar male voice answered the phone. About an hour later his terrified wife called the police. She told the emergency operator that she was alone in her apartment and her husband was outside, shouting threats, and trying to break down her door. The horrified operator heard sounds of the door crashing in, then screams and several gunshots. When the police arrived a few minutes later, they found that this seemingly quiet, low-key man had killed his wife, then himself.

Sex, love, and marriage figure into our greatest joys, our greatest suffering, and our greatest tragedies. According to one psychological survey, the ten most stressful life events are, in ascending order: gaining a new family member, sexual difficulties, a major change in the health or behavior of a family member, being fired or laid off, marriage, a major personal injury or illness, death of a close family member, marital separation, divorce, and the death of a spouse. Notice that eight of the stressful events on this list involve sexual relationships, marriage, and family. The other two center around job stress and personal health.[1]

Hate can erupt not only from a perception of being physically trapped, but through a sense of being emotionally trapped as well. A sense of emotional confinement is a powerful source of love-hate relationships. When we love others, we grow emotionally attached to them. As part of this process, we tend to become much more sensitive to their behavior toward us. If we feel betrayed or hurt by them, we may nevertheless remain trapped by our emotional attachment, which can include not only our continuing emotional ties but, in the case of many couples, the feelings we have for our children. Our pain shifts into the primitive neural system, and from these stressful feelings hate can develop. Love traps us in a painful relationship, and the pain creates hate that mingles with love.

Sadly, our most intimate relationships can combine elements of both love and hate. Sexual intimacy, marriage, and children directly involve the prime evolutionary imperative of reproduction and thus tend to heavily activate the primitive neural system, which is directly responsible for ensuring that this goal is met. Not surprisingly, these kinds of relationships tend to generate intense primal emotions— love, joy, anger, sadness, fear, hate—and can be emotionally stormy and stressful. They can easily slip into the simplistic, categorical, binary thinking of the primitive neural system: good-bad, right- wrong, love-hate, friend-enemy. These kinds of powerful and primitive emotions tend to be felt whenever we deal with situations that directly affect survival or reproduction, as with soldiers in combat or when we protect our children from imminent harm. This is an important reason divorce proceedings and battles over the custody of children often prompt such violent emotions.

Sex, in particular, is a volatile subject because it plays an unusually complex role in human societies. Sex represents one-half of the twin primal goals of evolution: survival and reproduction. But it is human culture, not our instincts, that defines the meaning and rituals surrounding sex. This is a mysterious and complicated process.

THE BRAIN'S MAPS OF THE BODY

How does your brain see your body? If you look in a full-length mirror, a normal reflection looks back at you. But that image is not what is etched on the outer surface—or neocortex—of your brain. There are two strips of cortex on each cerebral hemisphere that map the body in a unique way, reflecting our evolution and the functional importance of each of our body parts to our survival as a species. One is called the primary motor cortex. This area, which runs roughly from one ear across the top of the head to the other ear, controls the movement of the muscles in the body. The portion of this strip that lies on the surface of the left cerebral hemisphere generally controls movement on the right side of the body, while the portion on the right cerebral hemisphere controls movement on the left. Just behind this strip is a second strip of cortex—the primary somatosensory cortex—which receives sensations from the different parts of the body. On these brain maps our face is huge compared to the rest of our body—that is, the area of the cortex devoted to our face is much larger than the actual size of our face with respect to the rest of our body. Similarly, our tongue is enormous, as are our hands. Of our five fingers, the thumb dwarfs all the rest. Our feet are big. And we have very, very large genitals. In fact, the area of the somatosensory cortex devoted to the genitals is greater than the combined area dedicated to the chest, abdomen, and back.[2]

These are the brain's primary maps of the body, though the body is mapped in other brain areas as well. The reason for this odd mapping is at once fascinating and suggestive. The large hands with the especially large thumbs reflect the exceptional importance of the hands to our survival. Hands are the means we use to make our tools. With these tools we construct our culture and our civilization. It is the opposable thumb that gives our hands their power. The thumb of a gorilla or chimpanzee is relatively small and cannot work easily with the other fingers to create precise manipulation. This can make these primates seem comically clumsy when they are handling objects, though when they use their hands for what the primate hand originally evolved to do—climb trees—they are far more graceful and agile than we are.

Every complex animal species has a map of its body etched on the surface of its brain. The brain map of a rabbit, for example, reveals a small body and an oversized face and snout, because the face and snout are the primary areas a rabbit uses to explore its environment. The brain map of a chimpanzee has a disproportionately large tongue because with their tongues chimpanzees produce a series of calls used to communicate with each other. The representation of the tongue on the surface of the human brain, however, is much larger. Our complex language, which depends on fantastically rapid and complicated movements of our tongue, is absolutely essential for our cooperation and survival. The human tongue takes up an especially large area of the cortex because it contains a denser and more complex network of nerves for the purpose of sensation and control. Similarly, the map of our face is huge because we use not only our tongue and the other parts of the vocal tract to communicate through sound, we also use our face to enhance this communication with a vast repertoire of expressions: anger, fear, joy, disgust, and hatred, among many others. As Darwin and his successors have shown, many basic human expressions—such as smiling and frowning—are innate and are universally recognized and employed by all cultures. The large representation of our feet reflects the important and intricate role they play in another of our distinctive characteristics: walking upright. But why is the brain map of our genitals so huge?

HUMAN SEXUAL BEHAVIOR

By the standards of other species, human sexual behavior is highly unusual. Though sex, of course, is essential for the survival of the species, it can be costly, even dangerous, for any animal. Sexual activity takes away from time that could be spent finding the food necessary to stay alive. It can also serve as a distraction that can leave a pair of animals vulnerable to attack by predators. From an evolutionary point of view, we might expect that animals would have sex only when there is a good chance that it will lead to conception. And that is exactly the case for most species, including the vast majority of primates—sexual activity is brief and takes place only when the female is most likely to conceive. As dog owners know, when a female is in estrus or heat (ovulating and capable of conception), she signals nearby males either through chemical scents, by her behavior, or both. In some monkey species there are visual signals as well. The genital region may swell and change color. When this happens, sexual instincts are activated, and any males in the area will eagerly try to mate. When the female is not in heat, however, most species show little or no interest in sex.

For humans, the story is quite different. Our species is monogamous or slightly polygamous, with men and women pairing off in most modern societies, although the family grouping in some cultures consists of a male and several females. In this, we are like many other social species. But rather than being advertised, human ovulation is concealed. This is unusual. Many women have no idea when they are ovulating, which can make planning a family—or even conceiving, for some couples—exceedingly difficult. Female fertility in humans is low by the standards of other species. Even if a healthy young couple trying to have a baby makes love at maximum frequency, they have on the average less than a one in three chance of conceiving a child in any given month. Animal breeders count on conception rates at least double that. And with humans, one baby at a time is the norm—multiple births are unusual. With dogs, cats, and many other animals, multiple births are the norm.

One human sexual practice is particularly curious. Our sexual activity takes place primarily in private. Chimpanzees and practically every other social species mate in public and are totally unselfconscious about it. Private sex is the exception and usually occurs only when a subordinate male is trying to sneak away to mate with a female who is under the control of a dominant male. In virtually every human culture, however, having sex in public is considered offensive and shameful, and it is usually illegal. Sex is surrounded by many fears and taboos. When public sexual activity occurs, it is often associated with alcohol, drugs, or mental illness. Yet unlike other species, our interest in sex does not turn off when females are not ovulating. We can and do have sex—or refrain from sex—whenever we want and for whatever reasons we want. As the large map of the genitals engraved in our brain implies, sex tends to pervade our thoughts and behaviors almost all the time. It is a prominent feature of all human cultures. In the modern world, sex sells. We buy products from toothpaste to automobiles because they will supposedly make us more attractive to the opposite sex. Sexual issues become tangled up in our politics, our art, even our science: the scientific study of sexuality is often highly controversial. There is no mating season for humans. From youth through old age, as long as we are in good health, our sexuality permeates much of what we think and do.[3]

Human sexuality follows the exceptional pattern of most of our other behaviors. We have general tendencies but not specific instincts. Our interest in sex is innate, kicking in strongly at puberty.

But specific sexual practices vary from culture to culture and person to person. We must supply the meaning and the values within which sexual activity takes place, and variations in meaning lead to behaviors ranging from celibacy to promiscuity, and from having no children and using sex strictly for recreation to having many children and engaging in sex solely for procreation. Sexual activity is shaped by institutions such as marriage, whose structure is heavily influenced by religious and cultural systems of meaning.

There are many competing theories about the origin and purpose of human sexual behavior. This is an area of robust scientific controversy. But if we look back a hundred thousand years or so to the earliest members of our species, *Homo sapiens*, we may be able to glimpse the reasons for our unusual sexuality. Modern humans probably evolved in sub-Saharan Africa, although this is still a matter of some debate. Life in the African forests and on the savanna was harsh and dangerous. This was made doubly difficult by having extremely dependent children requiring many years of attention to become self-sufficient. It would take the utmost efforts of both a father and mother to raise, teach, protect, and provide for their children. But even that would not be enough. To ensure that their offspring survived to sexual maturity, the parents would have to work cooperatively with a larger group of adults. Anthropologists estimate that these early humans lived in a foraging band of twenty-five to fifty people. Collectively, they would hunt and gather food and protect themselves against predators and perhaps other bands of humans. It was in this fragile cocoon that parents would bring up their children.

From an evolutionary perspective in that precarious setting, a man and a woman would have somewhat different biological interests in their relationship. In order to make this long-term commitment, a man would have to be reasonably certain that the children he was helping to provide for were his own offspring. Otherwise, he would lose the opportunity to pass his genetic endowment to the next generation. This, of course, would not be an issue for women.

But before having a child who would be a tremendous drain on her time and energy in an unforgiving environment, a woman would have to be convinced that the father was willing to make the long-term commitment necessary to help her raise the child. Without that commitment, the child might not survive, and the mother, too, might die trying to care for the child. A woman would have a natural concern that a man might move on to another woman who had no children and who would be less of a drain on his resources. And childbirth itself is risky, largely because of the enormous size of the human brain contained within the newborn's skull. The average gorilla newborn weighs half the seven-pound weight of the average human newborn, and the two-hundred-pound gorilla mother is far larger than most women. Having a child would be a deadly serious commitment for early *Homo sapiens* and would require a powerful, long-term bond between a man and woman.

ESTABLISHING AND MAINTAINING PAIR BONDS

Because female ovulation is concealed and female fertility is relatively low, most human sexual activity does not lead to conception. It seems clear that sex among *Homo sapiens* is as much about establishing and maintaining pair bonds as it is about reproduction. Having sex in private creates a special bond between a man and a woman. There are all sorts of powerful emotions surrounding human sexuality, many with deep evolutionary roots. Male jealousy tends to center on fears of infidelity; female jealousy, on fears of abandonment. These types of jealousy continue to be sources of conflict, violence, hatred, and even murder—especially, but not exclusively, by males—in the modern world. In all cultures, sexual jealousy remains one of the most common motives for homicide. Our innate preference for private sexual activity is one important reason that having sex in public or even explicitly discussing sex in

mixed company is often surrounded by feelings of emotional discomfort, which can include shame or anger. Some comedians play
on this discomfort by using raw sexual humor to shock an audience.
It may be that the ancient portions of our brain tend to perceive public sexuality as threatening the pair bond that for most of the history
of our species was absolutely essential for successfully rearing a
child in an incredibly hostile environment. As always, however, cultural meaning plays a critical role in human behavior. Modern industrial societies are almost exclusively monogamous within the
institution of marriage. Bigamy is often punished criminally. But the
actual practice in any society varies depending on the values of individuals and groups. These variations can range from absolute, lifelong fidelity to flagrant adultery or serial pair bonding through
successive informal relationships or repeated divorce.[4]

A judge friend told me that though he had presided over the tri-
als of many vicious killers, he was most afraid for his safety during
divorce proceedings, particularly where custody of children was
involved. Sometimes this judge meets with the spouses in his chambers to try to negotiate a settlement. He said emotions at these meetings often become almost uncontrollable. He and the other judges
of his circuit have had buttons installed on their desks that they can
unobtrusively push to alert the bailiffs if things get out of hand. The
us-them division between divorcing spouses can be ferocious and
lead to inordinate hate. Similarly, police are statistically in maximum
danger of injury or death not when chasing armed criminals but
when they are called to a violent or potentially violent domestic
dispute.

More time spent working, a more hectic pace, lack of time for
intimacy (especially when you throw in the enormous commitment
necessary for raising children), lack of sleep—all can contribute to
love-hate relationships. One practical approach to avoiding feelings
of frustration, resentment, and hatred toward the relationship is better time management and parenting skills that result in greater productivity and an increased sense of control. Doing more in less time

can prevent a gnawing sense of frustration at being trapped by over-whelming responsibilities, which the limbic system interprets as a serious threat that tends to shift control of behavior to the primitive neural system and its fight-or-flight response. And greater produc-tivity can yield more time for being together, which means more time for the intimacy that creates and reinforces the bonds between two people.

Scientists have gone to great lengths to study the relationship between sexual activity and the brain. One experiment was de-scribed as follows: "The male subject was strapped to a chair-like device with his head painlessly immobilized. In this position it was possible to insert a fine microelectrode into the hypothalamus. The female subject was then strapped into another chair that was posi-tioned several feet away. The male was provided with a button that he could push to bring the chair bearing the female adjacent to his own. In this position the two were able to copulate without the male having to move his head. Recordings of neuronal activity were therefore obtained from the moment the male saw the female to completion of copulation. The highest neuronal activity (fifty impulses per second) was recorded from a neuron in the medial pre-optic area of the hypothalamus as the subject pressed the button to bring the female towards him. During copulation the discharge rate dropped and after ejaculation it ceased almost entirely. The specifi-cally sexual nature of the activity was confirmed by a control exper-iment in which the female was replaced by a banana."[5]

The subjects of this experiment were two macaque monkeys, but the findings seem to hold true for humans as well. The hypothala-mus plays a fundamental role in sexuality. The medial preoptic area of the hypothalamus mentioned in the experiment seems to be an important focus of the male sexual response. The hypothalamus is made up of a number of different nuclei—tiny clumps of gray mat-ter—that are wedged between the thalamus and the base of the brain. The medial preoptic area has a high concentration of recep-tors that are sensitive to male hormones. Female sexuality seems to center on another area of the hypothalamus: the ventromedial nucleus. Orgasm is accompanied by a massive release of dopamine followed by the release of oxytocin—a hormone related to endorphins—which tends to promote bonding. This helps explain how sexual activity in and of itself tends to promote pair bonding, allowing love and commitment to take root even in arranged marriages, which have been a prominent part of many cultures throughout human history. But the hypothalamus is just one component of a widespread system governing sexual behavior in humans that extends from the brain stem to the neocortex. This system is not under detailed instinctive control, which is why we vary enormously in our sexual values and behaviors.

Among the apes, modern human bonding resembles the monogamous gibbons. Male gorillas compete among themselves, often violently, for harems that typically include three to six females. Common chimpanzees are promiscuous, though males and females will sometimes pick their favorites. An estrous female chimp may mate with five or six males in succession, making the determination of paternity impossible. Pygmy chimpanzees are even more promiscuous. Orangutans are solitary and do not form pair bonds. Gibbons, however, maintain lifelong pair bonds despite having sex only every few years, when the female has completed raising her offspring and is again sexually receptive. But gibbons have powerful, specific instincts that cement their bond hormonally and neurochemically. Humans have general tendencies rather than specific instincts and can supply a rationale for their behaviors, something that instinct dispenses with in most other species. Differing human meaning systems can lead to chimplike promiscuity or gorilla-like harems.

As we have noted, our general tendencies include a fairly constant interest in sex and an inclination to have sex in private. Frequent, private sexual activity isolates the bonding couple from all other members of the group and would seem to allow an undistracted focus on each other that reflects the extraordinary need by our species to establish the long-term male-female relationships necessary to raise our exceptionally dependent and demanding offspring. The preference for sex in private may also reflect our unusually pervasive form of consciousness, which tends to make us acutely aware of what others are thinking and can distract from the concentration that human lovemaking requires. Human foreplay and lovemaking last much longer than any other social primate. The mean duration of copulation for gorillas is one minute; pygmy chimpanzees, fifteen seconds; and common chimpanzees, seven seconds. For us, the sexual bond is often deeply involved in our perception of life satisfaction. In survey after survey, people who say that their marriages are rewarding and sexually fulfilling report substantially higher levels of happiness and much lower levels of depression and discontent than those who are single, divorced, or separated.

The oversized map of our genitals engraved on the cortex of our brain represents much more than sex and reproduction: it represents the sexual bond that has kept our species alive and thriving for thousands of generations. It symbolizes the glory of our pair bonds, our willingness to sacrifice for each other and for our children, our ability to inspire each other, to teach and to learn, to love and, through love, share our sorrows and dreams. Much of our art, literature, and music celebrate the rapture and pain of love and lovers. The cortical map of our body reflects the way we interact within pair bonds. With our hands, we comfort and excite each other. With our complex language we communicate and share meaning and intimacy. Our faces express how we feel about each other. Studies of the electrical activity in the limbic system have revealed that the human amygdala, which is intimately involved in our emotions as well as our sexual behavior, reacts most strongly to words and faces.

Sex, love, and happiness form a momentous triangle of emotion and behavior. Sex and love require physical and emotional connection, and when this connection is made, the resulting joy can be delirious. Though sex may not involve love, evolution has designed sexual activity and sexual desire to have the power to lead us, even against our will, into a deep bond with another human being. This kind of bonding occurs in part subconsciously through a variety of neurochemicals and hormones. The most important appears to be oxytocin. According to neuroscientist Walter J. Freeman of the University of California at Berkeley, oxytocin "doesn't cause joy; it may cause anxiety, as it melts down the patterns of connections among neurons that hold experience, so that new experience can form. We become aware of this meltdown most dramatically as a frightening loss of identity and self-control when we fall in love for the first time. Bonding comes not with the meltdown but with the shared activity afterward, in which people learn about each other through cooperation. Trust emerges not just with sex, but also with shared activity. . . ."[6]

Romantic love involves desire, and desire is a form of intended connection. You may love someone, yet they may not immediately love you back. In that case there is love (unrequited) but no emotional reward (happiness). In fact, you may experience terrible anguish because of the potential rejection. Happiness appears when the actual connection is made with the object of your love—when the person returns your love. After making that connection, love fuses with joy. Yet if the connection is broken and your lover rejects you, your happiness ends even though your love may remain. Out of this mixture of love and pain may come anger and hate.

Happiness is the emotional reward for the connections that love strives for. The joy of romantic love can be supremely intoxicating, never more so than when expressed in a satisfying sexual relationship. The natural neurochemicals and hormones released by the deeper feelings of love and affection tend to keep us exciting to each other and counteract any tendency to habituate. Yet over the long term, our attraction to novelty and tendency to become bored may weaken the sexual and emotional bonds. A determined use of imagination and intimacy can keep a relationship fresh, however. Studies show that couples who share their innermost hopes, dreams, and desires tend to have the most durable romantic and sexual relationships. Sharing intimacies and secrets piques the imagination and tends to strengthen and refresh the connections between people. Routine is the enemy. In one study, for example, college students were randomly grouped into male-female pairs for the purpose of playing cards. None of the students knew each other prior to the experiment. Some of the randomly selected couples were coached by researchers in advance on how to unobtrusively play footsie under the table during a card game so that they could let each other know which cards they had. In other words, some of the couples were told to use a secret system to win the game when playing against another couple. Each male-female pair using the secret system played cards with another randomly selected male-female pair who had no inkling of what was going on. At the end of the experiment, all participants—those who used the secret system and those who didn't—were asked to rate the romantic desirability of their card-playing partners. The couples who shared the secret tended to rate each other as much more desirable than any of the other people they had met during the study. In contrast, the couples who knew nothing of the secret system did not tend to rate each other as particularly desirable. The only difference was this surreptitiously shared meaning, purpose, and connection.

Because human beings have a powerful drive for meaning, it is not surprising that couples whose relationships are the most enduring and sexually fulfilling overwhelmingly report that they share a deep sense of meaning and purpose—that both partners feel they have grown in the relationship and found meaning in their lives. For many couples, this sense of meaning involves a mutual concern for their children. But if their shared meaning does not grow beyond this, when the children leave home (if not before) the relationship may lose its rationale and collapse. Shared meaning involves shared intimacy, feelings, and experience. And like so many other human activities, sex involves an important element of playfulness as part of establishing and maintaining the bonds of love and commitment. Enjoyment tends to enhance our sexuality. At parties and celebrations and during other forms of playful activity we are more likely to sexually interact with others. Sharing meaning involves sharing fun as well as responsibility—happy couples usually socialize together, vacation together, and share other pleasurable activities. These often include elements of novelty: doing new things and seeing new places. Novelty tends to produce excitement and joy, which in turn can enhance sexuality, love, and bonding. This is why in many cultures newlyweds are encouraged to honeymoon in exotic places in order to begin their committed relationship under the most favorable possible circumstances.

THE MIX OF LOVE AND HATE

Yet the high divorce rate in the industrialized world is stark evidence that our understanding of the practical requirements of love, commitment, and sexual fulfillment is painfully limited. With our private lovemaking and our limitless eroticism, the human species has a strange combination of obsession with sex and extreme self-consciousness about it. Human sexual behavior is such a muddle that, according to one researcher, "If it were not for the fact that sex is pleasurable, we would not engage in it." There can be clashes between the primal attraction of the primitive neural system and the rational calculation of the advanced neural system. Love and hate can mix freely. And our closest relationships can not only be the source of emotional pain, but also physical danger, especially for women. A woman is most likely to be injured or killed by someone with whom she has an intimate emotional relationship. Battered women account for about a third of all women seeking emergency medical services, one-fourth of women who attempt suicide, just under a quarter of all pregnant women who seek prenatal services, and half of all women over thirty who are raped. Women are at least six times more likely than men to be the victim of crime in an intimate relationship. These statistics apply to women of all ethnic and economic backgrounds. Every year over the past decade, husbands, ex-husbands, lovers, and ex-lovers have committed more than a million violent acts against women, including a quarter of all rapes and assaults. In the year 2000, there were an estimated six million assaults against women including almost a million rapes and sexual assaults.

Love and hate exist on the opposite ends of the same axis within the primitive neural system. The two poles of the binary classification of like-dislike, when experienced at maximum intensity, lead to the emotions of love and hate. Love, of course, is the maximum intensity of "like." Our primitive neural system interprets that which we love as providing the maximum enhancement to survival and reproduction. In humans, love is also linked to meaning—that which we love gives our life maximum meaning. At its utmost intensity, love (like hate) involves stereotyping: positive stereotyping in the case of love. The saying "love is blind" captures this quality. Many of us have known people so deeply in love that they cannot see the faults of the object of their affection. Because hate involves negative stereotyping, we can also say that hate is blind. With hate, we see only negative qualities, and sometimes these qualities are exaggerated or even figments of our imagination. Our primitive neural system interprets that which we hate as providing the maximum threat to our survival and reproduction.[7]

One cannot be talked out of love any more than one can be talked out of hate. Both love and hate activate the primitive neural system and tend to become obsessive—obsessive attachment and obsessive dislike—in that the mind focuses a significant amount of its attention on the objects of love and hate because they are deemed to enhance or threaten survival and reproduction. A person who falls in love, for example, constantly thinks about his or her beloved. A person who hates may spend a similar amount of time brooding about the object of his or her hatred. With love, there are affection and tenderness. With hate, there are hostility and aggression. Both go beyond reason. Both can be blind. Hate is the most intense and long-lasting form of primal hostility. Love is the most intense and long-lasting form of primal affection. But just as hate can be modulated by the advanced neural system, so can love. When our more sophisticated capacities are activated, love moves beyond pure passion and becomes more refined and complex.

Love is an unlikely partner for hate, but we have evolved to create strong bonds of affection that, because of their importance, can sometimes be a source of enormous stress. When there is conflict or discord in this setting, we may feel trapped and frustrated— emotions that the primitive neural system can transform into intense, obsessive dislike. But our capacity for creating and choosing among meaning systems provides a buffer that can prevent hate from infecting love. The happiest couples tend to share a sense of meaning and purpose that carries them through the difficult times.

12

CHILDREN AND HATRED

PETER RUIZ DIDN'T KNOW that the violence had come full circle as he lay on his side, unable to move, with a bullet lodged in his pelvis. The twenty-two-year-old Ruiz was a campus security guard at Santana High School in the small San Diego suburb of Santee. Just about the time Ruiz was born, the nation experienced its first modern high-profile school shooting—in San Diego. On January 29, 1979, sixteen-year-old Brenda Spencer used a .22-caliber rifle to fire on the Grover Cleveland Elementary School from her family's house across the street. She killed the principal and a custodian and wounded eight students and a police officer. After pleading guilty to murder, she was sentenced to twenty-five years to life. In the intervening years, a succession of school shootings shattered the peace and security of towns and suburbs around the country. At a California parole board hearing in 2001, Spencer expressed regret for what she had done—to her victims and to the nation. "I know saying I'm sorry doesn't make it all right," she said. "With every school shooting I feel I'm partially responsible. What if they got their idea from what I did?" Her request for parole was denied. Yet Charles Andrew "Andy" Williams, who was new to the San Diego area, may never have heard of Brenda Spencer, at least not directly.

On Monday morning, March 5, 2001, Ruiz's week had started off as usual, herding kids into class. Around 9:20 A.M., during the fifteen-minute break between first and second periods, he heard a pop-popping noise and assumed someone was playing with fire-crackers in the boys' bathroom. As he approached the bathroom, frightened students ran past him without saying a word. When he walked in, he saw two students on the floor. One, bleeding from the back of the head, was motionless. The other shouted, "Get out! Get out!" Ruiz didn't see fifteen-year-old freshman Andy Williams or the .22-caliber handgun he was holding. Williams was hiding behind a partition in the bathroom, reloading.

Ruiz, a former football player who stands just under six feet tall and weighs 250 pounds, moved quickly to the nearby campus quad to call for help on his radio. Students were running everywhere, and Ruiz told them to stay clear of the area. "My main concern was the safety of the kids," he said. "I was trying to keep them away from the bathroom. Then I felt a big thump on the small of my back." He staggered about fifteen feet, then collapsed, unable to move his legs. He never felt the other two bullets that hit him from behind and passed right through his body, one piercing his right shoulder and the other his lower right back. He struggled over on his side and looked back to the bathroom. For the first time he saw Williams, standing at the entrance, holding the gun. "We made eye contact and he gave me a smirk," said Ruiz. "He never said a word. For that split second I thought he was going to come out and finish me off. But he went back into the bathroom and I heard more shots. I was out in the open, with nothing between me and him. He could've walked out and shot me again. I don't know why he didn't."[1]

When that morning was over, two students were dead and Ruiz and twelve others were wounded. The police found Williams in the bathroom. The meek-looking young man, barely five feet tall, later said that he carefully counted out forty bullets for the gun he had stolen from his father. He planned to use the last one on himself. The police got there first. Williams fit the profile of many of the modern school shooters, according to a U.S. Secret Service study. More than half have a history of feeling extremely depressed or desperate. Three-quarters show suicidal tendencies. Yet these young gunmen were not wild-eyed psychopaths. The study found that few were loners or bullies, and seldom had they been diagnosed with a mental illness. Instead, they were generally eaten up with hatred and fantasies of revenge. Revenge, in fact, was the most common motive for their attacks.

Williams made no secret of his hate and boasted to friends in the month before the shooting that there would be another Columbine. They laughed and thought he was kidding. Yet some of them became concerned enough to confront him. He insisted he was joking. Williams was a newcomer to Santee and, according to friends, had been constantly tormented. "Even the people who got picked on, picked on him," said sixteen-year-old Scott Wilke, a friend of Williams. "He would never defend himself at all. You could take the money out of his wallet, you could take the shirt off his back and throw it in the gutter and he would just walk away. He always said he would get people back but I never thought he would shoot people." The day before the attack, Williams reportedly told a twelve-year-old friend: "Tomorrow, I'm going to have a bunch of guns and I'm going to shoot a bunch of people. I'm going to shoot people down and you're going to watch."

The circle of violence that began at Grover Cleveland Elementary School returned to California little more than two decades later to devastate Santana High School. No one knew that it would soon make one more stop in the Golden State. Seventeen days later at Granite Hills High School in El Cajon—another San Diego suburb less than six miles from Santee—senior Jason Hoffman decided to take his pump-action 12-gauge shotgun to school. Shortly before 1:00 P.M. he parked his pickup on the street in front of the school administration building. The month before, Hoffman had had a disciplinary meeting with the school's assistant principal, Daniel Barnes, which seemed to end amicably. But when Hoffman saw Barnes standing just outside the administration offices, he pointed his shotgun at him and reportedly said, "I'm going to get you." Barnes dived through a nearby doorway as Hoffman fired three shots in quick succession, blasting out glass windows and injuring five people, three students and two teachers. "A bullet whizzed within inches of my head," said sophomore Chris Weston. An El Cajon police officer providing security for the school ended the rampage when he shot Hoffman in the jaw. All the wounded survived. At a preliminary hearing, teacher Elizabeth Murphy testified that as Hoffman lay on a stretcher waiting to be taken to the hospital, he looked up at her and said, "Good one, huh?"

Hoffman, it developed, had a troubled background. His parents, who divorced when he was young, first met at a place called the Big Noise Bar. His mother was a bartender, and his father was at that time a heavy drinker. The two began living together and Hoffman's mother, Denise Marquez, became pregnant with Jason. The relationship was stormy, and Marquez accused Jason's father, Ralph, of once throwing three-month-old Jason at her during a fight. When Jason was seventeen months old, his father was arrested during an incident in which he is said to have tossed the toddler repeatedly into a swimming pool. When the police came, Marquez told them that Ralph had been beating her head against the wall. Ralph Hoffman denied these allegations.

Both Jason's mother and father described their own upbringings as difficult. The parents of Denise Marquez were strict disciplinarians. Marquez lost a leg to cancer at age twelve. She said her father used to take her artificial leg and crutches away from her as punishment and lock them in the family car. Ralph told a family services caseworker that he never knew his father. When he was a year old, his mother married a man with seven children and a drinking problem. According to the caseworker's report, "Mr. Hoffman recalls the marriage between his mother and stepfather as being very violent.

He states that all of the kids had the hell beaten out of them and that the parents would use whatever they could get their hands on."[2]

As Jason grew up, he too exhibited violent impulses. Police arrested him at age fourteen for assaulting a student at another school. But at Granite Hills he was known for being a quiet student most of the time, though he had occasional angry blowups. One classmate reported that she overheard Hoffman saying, in a fit of rage, "I wish I could do Columbine all over again." In the months before the attack, Hoffman had been taking antidepressant medication.

HUMANS' EXTENDED CHILDHOOD

There is, of course, a danger of stereotyping and demonizing all adolescents because of a relatively small number of widely publicized incidents of violence. Most students, even those with serious problems, are never violent. Youth violence as a whole, in fact, has fallen significantly since the peak year of 1993. Nevertheless, among the young, "violent behavior remains alarmingly high," according to U.S. Surgeon General David Satcher. Scientists from many fields have launched massive studies to try to uncover the roots of such hatred and brutality. Why do people such as Andy Williams and Jason Hoffman resort to extreme violence while others don't? The answer, it appears, rests in part on how they see the world—the cognitive and emotional meaning they place on their lives and their experiences.

In the postmodern world there is a furious debate about the meaning of meaning—the kind of controversy that only our species would, or could, have. Is there such a thing as objective meaning, or is all meaning subjective? Is there an objective reality at all? There are whole schools of philosophy that deny we can truly know anything. Newborn children, however, are blissfully unaware of all this, and their drive for meaning is relentless. An infant not only observes and listens to his surroundings but begins babbling back. Before very long the babbling grows into the first half-articulated words, perhaps *mamma* or *dadda*. Each word embodies a meaning that is intensely important to the child and the source of boundless joy. These words grow into phrases, the phrases fuse into sentences, and the sentences expand into a sense of self and the internal and external narrative of one's life. The mastery of language is thus a primal human impulse that embodies our unique relationship to meaning. The child's struggle to speak and understand language is persistent, but success is not a certainty. In his or her first years of life, a child must be immersed in an environment in which language is being communicated. This is why deafness in a young child is so devastating, perhaps even more than blindness.

The mental agility of the human infant is in striking contrast to its utter physical helplessness. A baby zebra can walk within a short time after its birth. If it doesn't walk it doesn't survive. The human infant, however, is basically a fetus that has been forced prematurely out of the womb. It is as dependent as it can possibly be. By the standards of the great apes, the human newborn is only 60 percent developed. This is the compromise evolution has had to make because of the bulbous human brain. If a baby were born much later, its head would be too large for the birth canal. And at every period of human history except the most recent, with the development of modern surgery and cesarean sections, this would have been a death sentence for both mother and child. Among primates generally, childhood has lengthened, but among humans this lengthening has gone to extremes. The childhood of the chimpanzee lasts around six years. Human childhood doubles that—puberty does not occur until about age twelve. And within that childhood, the dependency of humans is much greater than that of chimpanzees. Once weaned from its mother's breast, the young chimpanzee can help gather its own food. But the young human after weaning remains completely reliant on its parents.

What is the purpose of this exceptionally long childhood? In short, to learn. Because humans rely on meaning rather than instinct, a child must be trained to master specialized tools and complex behaviors. Just developing the fine motor skills needed to competently handle the tool kit of the hunter-gatherer culture takes years of practice, something that is unnecessary for a great ape. A six-year-old chimpanzee is ready to handle almost all the activities that make up its way of life. But a six-year-old child in a modern society is years away from doing something as simple—for adults—as driving a car. Our extended childhood has led to other important changes in our life cycle. Most mammals, including chimpanzees, grow at a steady rate to adult size. In humans, however, this growth is retarded. Younger children stay smaller longer, and teenagers experience something highly unusual in the animal world: a growth spurt that increases their size by about 25 percent. Our smaller size as children may be an adaptation that promotes greater adult control over the child as it absorbs the body of cultural knowledge necessary for a reasonable chance of survival. Over the past few centuries, however, the complexity of culture in the industrialized world has, in effect, been artificially extending the age of maturity and independence far past puberty. To thrive in the middle and upper echelons of a technological culture requires years of education and training beyond that needed by a hunter-gatherer child. Despite the fact that a child's innate desire for independence usually peaks around age thirteen, young people in the modern world are usually not fully ready to support themselves and a family until they are in their late teens or early twenties, especially if they are pursuing advanced education and training. This puts parents and teachers in industrialized countries in an awkward position: they must control and educate full-sized teenagers and young adults. The problems caused by treating biological adults as little more than dependent children are a constant source of social tension. They fuel the rebellious elements of adolescent culture and can lead to emotional outbursts, even hatred, as teenagers—who may feel trapped by their dependency—clash with parents or guardians.

There are wide individual variations in the maturity of adolescents. Some thirteen-year-olds are more mature than some twenty-five-year-olds are. But imaging studies of the developing brain suggest that the impulse-control centers of the frontal lobes are the last brain areas to fully mature. These centers are still being wired into the early twenties. The limbic system, on the other hand, is largely mature by about age five, except for highly advanced areas like the orbitofrontal cortex. When the adult and adolescent pattern of brain activation is compared, there are often striking differences. When adults answer questions, the primary areas of activation tend to be in the cognitive areas of the neocortex. But when adolescents answer the same questions, the emotional centers of the limbic system, especially the amygdala, are often more strongly activated than the neocortex.

Young children exhibit another remarkable behavior that echoes throughout the human life cycle: a powerful response to play. Most young mammals, and even many birds, are playful and curious. As usual, however, humans carry this playfulness and curiosity to unusual lengths. The innate structure of the human brain motivates children not only to passionately master language but also to eagerly incorporate into their play something that most other species would find extremely strange: toys. Dolphins are playful, but they have few, if any, toys—unless we train them to play like us. The delight children experience in playing with toys is a reflection of our tool-based culture, for toys are a child's version of tools. For younger children, almost anything will do. They may be as interested in playing with the box a toy came in as with the toy itself. For older children, however, the more elaborate or novel the toy, the more fascinated they tend to be. We see this reenacted every year as millions of harried parents try to ensure that their children receive the trendiest toys for Christmas or Hanukkah.

Toys are not unprecedented in the animal world. Young ravens, for example, have been observed to pick up an inedible object—a small stone, for example—and carry it into the air. One bird will drop the stone and another will catch it before it hits the ground. Then that bird will drop the stone and the other bird will catch it. But no animal has the range and variety of toys and play behavior that we have. The only species even remotely comparable to us is the chimpanzee. Jane Goodall learned this firsthand shortly after setting up her original base camp at the Gombe Stream National Park in Tanzania. The band of chimpanzees she was supposed to be studying decided to study her. They ransacked her camp, carrying off most of the food and a good deal of the equipment for use as toys. The mischievous chimps were delighted at the success of their raid. "They climbed, jumped, swung and dangled from branches of trees," Goodall said, "chased round tree trunks, broke off and waved or carried branches, leaves, or fruit clusters, grappled with each other for an assortment of small objects, dragged and hit each other with branches, and so on." Chimpanzees love to play games like hide-and-seek and will make up new games when they are bored. A group of chimps at the San Diego Zoo was observed to play a version of blind man's bluff in which they would cover their eyes with a banana leaf or a bag and try to negotiate a climbing frame suspended fifteen feet off the ground. Researchers have not been surprised to find that young chimpanzees in captivity often find joystick-driven video games enormously fun.[3]

Children, too, love games, but they also incorporate their rapidly growing linguistic ability into their play in the form of stories, riddles, jokes, puzzles, and a wide range of other forms of entertainment. These activities have important consequences for human development. They polish our social skills and our motor skills and enhance our mastery of language and the world around us. The friendships we form with our playmates and companions can last a lifetime. And like the marauding band of chimpanzees at the Gombe National Park, which consisted of animals of all ages, humans don't stop playing when they grow up. Adults continue to play. As a matter of fact, we tend to divide our lives into work and play, and we often set as a goal for ourselves finding an occupation in which our work is like play. Like our primate cousins, we spontaneously initiate play with our children. Even the most sedentary adult normally enjoys roughhousing occasionally with his or her child or grandchild. And this playfulness carries over to our pets. Because we enjoy playing with our dogs, cats, and the other kinds of animals that keep us company, we tend to treat them as valued friends and companions, often loving them like children.

The Dutch historian Johan Huizinga dubbed the human race *Homo ludens* (playful man) not only because of our physical playfulness but because of our mental playfulness as well. "In a sense, all science, all human thought, is a form of play," said mathematician Jacob Bronowski. "Abstract thought is the neoteny of the intellect, by which man is able to continue to carry out activities which have no immediate goal (other animals play while young) in order to prepare himself for long-term strategies and plans."

As Bronowski observed, a key characteristic of play is the pursuit of a pleasurable activity for its own sake. One unusual dimension of mature human behavior is our inclination, like eternal children, to pursue activities because they are interesting and fun, not just because they are useful or profitable. We have hobbies, and we tend to treat our possessions as toys. A new car can be both a means of getting to work and a source of pleasure in and of itself. We daydream and amuse ourselves with our imagination because we find these kinds of activities intrinsically entertaining. We enjoy them.

THE RESULT OF A NEGATIVE EARLY ENVIRONMENT

The dark side of the incredible plasticity of the young brain is that it can be warped by the wrong kinds of stress. If a vulnerable young person is repeatedly exposed to abuse, neglect, and terror, the result appears to be a reprogramming of the primitive neural system's hypothalamic-pituitary-adrenal axis—which regulates the fight-or-flight response—placing it on a hair trigger. The result can be outbursts of aggression at the slightest cause. "The early environment programs the nervous system to make an individual more or less reactive to stress," said biologist Michael Meaney of McGill University. "If parental care is inadequate or unsupportive, the [brain] may decide that the world stinks—and it is better to be ready to meet the challenge." This kind of impulsive anger seems to describe Jason Hoffman. But what about Andy Williams, who had always appeared the epitome of nonviolence? Although his parents were divorced, there was no evidence that he had ever experienced the kind of early trauma that Hoffman had.

EMOTIONAL SHUTDOWN

Researchers have noted another reaction that may occur at any time if a susceptible young person is subject to long periods of extreme stress: emotional shutdown, especially toward "them"—those who are perceived as persecutors. In this case, sensitivity to others disappears. According to Bruce Perry of the Baylor College of Medicine, such "kids have a hard time empathizing with people. They tend to be relatively passive and perceive themselves to be stomped on by the outside world." If such an individual explodes, it is often with cold deliberation, which may explain the sardonic smile that many people saw that day on Andy Williams's face. Although these kinds of outbursts are primarily associated with males, there is a growing problem with female aggression. Deborah Prothrow-Smith of the Harvard School of Public Health pointed out that girls such as school shooter Brenda Spencer "are now twenty-five percent of the adolescents arrested for violent crime."

When neuroscientists use imaging techniques to probe the brains of violent adolescents, they tend to find the same pattern of activation that often appears in adult criminals: lower than normal activity in the impulse-control centers of the prefrontal cortex and higher than normal activity in the cingulate cortex, which is associated with obsessive thoughts. This abnormal activity in the cingulate cortex makes it clear why the easy availability of guns to troubled young people is so dangerous. Adolescents such as Andy

Williams are often contemplating not only homicide but suicide. As novelist William Styron pointed out, such a mentality constantly reviews every possible method for carrying out the plans he obsessively fantasizes about. A gun can be the ideal tool for quickly and decisively accomplishing the goals demanded not only by self-hate, but also by hate.[4]

WARPED MEANING SYSTEMS

There is one more important characteristic of school shooters— they tend to have eerily similar meaning systems. Within this frame of reference, their actions are perfectly justified. Almost every one of them believed at the time of their attacks that striking out was completely legitimate. They had no sense that their actions were extreme or grotesquely disproportionate. They viewed themselves as victims who had a right to defend themselves. "I killed because people like me are mistreated every day," said Luke Woodham, a chubby, bespectacled sixteen-year-old who stabbed his mother to death then gunned down nine of his Pearl, Mississippi, high school classmates, killing two, in an October 1997 attack. In this, we are reminded of the many hate-infested areas of the world in which both sides see themselves as victims and vehemently justify their violent attacks and counterattacks.

MEDIA

What effect does media violence have on adolescent antisocial behavior? The scientific correlation between media violence and actual, physical violence is surprisingly small, particularly when compared to other, more potent risk factors such as abuse, neglect, illegal drug use, gang membership, and access to guns. That is not to say there aren't cases in which media violence may precipitate physical violence. The brutal killing of Elyse Pahler by the three boys obsessed with the heavy metal group Slayer raised this disturbing issue. So did the March 2001 conviction of fourteen-year-old Lionel Tate for the murder of a six-year-old playmate, Tiffany Eunick. Tate's attorney argued that the boy, who was only twelve at the time of the killing, was imitating the violent moves of the professional wrestlers he idolized when he hurled Eunick's forty-eight-pound body into a metal staircase after asking, "Do you want to play wrestling?" Tate was tried as an adult and received a life sentence without parole, though there was widespread criticism of the severity of the punishment. The case serves as a warning that play instincts are capable of being distorted and turned violent. Some of the bloodiest video games are the biggest sellers. And popular forms of entertainment such as professional wrestling and ultraviolent movies, though carefully staged and choreographed, nevertheless represent the pure fight response in a form that both vicariously arouses the primitive neural system and may be difficult for the most impressionable young minds to distinguish from the real thing.

There are many hypotheses about how violence in the media—both in entertainment and through the reporting of sensational crimes and other news events—may affect vulnerable individuals. There appears to be a link between specific kinds of hate crimes and current events, particularly those events that can be misconstrued by the primitive neural system as singling out a group as a threatening "them." During the debate about gays in the military in the early 1990s, hate crimes against gays—which have remained appallingly high since the discovery of the AIDS virus in 1981—shot up even further. After a U.S. Navy reconnaissance plane collided with a Chinese jet in April 2001, hate crimes against Asians increased. And, of course, after the September 11, 2001, terrorist attacks there was a sharp spike in hate crimes against Muslim-Americans.

Another possible role of the media, either news or entertainment, is through publicizing novel cultural forms of violence that shape the aggression of those who are mentally unstable.

Robert Ressler, an FBI expert on mass murder, has argued that films such as the classic thriller *Psycho* may have contributed to an increase in serial killers. Ressler has noted, according to social psychologist Roy F. Baumeister, that "the spread of serial killing in the United States coincided with a historical shift in the film industry. Up through the 1950s, most horror movies featured supernatural villains such as Dracula and Frankenstein. Beginning in the 1960s, however, films began to depict ordinary people committing monstrous crimes. Alfred Hitchcock's *Psycho* was famous in this regard, because the bloodthirsty killer was the apparently quiet and friendly clerk in a motel. Ressler thinks that lonely, violently inclined individuals scattered around the United States may not have been inspired to identify with Dracula, and so watching the earlier horror films had little effect on them. But when they began to see ordinary people killing victims in the movies, something clicked. These films planted something in their imagination and made them begin to think about how they might do similar things. Ressler's argument does not mean that movies planted the urge to kill. Instead, he thinks that these people may have had vague violent urges that remained shapeless and ambiguous for a long time. Movies enabled these people to imagine themselves tormenting and killing people. Imagining something is an important step toward actually doing it. For that reason, Ressler thinks that the modern epidemic of serial murder coincided with the rising popularity of horror films that feature violent acts by seemingly ordinary people."[5]

Serial killings have become a staple Hollywood plot device. Each popular new serial killer movie may reinforce this cultural form of violence in the minds of a tiny group of vulnerable individuals. Similarly, the widely publicized accounts of Brenda Spencer's attack on Cleveland Elementary School in 1979 might have begun to establish the school shooting as a new cultural form of violence. Saturation coverage of every major school shooting since then may have reinforced this cultural model in the minds of a scattered minority of troubled young people brooding on thoughts of hatred and revenge.

Especially since the killings at Columbine High School, there has been a wave of threats against schools around the country, causing major disruptions in many school districts. Most of these threats have been pranks, but law enforcement authorities have taken hundreds of them seriously. As we have seen, Andy Williams and Jason Hoffman were reported to have made Columbine-related threats before their attacks. A copycat phenomenon seems to be at work. After each new shooting, threats and rumors spread, especially on the Internet, which appears to have substantially amplified the negative effects of these tragic events. Within this swirl of publicity and concern, the next shooter may begin making his plans. Even if they knew nothing about Brenda Spencer, Williams and Hoffman may have been influenced by the violent trend she began.

With worrisome regularity, therapists encounter people who are susceptible to media violence. Eric Harris and Dylan Klebold were obsessed with violent video games and films. Richard Restak described one of his patients—a former prison guard—whose entire life had been marked by excessive aggression. "If I see a violent movie," the man said, "I want to get dressed and walk the streets in the toughest section of town, just hoping somebody tries to attack me."[6]

In a January 2001 report, Surgeon General Satcher concluded that, "a substantial body of research now indicates that exposure to media violence increases children's physically and verbally aggressive behavior in the short term," and a less extensive body of research has shown a "small but statistically significant impact on aggression over many years." The report noted that studies do not demonstrate a consistent connection between the media and extreme acts of violence such as murder and rape.[7]

Clearly, much more study is warranted, particularly as we gain a better understanding of the detailed brain mechanisms involved in violent behavior and how they might be affected in those who are mentally unstable. Some researchers have pointed out that given the huge audiences that the media attract, even a small effect could produce a significant amount of violence. "If you consider the country as a whole, you're going to have more violence than would otherwise have occurred," said Leonard Berkowitz, a professor of psychology at the University of Wisconsin and one of the chief authors of the surgeon general report's media section. "It's a question of what kind of society we want to live in, and I think that these movies and this television programming just make society a little nastier."

We should, however, not only be concerned about the direct effect of the media on violent behavior, but the indirect effect as well. The media and those who garner a disproportionate amount of media attention—including notorious criminals—can play a role in coarsening social behavior, especially among the young. As the surgeon general's report suggested, media depictions of hostility and violence may exacerbate forms of verbal and physical aggression that include teasing and bullying. Given the pathological reaction to such incivility by people such as Andy Williams, the media may help create an atmosphere that occasionally ignites explosions of extreme hatred and violence among the unstable few. As society becomes coarser and more aggressive, the most vulnerable individuals are ever likelier to be pushed over the edge.

GENDER DIFFERENCES

Two days after the attack at Santana High School, a fourteen-year-old girl at a Roman Catholic school in Williamsport, Pennsylvania, was accused of shooting another eighth-grade girl while the two were in the school cafeteria. After wounding her victim in the shoulder, the accused attacker, whose name was not released, is reported to have pointed the handgun at her head and threatened suicide. She was persuaded to drop the gun by a male classmate. This was one of the first school shootings by a female since the Brenda Spencer case in 1979. But the Harvard School of Public Health's Prothrow-Smith sees a link to popular culture in the rise in violent crime among female adolescents. "This follows the media portrayal of girl superheroes beating people up," she said.

Studies suggest possible reasons that boys (and men) may have more trouble with impulse control and aggressive behavior than girls (and women) have. Female hormones seem to stimulate the growth of the hippocampus, which has major responsibilities in learning and memory. Male hormones, in contrast, seem to stimulate the growth of the amygdala, a key area that modulates anger, hate, and aggression. Males may also tend to have lower serotonin levels than females have. In primates, serotonin deficits in areas of the limbic system such as the amygdala and orbitofrontal cortex have been associated with poor social behavior and increased aggression. Boys are much more susceptible to many brain-related disorders. Twice as many boys as girls have autism. Three times as many boys are in special education. And ten times more boys are diagnosed with attention deficit hyperactivity disorder. In addition, meaning systems in most cultures tend to make it easier for girls to relieve stress by talking to others about their problems. In the end, not only do males commit the preponderance of violence against others, including hate crimes, they also dominate many categories involving self-hate and self-destructive behavior. The vast majority of suicides, including adolescent suicides, are committed by males. Females tend to make more suicide attempts than males, but males often use more lethal methods of killing themselves and, thus, are far more likely to succeed.[8]

Today, there remain unanswered questions about the role of culture in the wiring of a child's brain. Does a cultural environment that features large amounts of primitive violence, sex, and stereotyped thinking tend to overstimulate the primitive neural system and understimulate the advanced neural system, which thrives on complex meaning, complex emotions, and complex modeling of the world? Can such an environment result in the inadequate development of the prefrontal impulse-control centers of some children? These are topics that will require further research. We do know, however, that the lack of an enriched environment at every stage in life, but especially early in life, has a definite negative effect on brain development. Experiments with rats have consistently shown that those raised in an enriched environment that is complex and challenging have a thicker, more densely wired neocortex. Even older rats who are introduced into such an environment experience substantial cortical development. This may help explain why studies have suggested that many children from less advantaged backgrounds are significantly helped by Head Start–style preschool programs, which seem to significantly lower later dropout and crime rates. Other promising programs are those that focus on at-risk families and teach family management and parenting skills. These programs assist parents in providing a more enriched environment for their children. All this bolsters the advanced neural system, which should be at the heart of efforts to break the cycles of violence and hate that can lock both individuals and societies into an obsessive concern with past wrongs and stereotypes.

During a routine bed check shortly after 1:00 A.M. on October 29, 2001, Jason Hoffman was found dead in his jail cell. The eighteen-year-old had looped strips of a bed sheet around the grillwork on an air vent and hanged himself. He left a one-page note full of doodles and profanity that described the despair and anger he felt. Hoffman was awaiting sentencing after pleading guilty to one count of attempted murder and five counts of assault with a deadly weapon in connection with the attack on Granite Hills High School in El Cajon. He was facing a possible sentence of twenty-seven years to life in prison. Hoffman had spent time in a padded suicide-watch cell, but he had been cleared by a doctor to return to a regular cell. His lawyer, William LaFond, a prominent San Diego defense attorney, said Hoffman's mother was devastated by her son's suicide. But LaFond said he was not surprised by what Hoffman had done because "nearly every juvenile I've represented in a murder case has tried to kill himself."[9]

13

STEREOTYPING, CATEGORIZING, AND GENERALIZING

THE GAME MANUFACTURER NINTENDO knew something was wrong when Japan's embassies all over the Arab world began responding to a stream of inquiries from concerned parents and government officials all asking the same question: Does "Pikachu" mean "I am a Jew" in Japanese? Pikachu, as every child knows, is the most popular animated character of Japan-based Nintendo's Pokémon phenomenon, which includes cartoons, toys, trading cards, comic books, clothing, and video games. Pokémon mania swept Arab countries in 2000. But this was about the same time that the Arab-Israeli conflict was erupting into the Palestinian uprising known as the second *intifada*, and rumors started surfacing that Pokémon was part of a Jewish plot against Islam. Some said the word *Pokémon* means "there is no God in the universe."

"It has been proven that this toy is part of a Jewish plan to corrupt the minds of our young generation because it alludes to blasphemous thinking, it mocks our God and our moral values, and is therefore extremely dangerous for our youth," charged Sheik Abdel Monem abu Zent, a leading anti-Pokémon activist and former member of parliament in Jordan, though he acknowledged that he was personally unfamiliar with the make-believe world of good and evil that Pikachu inhabits.

Japanese officials and representatives of the game's manufacturer patiently explained that Pokémon is short for "pocket monster" and that the names of each of the 250 or so different types of Pokémon creatures were perfectly innocent and not code words for such phrases as "Be a Jew." These rumors apparently began with an unsigned leaflet written in poor Arabic that was circulated in Saudi Arabia and other Arab countries. The leaflet blamed Pokémon for undermining Islamic morality and charged that it was part of a Jewish conspiracy. Until then, Pokémon had simply been the same delight to children and annoyance to parents that the rest of the world experienced after Nintendo introduced it as a video game in 1995 and it took off as a multibillion dollar craze. Countless Arab children became obsessed with collecting and trading Pokémon cards. One popular Arab magazine dubbed it the Pokémon virus and observed: "It is the burden of this age which has hit tens of millions of children worldwide. . . . They neglect their studies and prevent their parents from getting close to the television to change the channel, which is broadcasting a Pokémon series."

Though many found the conspiracy theory ludicrous, it became caught up in anti-Israel, anti-Semitic hysteria. Because religious meaning systems are so important in this part of the world, the religious establishment was soon in the thick of the controversy. Muslim leaders in Saudi Arabia, Oman, Qatar, Dubai, Jordan, and Egypt issued fatwas, or edicts, declaring that Pokémon was unacceptable to Islam. A Saudi edict urged "all Muslims to beware of this game and prevent their children from playing it so as to protect their religion and manners." The edict went on to say that most of the Pokémon cards feature "six-pointed stars, a symbol of international Zionism and the state of Israel." A fatwa in Dubai claimed Pokémon "clearly contains gambling" and "is based on the theory of evolution, a Jewish-Darwinist theory, that conflicts with the truth about humans and with Islamic principles." Pokémon merchandise was removed from store shelves. Schools set up centers to collect Pokémon material for disposal.[1]

This was not the first time Pokémon had run into trouble. In the United States, Nintendo withdrew a card containing an image that appeared to resemble a swastika after complaints from some Jewish parents and the Anti-Defamation League. A Christian church in Mexico called the game demonic. But the speed with which Pokémon was rejected in the Arab world was unprecedented. It reflected an atmosphere of extraordinary hostility toward everything remotely considered Jewish that intensified when the Palestinian uprising began in September 2000. The most popular song in Egypt after the start of the second *intifada* was titled "I Hate Israel" and made a superstar out of an unknown singer named Shaaban Abdel-Rahim. "You know the situation, the chaos and problems between the Palestinians and the Jews," said Abu Laila, an academic associated with Al Azhar University, the prestigious center of Islamic learning in Cairo. "The situation is so sensitive."

HATE CONTAGION

Without firm neocortical control, hate not only takes root, but also spreads. Specific, rational dislike can be transformed by the primitive neural system into obsessive hatred, and hate easily enlarges beyond its initial bounds because its core mechanism involves stereotyping and generalization. Demonizing opponents can lead to limbic paranoia with absurdly generalized thinking, loose associations, and the rapid spreading of hatred among susceptible groups—a kind of hate contagion. Under the sway of hate, a crowd of ordinary people can turn into a bloodthirsty lynch mob, as the world saw in horrifying detail in April 1992 when Los Angeles erupted in a racially charged rage after the four officers charged with beating Rodney King were found not guilty. Whenever we feel threatened, our primitive neural system filters the threat through the general and middle-level categories it understands. Primitive awareness tends to define a threat broadly by generalizing from any traits it notices: ethnicity, religion, skin color, national origin, ideology, class. If unchecked by the advanced neural system, hostility toward one group—Chechen guerilla fighters, for example—can easily broaden to become hatred of all Chechen men, women, and children. Similarly, outrage at Osama bin Laden and his Al Qaeda terrorists can expand to become animosity toward a much larger group: all Muslim- or Arab-looking men, women, and children. (The whole notion of "Arab-looking" is itself a stereotype.)

Hate, like fear, spreads in two ways via the primitive neural system: subject contagion and object contagion. Subject contagion refers to the rapid spreading of hatred through a population of individuals who feel angry or threatened. Because hate is an emotion that marks perceived dangers to survival and reproduction, our primitive neural system—especially when primed by existing hostility—is tuned to detect all aspects of an alleged threat, even when they are rationally ridiculous. Object contagion describes the tendency of the object of hatred to expand in scope. The primitive neural system lumps things into broad categories that are prone to rapid enlargement. Hatred of the policies of the Israeli government becomes hatred of all Israelis. This, in turn, grows to become hatred of Jewish people everywhere. Then, on the flimsiest evidence, "Israeli" or "Jewish" can be linked to anything remotely associated with these categories. In our example, a few poorly written leaflets were enough to rapidly infect millions of people with the belief that Pokémon represents another dimension of the supposed threat that Israel poses to Arabs and Islam. Hatred of Israel, which in many parts of the Arab world had already spread to Israel's major ally, the United States, now expanded to include hatred of Pokémon.

This kind of religiously fueled bigotry is not without its critics among Muslims. The Muslim Public Affairs Council, a U.S. organization based in Los Angeles, has long been a critic of such intolerance. "The decision to ban Pokémon on religious grounds in some Arab Muslim countries exposes the reduced level of thinking in the Muslim world," said Salam al-Marayati, the council's director. "With the sheiks, it is a Jewish conspiracy that fuels why children are glued to the TV, not bad parenting. It is an easy fix to distract leaders of Muslim countries from the real issue of their social ills, namely the paralysis of free thinking as a result of their authoritarian governance." While al-Marayati criticized the stereotyping of Jews, he also criticized the stereotyping of Arabs by the U.S. entertainment industry, pointing out that there have been far too many movies and television programs "involving dark Muslims praising the Lord for setting off nuclear bombs against white America. . . ." Al-Marayati concluded: "The two victims of the madness are free thinking and religion. Judaism, Islam, and other divine religions will flourish in spite of the hatred. Freedom of expression will also prevail."[2]

Pokémon paranoia is an absurd manifestation of a profoundly disturbing mind-set with deadly consequences. There is a surprisingly widespread belief in many Muslim countries—based on nothing more than a preposterous rumor—that thousands of Jewish workers were warned to stay away from their jobs at the World Trade Center on September 11. Because of this persistent rumor, many Muslims have concluded that the September 11 attacks were engineered by the Israeli intelligence service, Mossad, or perhaps by the CIA as a pretext for an all-out American-Israeli attack on Islam—a theory that persisted even after the release in December 2001 of a videotape recovered by allied forces in Afghanistan that shows bin Laden recounting his role in the attack. Many in the Arab world dismissed the tape as a fabrication. This illustrates how prejudice and hatred can distort even the most basic perception of reality, making rational dialogue extraordinarily difficult as thinking descends into primitive us-them stereotyping, paranoia, and distrust. Throughout human history, these kinds of distortions have been an all too frequent source of calamitous misunderstanding.

Prejudice warps human relations in large ways and small. On the day of the Oklahoma City bombing in 1995, many assumed this despicable act was the work of Arab terrorists. A number of individuals were detained and aggressively questioned at airports and other U.S. ports of entry simply because they fit the profile of "Arab" or "Muslim." After September 11, where to draw the fine line between prudent investigation and harassment became an issue of urgent importance. African-Americans have complained for years about a particular form of stereotyping: racial profiling. They speak ruefully of driving while black, shopping while black, and walking while black—"offenses" that may result in unwanted surveillance by police and others. Generalized racial or ethnic profiling, like all such broad categorizing, is a problem because it tends to use race or ethnicity as a predictive factor. By implying that blacks and Hispanics, for example, are more likely to engage in criminal activity, profiling can stigmatize all blacks and Hispanics and put them under suspicion, though the vast majority are honest and law-abiding. This leads not only to disproportionate numbers of traffic stops by police, but also offensive surveillance in stores as well as other forms of demeaning harassment. Again, this goes back to the primitive neural system's innate tendency to stereotype where a perceived threat is involved. It takes constant neocortical effort to combat this tendency. Racial profiling is an example of the kind of primitive generalization that can fuel prejudice and hatred not only on the part of those who do the profiling but among those who are profiled as well.

Us-them prejudice can infect our thinking without our clearly being aware of it. One test of prejudice—the marriage test—can be framed in terms of a thought experiment that seeks to highlight unacknowledged stereotypes. Would you want to marry, or want your children to marry, someone who falls into one of the following categories (try to respond to each with just a first impression): Asian, Hispanic, Native American, Caucasian, African-American, Catholic, Protestant, Jew, Hindu, Muslim, bisexual, heterosexual, liberal Democrat, conservative Republican, fundamentalist, mentally ill, elderly, poor, uneducated, homeless, obese, alcoholic, physically disabled, drug-addicted, convicted felon? The potential list is endless. Your first impression, positive or negative, is probably being generated by your preconscious alerting system. If you feel negative or hesitant about a particular category—even though you may think this feeling is quite rational—there could be an element of stereotyping and prejudice (primitive prejudging) involved because, in the real world, each case and set of circumstances would be quite different. A truly nonprejudiced approach would be to withhold judgment based on a one-word description and carefully assess each person given the totality of the circumstances. A convicted felon, for example, might have committed the offense decades ago as a teenager protesting racial discrimination. Because marriage involves a prime evolutionary imperative—reproduction—it usually brings to the surface all hidden sensitivities. A major indication of the true decline in racial and ethnic prejudice in America is the increasing rate of intermarriage among all ethnic groups.[3]

The primitive neural system easily generates prejudice and stereotypes. Yet our goal is not to totally eliminate it from our lives—which would be impossible—but only to keep it from inappropriately controlling us. The primitive neural system is the source of primal emotions such as joy, fear, love, and anger. It is the foundation of a rich emotional life. We should welcome its ability to protect us from harm whenever we instinctively jerk our hand away from a hot object or jump back from a potential threat. But we must also zealously guard against tendencies that are no longer adaptive in the modern world, especially when the primitive neural system attempts to rule our lives through emotions such as hate and obsessive fear, which often involve unfair stereotyping and categorical thinking.

SEVEN CHARACTERISTICS
OF THE PRIMITIVE MIND

Psychologists have identified seven major characteristics of the primitive mind. The first of these is associative thinking. The primitive neural system tends to causally link phenomena that have only a superficial association, especially in time and space. This is a primary source of superstitions and taboos. If you receive a traffic ticket on Friday the thirteenth and then your car breaks down, you may actually begin to believe that this is an unlucky day. The amygdala and hippocampus seem to take a mental snapshot of all the circumstances surrounding an event that is out of the ordinary—good or bad. Then the primitive neural system tries to make causal connections between the event itself and elements of the surrounding circumstances, particularly elements that are themselves novel or unusual (here, the fact that your series of misfortunes happened to fall on a Friday the thirteenth). This kind of primitive analysis is an example of misplaced causality, which is a hallmark of the primitive mind. Friday the thirteenth actually has nothing to do with any associated bad luck, but the primitive neural system nevertheless tries to make a causal connection because of a cultural superstition that is completely arbitrary. In some cultures, for instance, a black cat walking across one's path is considered good luck. In other cultures, it is considered bad luck. Studies of these kinds of superstitions have found that—over any large population of individuals—there is a random distribution of positive and negative experiences associated with phenomena (such as Friday the thirteenth) that are considered lucky or unlucky.

One exception, however, is when the perception of good or bad luck becomes a self-fulfilling prophecy. If you believe that Friday the thirteenth is an unlucky day and that happens to be the day you have to make a major presentation, your fear may cause you to do a poor job. Sports figures often have lucky objects or may go through rituals or routines that are designed to bring them luck. Sometimes such primitive thinking may have the effect of relaxing an athlete and making him or her more confident. But not always. Basketball great Michael Jordan, during his not especially successful fling with baseball, admitted to wearing his basketball shorts under his base-ball uniform for good luck. If a team goes on a winning streak, team members may refuse to wash their uniforms as long as they continue to win. They have made a primitive association between their vic-tories and their uniforms. The primitive mind can see in a four-leaf clover, a crystal, or a rabbit's foot magical power that is the cause of good luck. This reflects a primitive desire for control of the forces around us. But science and other disciplines, using the advanced neural system, have developed processes for teasing out the actual causes of events, which give us real control.

A second characteristic of the primitive mind is generalized thinking. We have explored the limited ability of the primitive neu-ral system to grasp uniqueness. Thus, if one snake poses a threat, there is an innate disposition to see all snakes as threatening. This tendency to engage in another logical fallacy—hasty generaliza-tion—can have catastrophic consequences when combined with hatred. We have seen how Russian forces fighting in Chechnya tend to see the enemy not just as the Chechen rebel fighters but as the entire Chechen people. This has led to the slaughter of thousands of innocent men, women, and children. Osama bin Laden doesn't limit his attacks to the governments of Israel and the United States—whose policies he abhors—but to all "Jews and crusaders." We see the same kind of primitive generalization and stereotyping over and over in genocidal conflicts. The limbic system is capable of lumping other human beings into enormous threat categories based on sweeping characteristics such as race, ethnicity, religion, nation-ality, and so forth. And when the primitive neural system fully takes control of thought, feeling, and behavior, there is an impulse to try to destroy the entire category: all Chechens, all Serbs, all Croats, all Jews, all Gypsies, all Hutus, all Tutsis. When confronted with hated enemies the primitive mind often has a simple but terrifying response: kill them.[4]

This leads to the third major characteristic of the primitive mind, which is categorical thinking. Not only does the primitive neural system reason in terms of stereotypes, it assesses those stereotypes using a kind of either-or logic—someone or something is either good or bad, a friend or an enemy, one of us or one of them, superior or inferior. Unique individuality is lost on a racist or bigot, or on those consumed by other forms of hate. Associative thinking, misplaced causality, generalized thinking, and categorical thinking make it plain how easy it is for hate to spread: a children's game such as Pokémon can abruptly be perceived as a vehicle for corrupting Arab morality and religion. Associations like this seem irrational to the advanced neural system, yet they are completely consistent with primitive logic. And if you talk with someone who honestly believes this kind of thing, he or she will assure you with great sincerity that he or she is being perfectly reasonable.

We exist simultaneously in two worlds: advanced and primitive. As our thought processes shift from the advanced to the primitive neural system when confronted with a serious threat, ideas that once seemed preposterous can suddenly make sense. In the hysteria following the December 7, 1941, attack by the Japanese on Pearl Harbor, a large segment of American society—including the highest government officials—became convinced that Japanese-Americans posed an imminent danger to national security, even though virtually no credible evidence supported this belief. These law-abiding citizens were rounded up and placed in internment camps for the duration of the war. This clearly unconstitutional policy was nevertheless upheld by the United States Supreme Court, much to the court's subsequent regret. Memories of that period are still painful to Japanese-Americans, and the pain was revived by the release of a major Walt Disney film, *Pearl Harbor*, over the 2001 Memorial Day weekend. Some Japanese-Americans were concerned that the movie would revive anti-Japanese prejudice and they would once again be blamed for the surprise attack that claimed the lives of more than two thousand American military personnel. The fear made fourteen-year-old Kristy Ito of Los Angeles hesitant to see the film. "I think if I go, there are people that are going to be racist," she said. "They might say, 'Hey, there's a Japanese girl.' I'm scared people are going to hate us more now." Although fears about the film proved largely unfounded, many Japanese-Americans can recount incidents from their childhood in which they were teased or bullied about the Japanese role in World War II. Many Muslim-Americans, in light of the September 11 attacks and the war in Afghanistan, fear that they may have to endure the same kind of harassment for decades to come.[5]

The primitive mind has other qualities that tend to subvert advanced rationality, including a fourth characteristic that can be described as personalized thinking. Here, everything is related to one's own emotional needs and desires. The primitive neural system contains stereotypes about ourselves as well as others. These stereotypes may incorporate our insecurities. Personalized thinking can lead to extreme sensitivity and overreaction to criticism. If, for example, your boss makes suggestions about how a report you have written could be better organized, your primitive neural system may misinterpret this as a general attack on you for being a disorganized person. This might lead to an emotional overreaction and an irrational obsession with comments that were intended to be objective, specific, and helpful. The result could be feelings of hatred or self-hate. Personalized thinking tends to suppress empathy for others and focus only on oneself and one's perceived emotional needs.

The capacity for empathy is centered in the orbitofrontal portion of the prefrontal cortex, one of the most advanced areas of the brain. Many of the attributes of the primitive mind result from disabling such advanced capacities. A fifth characteristic—thinking fixated on either the past or the immediate present—is another of these attributes. The prefrontal cortex allows us to spin sophisticated

scenarios that look ahead to future possibilities. We can then analyze and choose from among these potential scenarios using
advanced neural choice. But the primitive mind tends to interpret
everything from the perspective of its current situation, wants, and
needs. As part of this assessment, it considers past grievances, plea-
sures, and pains. Because it engages in little reflection or anticipa-
tion, the primitive mind often chooses quickly, reacting impulsively
and emotionally. We see this in children and adolescents, whose prefrontal areas have not fully matured. This present- and past-oriented
behavior is consistent with the kind of database of emotional
responses compiled by the amygdala. Remember that the amygdala's
responses, once formed, are highly resistant to change. If we are
afraid of snakes due to some past negative experience, our current
fear response tends to be deeply ingrained and hard to change. Similarly, entrenched hatred in places such as the Balkans is extremely
difficult to change and can persist for centuries as each generation
of children absorbs it.

The final two characteristics of the primitive mind—selective
memory and state-specific reactions—also reflect drastic limitations
on mental flexibility. Neuroscientists have discovered that maintaining a complex mental agenda that allows us to flexibly shift from
one mental state to another (for example, being tender with our family and businesslike with our coworkers) is centered primarily in the
prefrontal cortex. The primitive neural system, in contrast, tends to
maintain an obsessive focus. If someone with a snake phobia is told
while on a camping trip that a snake has been spotted, he or she will
have a hard time thinking about anything else. State-specific reactions and selective memory are most dramatically illustrated in
severe depression, which drastically cuts back on neocortical activity. In state-specific reactions, all one's responses to a current situation are related to the current emotion or mood. People suffering
from depression are often so ensnared by their dark, painful mood
that they cannot even imagine what it is like to be joyful. They also
suffer from selective memory in that they tend to dwell on painful

episodes in their past and find it difficult to recall happier times. The opposite condition might be experienced by someone who is pleasantly intoxicated and sees the world through rose-colored glasses. All of his or her thoughts, feelings, and memories are happy ones. Alcohol tends to depress the frontal lobes, freeing the primitive neural system. For some, this can be a pleasurable experience. For others, negative emotions are released that can lead to anger and violence.

THE NEURAL SYSTEMS' STRUGGLE FOR CONTROL

The primitive neural system and advanced neural system each contain a model of the world. Lodged in the primitive mind are our primal fears and desires, likes and dislikes, and instinctive drives designed to promote our survival and reproduction. The primitive neural system is designed for speedy responses to threats and opportunities. The advanced neural system contains a far more sophisticated model whose potential for detail and complex meaning is virtually unlimited. It can reflect and elaborate at its leisure, contemplating everything from elementary particles to the entire universe and casting its thoughts billion of years into the future or billions of years into the past. Unlike the primitive neural system, it also contains a model of the self that is the basis of consciousness. There is a constant competition between these two systems for control of our thoughts, emotions, and behavior. Do we react to an annoyance with explosive anger or by putting it in perspective and laughing it off? The orbitofrontal cortex, which is by far the most advanced portion of the limbic association cortex, is an important bridge between these two systems. Through it, the advanced neural system can shape or suppress the impulses of the primitive mind, though success will vary depending on the strength of the primitive urges.[6]

The enormous capacities of the advanced neural system, however, are just that—capacities. They are tapped only if an individual mind undergoes the kind of education, training, and constant
challenges that build up the complex circuitry necessary to unleash
this advanced potential. The primitive neural system can easily
overmaster an immature or poorly developed advanced neural system. And the untrained advanced neural system is itself perfectly
capable of engaging in hasty generalization, stereotyping, misplaced
causality, categorical thinking, and other forms of flawed mental
processing. The major difference, however, is that when the advanced neural system realizes it has made a mistake, it can rapidly
alter the course of its thinking, whereas the primitive neural system
has a much more difficult time changing its mind.

THE HATE TRAP

Hate tends to lock us into the blame game, as we spar with adversaries for whom we have little empathy or understanding. Hate shuts
off empathy for the hated. And violence among antagonists who
resent and hate each other can begin a cycle of rage and retaliation
that is enormously difficult to stop. Hate can obsess us with past
wrongs because the pain that those wrongs cause us remains so
vividly in memory. Because the primitive neural system deals
directly with survival and reproduction, whenever it perceives a significant danger, it turns up our memory mechanism so every detail
of the threatening situation is etched deeply in our mind. This can
precipitate serious mental problems such as posttraumatic stress disorder, which may be accompanied by frighteningly realistic flash-
backs to a traumatic event. The human brain is insensitive to pain,
which allows neurosurgery to be carried out with only a local anes-
thetic. Neurosurgeons have found that when they electrically stimulate areas of the temporal cortex that overlie the amygdala, patients
sometimes report feeling as if they are reliving a past experience in

an incredibly realistic way. But if a society is constantly reliving the most painful possible events in its past, it can become consumed by the desire for revenge. This is what has occurred too frequently between the Israelis and Palestinians, for example, who are struggling to find some accommodation in the same small region of the world. It happened again with the outbreak of the second *intifada*— the frustrating aftermath of negotiations that came tantalizingly close to breaking the impasse between them. Each side blamed the other. But once the cycle of rage and reprisal began, though many people could clearly see the inevitable downward spiral, it became enormously difficult to stop. This was not simply a matter of logic or reason. The primitive mind had taken over.

During an especially intense period of violence, Tom Segev, a columnist for the Israeli newspaper *Haaretz*, quoted a passage that Bernard Montgomery, a British general, wrote from Palestine a few months before the outbreak of World War II: "The Jew murders the Arab and the Arab murders the Jew. This is what is going on in Palestine now. And it will go on for the next fifty years in all probability." Segev then observed: "More than sixty years later, old Monty's prediction seems as relevant as ever. The same elements of the conflict that led the British to end their thirty-year rule in Palestine still determine the situation today. Only unlike the British, the Israelis and Palestinians have nowhere to go; they are doomed to share the land and work out some sort of settlement that would at least make it possible for them to live together without violence or oppression, if not in full peace."[7]

But vengeance and animosity are formidable obstacles to rational accommodation. During that same period of the *intifada*, Israeli novelist David Grossman summed up the problem: "Each day more people join the ranks of the dead and wounded, of the haters and the despondent. Each day the appetite for revenge grows. . . . Instead of pursuing a 'peace of the courageous,' both sides are busy keeping a bloody, you-killed-me-I'll-kill-you balance sheet. The principal objective is to avenge yesterday's murder while minimizing the enemy's retaliation tomorrow. Without noticing it, Palestinians and Israelis are reverting to the pattern of an ancient tribal war, eye for an eye and tooth for a tooth."[8]

Remember what fifteen-year-old Kip Kinkel wrote in his journal before murdering his parents and shooting his classmates in Springfield, Oregon: "Hate drives me. . . . I am so full of rage. . . . Everyone is against me. . . . As soon as my hope is gone, people die." This encapsulates a pattern of emotional response that we see too often in outbreaks of savagery: hate, rage, paranoia, hopelessness, blame, and violence. With its brooding and obsessive qualities, and its drive to identify, through scapegoating and false perceptions, the catalyst of a perceived wrong, hate traps us in the past. It shatters trust and crushes hope, both of which look to the future. Yet within the recesses of the mind lie the tools necessary to heal mistrust and soothe despair. Our evolutionary development is both the problem and the solution.

14

SEEKING JUSTICE, NOT VENGEANCE

HATE IS PERSONAL. So is vengeance. Justice is not. In some other time and place, former Ku Klux Klan member Thomas E. Blanton Jr. might have been killed as an act of revenge. For Blanton had long been suspected of being one of the men who planted ten sticks of dynamite at the back door of the 16th Street Baptist Church in Birmingham, Alabama. The bomb exploded on the morning of September 15, 1963, killing four young African-American girls who were in a downstairs lounge preparing to go to Sunday school. Birmingham at that time was the center of the struggle for civil rights led by Martin Luther King Jr., and it was King who delivered the eulogy for eleven-year-old Denise McNair and for Carole Robertson, Cynthia Wesley, and Addie Mae Collins, all fourteen. "These children—unoffending, innocent, and beautiful—were the victims of one of the most vicious, heinous crimes ever perpetuated against humanity," he said. The Birmingham church bombing was the single deadliest act of violence against the civil rights movement.

But there were no public calls by King for vengeance or vigi-
lantism. His movement was dedicated to the principle of nonviolence. He was committed to using the rule of law through the courts
and Congress to change the practices of segregation and discrimination that disenfranchised and impoverished black Americans.
When intense dislike is subsumed by the primitive neural system, it
is transformed into hate, with its obsessions and stereotypes, and
can become the source of rage and violence. But if dislike remains
under the control of the advanced neural system, primitive limbic
impulses can be shaped into far more sophisticated, powerful, and
effective forms of motivation. Unlike hate, rational dislike can be
quite complex and specific and can include such potentially useful
emotions as constructive anger, which is often expressed as outrage
or moral indignation and acts to energize individuals or groups to
take corrective action. There is no question that the murder of these
four young girls sparked both rage and outrage. But righteous indignation won out over hatred, and the civil rights movement went
forward. In large part because of the national outcry over this act of
unadulterated hatred, the civil rights movement received widespread
support and Congress passed the landmark Civil Rights Act of 1964.
King's approach epitomized a key strategy for curbing and eliminating hate: seek justice, not revenge. Justice, however, was long in
coming for Thomas Blanton.

JUSTICE UNDER THE RULE OF LAW

The rule of law is one of those extraordinary social innovations
whose origin is something of a mystery. It may have been invented
many times in many places. The invention of writing may have nur-
tured it. Written laws were an attempt to systematize social relationships and rein in the practice of revenge and retaliation, which
was destructive of the order required by a settled, agriculture-based

society. The Code of Hammurabi, which dates back almost four millennia, is one of the oldest preserved legal codes. Hammurabi was the ruler of a very early civilization in the Tigris-Euphrates valley.

"Two wrongs don't make a right," said Elliot Dorff, a professor of philosophy at the University of Judaism in Los Angeles. "Revenge doesn't just affect two people; it affects everybody. It adds a tear to society. It brings you to a lowered state." As we have seen, hatred and violence have no natural limits and can escalate rapidly to mass killing, genocidal destruction, and increasingly virulent retaliatory acts. Because of this, a system of order had to be devised to control these brutal behaviors. Thus was born the idea of justice.[1]

Justice is imposed not by the individual but by the group. In the modern setting, this means the state. When a serious infraction is committed—what we now call a violation of criminal law—the offended party is technically the state, representing society as a whole, not the victim. In a criminal case, it is not the victim versus the accused but the state versus the accused. The defendant is charged with violating the laws of the state, not offending an individual. In fact, because the state is the aggrieved party, the victim does not technically have the right to drop the matter. That is the state's decision. The victim's cooperation is necessary solely to help the state meet its burden of proof. In the Anglo-American system of criminal law, that burden is proof beyond a reasonable doubt.

As the idea of justice evolved over the millennia, people realized that only if society took over the role of dispensing punishment could primitive emotions such as hate and vengeance be controlled. Because hatred spreads easily, not only is the accused a potential object of revenge, but so are his family and friends. The accuser, too, risks retaliation. Cycles of violence, represented by blood feuds and vendettas, feed on this kind of back and forth. Hatred, of course, has not disappeared in a civilized setting, and retaliation can still be a problem. The state generally devotes substantial resources to protecting not only the accused but also the accuser, sometimes going to extraordinary lengths to prevent reprisals as with the federal witness protection program in which an endangered witness may be given a new identity.

In ancient systems of justice, the ruler as the embodiment of society exacted the penalty. This was a way to stop the cycle of violence by having someone too powerful to retaliate against impose punishment. In most modern states, sovereignty does not reside in one person but in society as a whole. So systems of justice seek to rationalize procedures and put the administration of justice in the hands of many people: law enforcement, prosecutors, judges, juries, layers of appellate courts, and the prison system. The rule of law seeks to break the cycle of violence in criminal cases by imposing punishment, including death where it is allowed, in the name of the entire society according to specific, uniform rules and procedures overseen by disinterested parties—a judge and jury in the Anglo-American system—thereby placing the administration of justice as far as possible within the advanced neural system. The procedures are most elaborate for criminal law, which includes the most serious and violent offenses that tend to prompt the most extreme emotions. And because the entire society imposes punishment, it is more difficult for the family and friends of the accused (or the accused himself) to focus on one person for purposes of revenge. Thus, justice under the rule of law with its formal, rational procedures seeks to exclude, as far as possible, primitive emotions such as hate from governing the process of punishing wrongdoers. The purpose of justice, like the purpose of vengeance, is to punish and deter. But it seeks to achieve these goals in ways that enhance the social order rather than undermine it. Whereas codes of justice make precise distinctions and center around specific charges with clearly defined elements, hatred and revenge engage the primitive neural system with its stereotypes, generalizations, and limitless anger.

When there is confidence in a fair judicial proceeding, it is easier for individuals to keep their reactions to traumatic events in the advanced neural system as well. Peter Ruiz, the security guard who was shot three times by Andy Williams at Santana High School, made an amazingly rapid and complete recovery from his wounds. He expressed no anger toward Williams, who was charged as an adult. "I just don't think I was singled out," said Ruiz. "Andy just saw me there and shot. He had never given me any trouble. There's nothing I can do to change the past. I can only go forward."[2]

WHEN THE RULE OF LAW IS NOT EFFECTIVE

Where the rule of law is effective, it can peacefully resolve the most heated disputes that might otherwise cause civil discord and violence. Blood feuds and revenge killings are largely eliminated. But sometimes the rule of law is not effective. It can be undermined by corruption or prejudice. This was the case in the Birmingham of 1963 and makes the nonviolent response to the murder of four little girls all the more remarkable. King called Birmingham "the most segregated city in America," and African-Americans had no confidence in the fairness of its justice system. The dynamiting of the 16th Street Baptist Church was only the worst of a series of racist bombings that had earned Birmingham the nickname "Bombingham." And the city's public safety commissioner, Eugene "Bull" Connor, was notorious for turning police dogs and fire hoses on peaceful demonstrators.

Within days of the church bombing, the FBI had identified four suspects, all extreme segregationists and members of the Ku Klux Klan: Robert E. "Dynamite Bob" Chambliss, Herman Frank Cash, Bobby Frank Cherry, and Blanton, a former Navy mechanic. Witnesses reported that before the bombing they had seen four white men in a 1957 Chevrolet outside the church. The automobile, with a Confederate flag on the antenna, matched the description of the car

Blanton drove. Despite this and other evidence gathered through wiretaps and informants, then–FBI Director J. Edgar Hoover decided not to pursue the investigation. He said a jury of all-white men, which would in all probability hear the case, would never convict the four Klansmen. Like the bombing itself, this decision was greeted with outrage and became a lingering cloud over Birmingham, despite the strides toward racial healing that were made in subsequent years. The city grew into a banking and high-technology center with a wide range of groups established to promote racial harmony. A white lawyer drafted a statement renouncing bigotry that became known as the Birmingham Pledge and has been signed by nearly a hundred thousand people, including Bill and Hillary Clinton. It reads in part, "I will strive daily to eliminate racial prejudice from my thoughts and actions." Nevertheless, the cloud remained. "Everybody links Birmingham to that bombing," said Bernard Kincaid, who was elected the city's second African-American mayor in 1999. "But what has been holding us back was not so much the act itself, however atrocious, but the idea that the men who killed those girls were walking around free."[3]

A major problem with the rule of law occurs when there is a breakdown of civil society that calls into question the social order itself, as in the case of a civil war. This occurred in the Balkans with the collapse of the Communist government of the former Yugoslavia following the fall of the Soviet Union. Government institutions began to implode as different ethnic groups scrambled for power in the ensuing chaos. Bloody ethnic wars erupted as hatreds were released that had been dormant for decades. The Balkans continue to be highly unstable because the most extreme elements of each ethnic group focus on past grievances and betrayals, refusing to contemplate the idea of multiethnic societies. Instead, they seek to rearrange borders so that homogeneous ethnic states can be formed. This is the root of ethnic cleansing in which different groups forcibly try to rearrange the ethnic map. If tensions in the Balkans are ever to ease, a sense of common humanity will have to transcend ethnic identity, and the social order will have to be reconstituted in ways that inspire confidence in every citizen.

Perhaps the greatest unresolved issue with the rule of law is the problem of conflicts between actual or potential nation-states. Despite the growth of international law and international institutions such as the United Nations, there is no generally recognized system of justice for arbitrating major disputes between nations. This includes terrorist organizations that are supported, openly or secretly, by one or more nations to be used as weapons against other nations. In the aftermath of September 11, the United States had to pull together an ad hoc and fragile coalition of nations to assist in dismantling and bringing to justice the Al Qaeda network and the Taliban leadership of Afghanistan that supported it. In international relations, force is still the ultimate arbiter and, without intelligent supervision, can quickly degenerate into hatred and extreme violence, whose intensity may range from occasional acts of aggression to all-out war. This is the problem in the Middle East, where the state of Israel faces the incipient state of Palestine. Nationalism and national rivalries have been the cause of belligerent us-them divisions, enmity, and conflict for centuries. Without a recognized system of international justice, these rivalries must simply play themselves out—sometimes violently, sometimes through negotiation. An independent arbiter trusted by both sides can occasionally be helpful. The United States has attempted to play this role in the Middle East. But even a superpower cannot overcome deep-seated suspicion and hatred, as became obvious in the shockingly violent sequel to the breakdown of the negotiation process mediated by President Clinton. Two veteran observers of the Middle East peace process summarized the causes of the collapse of the 2000 Camp David summit and the subsequent outbreak of fighting in the following way: "For all the top Israeli and Palestinian mediators' public talk of how well they knew one another, of the way they could ask after one another's children, there remained deep mistrust at all levels of society and a lack of basic empathy. The two peoples clung to their stereotypes of one another."

A CYCLE OF VENGEANCE

The image, caught by a French television crew on September 30, 2000, seared the conscience of the world: twelve-year-old Mohammed Durra crouching behind his father, who was vainly trying to shield the boy from harm after the two were caught in the cross fire of a gun battle between Israeli and Palestinian forces early in the second *intifada*. Mohammed was eventually shot to death and his father seriously wounded. The hatred that had been building on both sides seemed to solidify and the pattern of attacks and counterattacks—a cycle of vengeance—locked into place. Interest in each other's children had been one of the fragile elements out of which Israeli and Palestinian negotiators had built a delicate web of trust. The death of children, which provokes the most powerful primal emotions, helped destroy that web.

Most of the dead in the second *intifada* were Palestinians. But Israeli children died, too. One of them was ten-month-old Shalhevet Pas, who was laid to rest on April 1, 2001. She had been shot dead in her stroller by a Palestinian sniper as her parents wheeled her into a playground at the center of one of several Jewish enclaves in the West Bank city of Hebron. Her father was injured by the same bullet. The child's death quickly became a major political issue. Israeli settlers in Palestinian areas have borne the brunt of Palestinian attacks. They live in highly controversial settlements that are bitterly resented by the Palestinians. And the four hundred Jewish settlers among the more than one hundred thousand Palestinians in Hebron are considered the most vulnerable. The hills of Hebron, which are Palestinian land, look down on the Jewish areas and are the source of periodic sniper attacks. The Hebron settlers demanded that the Israeli army reoccupy the hills. At Shalhevet's funeral, her sobbing aunt, Ayelet Zarbiv, delivered a fiery eulogy. "Shalhevet, your blood is shouting for revenge," she said. "We'll take revenge yet, Shalhevet. We'll not forgive. We'll not forget."[4]

The death of the child began a weeklong rampage by Hebron's Jewish settlers, considered some of the most militant in Israel. Their cries of "Death to Arabs!" matched the cries of "Death to Jews!" from mobs of Palestinians. They ransacked and burned Palestinian-owned stores, spray painting the Star of David on some. As they tried to invade other Palestinian neighborhoods, Israeli soldiers pushed them back. Many of the settlers then turned on the soldiers, calling them Nazis and dogs and pelting them with eggs and rocks. Seven settlers were arrested, and two soldiers were hospitalized. Nothing really changed, however. The eye-for-an-eye violence continued.

More than a month after the killing of Shalhevet Pas, the central Sharon Mall in the Israeli coastal town of Netanya was crowded with shoppers. It was a Friday, and families flocked to the mall preparing for the Jewish sabbath. A few people noticed a skinny man with a mustache wearing a bulky blue coat—attire that was out of place in the heat and humidity. Someone became alarmed and notified the authorities. Security guard Lior Kamisa was one of those who rushed to the scene. When he saw the man at the entrance to the mall, he immediately feared that underneath the blue coat was a belt of explosives. "I looked him in the eye and he blew himself up," Kamisa recalled later from his hospital bed. "He just exploded and disintegrated right in front of me." The enormous blast killed six people and wounded a hundred other adults and children. Sixty-year-old Shalom Zioni was on one of his regular walks to the mall, a form of exercise that is part of his therapy for recovering from a stroke. He had nearly reached the mall entrance. "If I had been able to walk faster, I would be dead now," he said, weeping. "Every time I close my eyes, I see a vision of red. I see people without arms and legs."

The radical Islamic group Hamas issued a statement claiming responsibility for the bombing, saying that Israel was "reaping the suffering it has sown." The suicide bomber was reported to be twenty-one-year-old Mahmoud Ahmed Marmash, who lived in the West Bank town of Tulkarm, which lies ten miles east of Netanya. He was said to have left sweets for his family before traveling to Netanya. Many Palestinians were at Friday prayers when the attack occurred. The bombing was announced over loudspeakers at mosques as prayers concluded. The news was greeted with roars of approval. The Israelis responded within hours. F-16 jet fighters and helicopter gunships attacked targets in Gaza City and throughout the West Bank. It was the first time Israeli warplanes had flown against targets in the West Bank and Gaza since the 1967 Middle East war.

The hostility and cycle of revenge that are so common among many Israelis and Palestinians seem almost incomprehensible to an outsider. That is not unusual in these kinds of situations. The stereotypes, prejudice, and hatred that are part of the unique history of each conflict are foreign to those who are not participants. Visitors from countries such as Sweden and Norway often comment on the bizarre American preoccupation with race. To an outsider visiting Northern Ireland, the Protestants and Catholics seem to share more similarities than differences. Yet if you talk to extremists on either side of hate-filled conflicts, they will tell you with perfect sincerity how loathsome their opponents are. Their rationales often include decades, even centuries of grievances.

Hate and revenge are obsessed with the past. People think they are being rational when, at bottom, they are not. At the core of their rationalization is primitive hostility. To absorb this hostility one must be immersed in it and have some stake in it. If an American Catholic moved to Northern Ireland and felt threatened by Protestant militias, his or her primitive neural system would tend to automatically become tuned to the obsessions, stereotypes, and hatred that animate this conflict on the Catholic side. It would take an aggressive and constant intervention by the advanced neural system to prevent this subconscious tuning. Children who grow up in such an environment tend to absorb the hatred around them and the sense of a need for vengeance as effortlessly as the air they breathe, thus perpetuating them for another generation. There are ways to prevent this from happening, but they are often unrealistic.

Because of differing rates of neocortical and limbic development, children go through different stages of susceptibility to hate. Until about the age of five (the exact age will vary somewhat because individual rates of brain development vary), children are essentially immune to hatred and other kinds of bigotry based on skin color, ethnic origin, religion, and other relatively abstract criteria. The young brain is not yet capable of fully grasping these distinctions. However, by the seventh year of life, notes Richard Restak, children gain "the ability to see where they fit into the huge and amorphous world around them. Living things are distinguished from nonliving things. Objects and people are understood as belonging to separate categories. The pet cat is an 'animal' and at the same time a 'living thing,' a 'companion,' and a 'friend.' The child learns the hierarchies into which categories fit." Unfortunately, this miracle of logical thinking is also the time when children can fully absorb from their surroundings explicit and implicit messages about who is superior and who is inferior, who is a friend and who is an enemy, who can be trusted and who should be hated. If children are completely removed from a climate of prejudice before they enter first grade, however, they tend not to internalize the hatred they have been exposed to. Except for adoption, such a complete removal is usually neither practical nor fully possible. Even if the entire family moves away from a prejudiced environment, the child's parents, guardians, or older siblings will often retain the prejudices of the former environment, which will influence the child after age five. Nevertheless, even if other family members retain their biases, young children who have been removed from a prejudiced environment and grow up in a nonprejudiced environment will tend to have a significantly less biased outlook than their peers who remain behind. This is because the nonprejudiced environment does not reinforce, and often counteracts, the prejudices of the parents. By the third generation, these prejudices may have completely disappeared. Aside from emigration, however, leaving an environment of hate is not a realistic possibility for most people. The alternative is to rebuild that environment from the ground up so that hate is eliminated. This, of course, is a Herculean task.[5]

BREAKING THE CYCLE OF VENGEANCE AND VIOLENCE

The moment that transformed Yitzhak Frankenthal's life occurred in southern Israel in 1994. His eldest son, Arye, who was serving in the Israeli army, was hitchhiking back to his base. He was picked up by a group of Palestinian Hamas extremists posing as Jews. When the Palestinians went for his gun, Arye fought back and injured one of his attackers. But they were able to wrest the gun away and shoot him three times in the head. He was dead at nineteen. People can react to such horrors in many different ways. Some seek revenge. Others sink into depression. Still others try to find some sort of constructive meaning in such a tragedy and use it to change things for the better, as did James Brady—who suffered serious brain damage when he was struck by a bullet from John Hinckley's gun—and his wife, Sarah, who have devoted themselves to the cause of gun control. Yitzhak Frankenthal is also such a person. Ever since the killing of his son, he has fought not for vengeance but for a resolution of the Israeli-Palestinian conflict based on reconciliation, dialogue, and peaceful coexistence. He remained a steadfast supporter of peace throughout the numbing violence of the second *intifada*. "Peace will come. There can be no question about it, and no one can stop it," said fifty-year-old Frankenthal in April 2001. "The only question is how many people will have to die to achieve it."

Frankenthal, an Orthodox Jew, is still angry about Arye's murder. But he tries to use the drive this gives him for a higher purpose. He is under no illusions about the brutality of the Middle East conflict. "I do not love Palestinians. They killed my son," he said. "My sympathies are 100 percent with the Israelis. But I have respect for Palestinians as a people and give to them the dignity that I would give to an Israeli." After Arye's death, Frankenthal, a stocky man with thick gray hair, dropped out of his ice cream–making business and joined a religious antiviolence group that Arye had belonged to, eventually becoming its leader and an impassioned crusader for peace. He then formed an extraordinary organization, the Parents Circle/Family Forum. It is made up of 190 Israelis and 140 Palestinians who have lost a relative, usually a child, in the Israeli-Palestinian conflict. Some of the dead loved ones on the Palestinian side were suicide bombers. "If *we* can sit together, if we don't want revenge, if we can open a new page," Frankenthal said, "then anyone can."[6]

Over the years, delegations made up of both Israeli and Palestinian members of Parents Circle have met with the leadership of both sides of the conflict, urging peace. But the second *intifada* made any kind of meetings between Israelis and Palestinians almost impossible. Adib Mahana, a Palestinian from Gaza who has become Frankenthal's partner in organizing grieving families, described the extremely tense atmosphere since the *intifada*. "I have received telephone threats from people over my contacts with Israelis," he said. "They told me I was traitor. 'Look at what is happening,' they say. 'How can you talk to them?' But I knew going in that anyone choosing this path would have to endure these kinds of reactions. I remain convinced there is no other way." One primitive characteristic of hatred is its intolerance of dissent. Frankenthal, too, has been threatened and criticized for associating with "murderers and traitors," but he has refused to be silent. At the height of the *intifada*, he ran a controversial series of newspaper advertisements. Each one showed a graphic photo of a young person killed in the conflict with a plea from a parent of the dead youth to end the violence.

Frankenthal worries that neither side is prepared to make the concessions necessary for a final and lasting reconciliation. But he presses on. "If it takes twenty years, God forbid, to make peace," he said, "then today we are closer than yesterday."

By the early 1970s, attitudes in Birmingham, Alabama, had begun to change. A young Alabama attorney general, William J. Baxley, reopened the bombing case and targeted "Dynamite Bob" Chambliss, who was believed to have masterminded the attack on the 16th Street Baptist Church. Chambliss was convicted in 1977 and died eight years later while still in prison. The case against the other three men was weaker, but the failure to prosecute them remained a source of friction. In 1994, one of the remaining suspects, Herman Frank Cash, died. Three years later, the FBI believed it had its case against the remaining two suspects. Bobby Frank Cherry and Thomas Blanton were indicted on four counts of murder. The seventy-one-year-old Cherry was initially dropped from the proceeding when a judge ruled that he was not mentally competent. Sixty-two-year-old Blanton went to trial in April 2001, and the case drew worldwide attention.[7]

The most damaging evidence consisted of secretly taped conversations that were made within a year of the bombing. The bulk of the conversations were between Blanton and another Klansman, Mitchell Burns, who had become a paid FBI informant after he was shown autopsy photos of the torn bodies of the four little girls. Although Blanton never explicitly admitted being part of the church bombing, he made a number of apparent references to it on the tapes, which contained a constant stream of racist invective. "They ain't going to catch me when I bomb my next church," he said at one point. "I like to go shooting, I like to go fishing, I like to go bombing," he said at another. The jury of eight white women, three black women, and one black man took only two-and-a-half hours to return verdicts of guilty on all four counts of first-degree murder. The jury forewoman couldn't stop crying as she read the verdicts. Blanton was sentenced to life in prison. After the verdict, Mayor Kincaid said his city can now "look ahead and stop reliving September 15, 1963. Birmingham is a calm, peaceful place. Especially today."

The case against Cherry was eventually reinstated. In May 2002, he was found guilty of murder thirty-eight years after the 1963 church bombing, proving that justice delayed is not necessarily justice denied.

15

EMPATHY, UNDERSTANDING, AND FORGIVENESS

THE RACE SPANNED FOUR HUNDRED METERS and fifty thousand years in just under fifty seconds. When it was over, Cathy Freeman sat down on the track, soaking in the adulation of more than a hundred thousand people. It was the 2000 Summer Olympics in Sydney, and the two-time defending world champion in the four-hundred-meter sprint had just become the first of Australia's Aboriginal people to win an individual Olympic gold medal. Wave after wave of deafening cheers swept through Sydney's Olympic Stadium. It was one of the longest standing ovations in sports history. From the moment Freeman appeared for the race until the moment she left the stadium, the crowd was on its feet applauding and shouting its approval. "I was totally overwhelmed," Freeman said. "I could feel the crowd totally around me, over me. Happiness absorbed into every pore of my body. It was beyond words."

Walking to the stands after her victory, she hugged her mother and took a blue, white, and red Australian flag that was knotted with another flag colored yellow, black, and red. It was the Aboriginal flag—yellow for the sun, red for the rust-colored land in the center of the island continent, and black for the indigenous people that have lived there for perhaps fifty thousand years. Her space-age, hooded running suit bore the Australian colors of green and gold, but her running shoes were yellow, red, and black. She ran her victory lap, barefoot, waving the two flags. "My family is very proud of its Aboriginal heritage," she said. "What I'm about, really, is just being free to be who I am in my own country." Though people had made a symbol out of her, her message was simple: "I would just like for young Aboriginals to think that they can live in a world of unity of all people and religions."[1]

Ten days earlier, Freeman, clad in a snow-white running suit, had been chosen to light the Olympic torch at the spectacular opening ceremonies that prominently featured Aboriginal songs, dances, and customs. The Sydney Olympic Games were a moment of reconciliation between blacks and whites in Australia, who have had a long and troubled history, not unlike the history of most indigenous peoples in areas colonized by Europeans over the past five centuries, including the Americas. From the moment serious colonization of Australia began in 1788, Aborigines were largely viewed as "them," treated with hatred and contempt, and deemed little better than wild animals to be hunted and killed. Nineteenth-century novelist Anthony Trollope expressed the prevailing view: "Of the Australian black man we may certainly say that he has to go. That he should perish without unnecessary suffering should be the aim of all who are concerned in the matter." The Aboriginal people of Tasmania, an island two hundred miles off Australia's southeast coast, were completely exterminated through killing, mistreatment, and disease. The last full-blooded Tasmanian man, William Lanner, died in 1869, and the last Tasmanian woman, Truganini, died seven years later. The two were considered curiosities because some scientists believed the Tasmanians were the missing link between humans and apes. We know today that their genes were virtually identical to those of the scientists who studied them.

Australian Aborigines fared little better. From 1788 to 1921, their population dwindled from about three hundred thousand to sixty thousand. In the 1920s, however, their treatment began to improve slightly. By the year 2000, the number of Aborigines had increased to 386,000, about 2 percent of the Australian population. But they remain the poorest segment of society, with an average life expectancy twenty years less than other Australians. Even worse, to many Aborigines, was the "stolen generation." In an effort to speed Aboriginal assimilation, the Australian government from 1910 to the 1970s sanctioned a policy of forcibly removing thousands of Aboriginal children from their homes—estimates range up to one hundred thousand. These children were given to white families to raise. Two months before the Olympics, Freeman revealed that her grandmother had been one of those given to a white family. "The fact is, parts of people's lives were taken away, they were stolen," said Freeman. Her grandmother had not even been told the date of her birth.

Freeman has become a powerful symbol of hope for both blacks and whites during a period of increasing national reconciliation. In recent years, the Aborigines' claim that they were unfairly dispossessed of Australia by European colonists has been given at least partial judicial and political recognition, and they have been awarded 15 percent of the continent, though most of it is in the remote Northern Territory. Several billion dollars are being spent to improve their living conditions and social services. Many believe that much more must be done.

ERASING US-THEM DISTINCTIONS

Freeman is one of the most popular figures in Australia, and her views and example carry great weight. There is an intense identification with her and pride in her achievements. And because she is an Aborigine, this has helped bridge a vast us-them divide between the Aboriginal population and the rest of Australia. Why? Freeman represents one of the most important findings of social psychology. Just as the primitive neural system has subconscious mechanisms for creating us-them divisions, it also has subconscious mechanisms for erasing them. When a collection of individuals that has a shared sense of meaning undertakes a cooperative effort to achieve a common goal, us-them divisions tend to disappear and a single us-group can take their place. Those who were once "them" become part of "us." Stereotypes, prejudice, and hatred—which are often based on us-them distinctions—can drastically decline or disappear. And people don't have to take part directly in the cooperative effort in order for this mechanism to be triggered in their primitive neural systems. They can participate vicariously. Cathy Freeman illustrates why sports has become one of the most powerful methods for dissolving us-them divisions.[2]

The integration of amateur and professional sports in the United States and the identification of millions of people of all ethnic backgrounds with stars such as Jackie Robinson, Arthur Ashe, Magic Johnson, Michael Jordan, and Tiger Woods have been extraordinarily important in reducing racial divisions, stereotypes, and hatred. Sports is unusually effective because people identify with the common goal of the athlete—victory—and this activates a primal mechanism designed to mold otherwise indifferent or antagonistic human beings into an us-group capable of achieving mutually important goals. We see this throughout history. As we saw again after September 11, when a nation is militarily attacked, internal rivalries and divisions often drastically diminish as the country unites around the common goal of survival and victory. Patriotism—a core element of the nation-state and one of the most powerful emotional forces in the modern world—is built on a cooperative effort to achieve the common goal of building a successful society. The primitive neural system tends to interpret a cooperative effort to achieve a common goal of perceived importance—even winning a sports championship—as either enhancing the group members' survival and reproduction or fending off a threat to these primal goals. Athletic competition provides exceptionally intense emotional experiences, both positive and negative, because the primitive neural system interprets it as far more significant than it actually is. Our limbic system seems to identify with the success of a favorite sports team with the same intensity that early hominids would have had in identifying with the success of their small hunter-gatherer bands in the life-or-death struggle on the African savanna. Cathy Freeman became part of this powerful process in Australia. As one of the leaders of the Australian Olympic team, she was part of a cooperative effort by Australian athletes to bring honor and victory to the host country in a competition with the rest of the world. There was wide agreement in Australian society about the importance of this goal and intense identification and empathy with Freeman as one of the leaders in the effort to achieve it. Australian newspapers commonly referred to her as "our Cathy."

As always in human culture, the actual manifestation of this psychological process can be quite complex. Athletes who are the first to integrate a previously segregated sport frequently face extreme hostility. And sports figures such as the great and colorfully outspoken boxer Muhammad Ali can at times be highly divisive. But for those who love a particular sport and appreciate outstanding performance—even people riddled with bigotry and hate—the athletic excellence of an individual such as Ali tends to activate a primal fascination and sense of identification that, in the long run, often overcomes us-them divisions.

This subconscious process requires three basic elements: shared meaning, common goal, and cooperative effort. First, there must be a shared system of meaning between athlete and fan. In simplified terms, the creation of meaning requires the generation of categories, the linking of these categories together in some coherent pattern, and the ranking of these categories in relative importance. Take baseball, for example, which like all sports is a completely arbitrary collection of rules and practices. Baseball creates certain categories that constitute the meaning of the game and its surrounding environment. Within this system, "strike four" or "ball five" has no meaning. Similarly, in basketball or soccer, striking the ball with a bat has no meaning. In baseball, a home run is generally valued more than a single, though this depends on the context—when the score is tied, a single at the bottom of the ninth inning with the bases loaded will win the game just as surely as a home run, though most fans would probably feel a home run would be more dramatic and satisfying. Within this system of shared meaning, the common goal of a baseball team is to win games, win the pennant, and win the World Series. The cooperative effort includes different roles and responsibilities for each of the nine players: the pitcher and catcher, four infielders, and three outfielders. Others also have a role, including the manager and the fans, who loyally support the team, share a sense of its importance, and identify with its cooperative effort to achieve the common goal. This vicarious identification comes from the frontal lobes: the prefrontal association cortex allows us to imagine ourselves actually playing the game, and the orbitofrontal cortex enables us to experience the appropriate emotions. To an outsider, or someone unfamiliar with the game, the team and its fans can seem like a closed group—"them." To the team members and their supporters, other teams also tend to become "them," because they are rivals for the same goal. But the players and fans of every team share a meaning system—or common understanding—that esteems the importance of the game and values excellent play. Thus, millions of fans of unsuccessful teams will watch the World Series with interest because of their shared appreciation of the game. There is a larger us-group made up of all the players and fans of a particular sport.

International athletic competitions such as the World Cup, the Olympics, and the Tour de France can be important sources of regional, national, and international unity. But the three critical elements—shared meaning, common goal, cooperative effort—must be present for this primitive process to work at maximum effectiveness. Imagine, for example, an Italian soccer player who has joined an American football team because he is an excellent field goal kicker. If the soccer player has grown up living and breathing soccer, he might be kicking field goals in America primarily for the money. And if his team wins the Super Bowl, the meaning to him and the bonding with his teammates will tend to be far less (in his mind) than if he had helped win the World Cup. In contrast, American football players on the team who have grown up watching the Super Bowl and dreaming of playing in it will tend to have a far deeper sense of shared meaning and tend to experience greater bonding with fellow players who share this meaning, even though all (including the soccer player) have shared in the common goal (winning the championship) and the cooperative effort to achieve it. The only variable here is the degree of shared meaning.

This mechanism for diminishing us-them divisions is particularly important when it comes to hatred because it counteracts one of hate's major characteristics: an obsession with past wrongs. A common goal, whether winning a championship or winning a war, by definition looks to the future and tends to pull the mind away from the past. If you've ever been in a city in which an admired sports team is on an unexpected winning streak, you've probably observed the optimistic attitude expressed by huge numbers of people and their excited focus on the next big game. They tend to forget their problems. As we have discussed, during wartime when a nation is unified behind the common goal of victory, the suicide rate tends to drop significantly. Antagonistic individuals and groups should, wherever possible, find ways to cooperate in achieving common goals of mutual importance, a valuable step in curbing and eliminating hate. Potential forms of cooperation may be economic, social, political, technological, or scientific. The possibilities are limited only by our imagination. One opportunity to cooperate is during natural disasters when nations can put aside their rivalries to help each other for humanitarian reasons. The act of saving helpless victims of an earthquake or flood can activate the empathy of everyone involved. It moves people toward an us-us perspective, in which we recognize both the common humanity of all and the unique importance of each individual.[3]

The strategies and approaches discussed throughout this book—be specific, empathize, communicate, negotiate, educate, cooperate, put things in perspective, avoid feeling trapped, immerse yourself, and seek justice rather than revenge—are not only an approach to combating hate but also a way of detecting its presence and intensity. Hate is uncommonly dangerous because it combines a whole array of behaviors that tend to create and perpetuate animosity and misunderstanding in places such as the Middle East. These can be conceptualized as the opposite of each of the aforementioned strategies. Consider the first step: be specific. Rather than being specific, those who hate tend to generalize and stereotype the objects of their hatred so that contradictory evidence, nuances, and gray areas are ignored. There is an overwhelming tendency to create primitive us-them divisions. After the outbreak of the second *intifada*, the word *Arab* became for some Israelis what the word *Jew* is for many Palestinians: a linguistic stereotype of the despised enemy. When hate exists, there is usually little or no empathy for the hated. There may even be perverse empathy—delight in the suffering and pain of one's adversaries. Communication, if it exists at all, usually takes the form of hurtful language, including insults, hate speech, and various forms of psychological warfare. Hate can twist even positive emotions into psychological weapons. Laughter becomes sarcastic, derisive, cruel, and dehumanizing; joy becomes perverse and sadistic. Negotiation, if any, is usually not in good faith and is simply an opportunity for one party to try to gain an advantage over the other. The hater often chooses to remain ignorant of that which he hates and is willing to believe the most outrageous lies about the object of his hatred. We saw this in the Pokémon case and the treatment of Japanese-Americans during World War II. Genuine cooperation is usually out of the question. At best, it is difficult to arrange and extremely fragile—subject to rapid and complete breakdown, as we saw at the outset of the second *intifada*. Those who hate tend to obsess about past injuries as well as the current and future threats they perceive. They have difficulty stepping back and putting things into a larger perspective that transcends their personal anger and mistrust. Because of this obsessive thinking, there is a tendency to feel trapped in a zero-sum game that can be escaped only by the destruction of one's adversary. Those who hate tend to have a minimum of contact—or no contact at all—with those who are hated and feared. There is a strong, almost phobic reluctance to immerse oneself with members of the out-group. Observers frequently note, for example, that Israelis and Palestinians have very little interaction as social equals. And after the second *intifada* began, many on both sides became consumed with seeking revenge, not justice.

An us-us strategy, however, must be managed by the advanced neural system and not the primitive neural system. The goal is to recognize that humans form many groups, but that the members of every group have a core of humanity that cannot be forgotten or stereotyped away. Though an individual or group can be wrong, even commit barbaric acts, no one should ever be dehumanized. Not only does dehumanization tend to suppress the advanced neural system—which may be the source of your most effective response to a ruthless adversary—but primitive hatred may push you into the same kind of savagery. An us-us perspective is designed to eliminate hatred, but not conflict or disagreement, which can serve a useful purpose as long as they flow from the advanced neural system. In fact, principled disagreement guided by reason is an indispensable method for debating important issues and crafting solutions. We don't demand that candidates in a presidential election agree on everything. We expect a robust debate. An us-us perspective, however, would carry on such a debate without stereotyping or demonizing an opponent—an all too frequent tactic that, in the long run, places dangerous stresses on social cohesiveness. These pitfalls could be avoided if the voting public, in an ideal world, insisted that candidates engage in specific arguments and criticisms and display mutual empathy, genuine communication, informed discussion, cooperation where appropriate, and a sense of perspective and optimism.

Although an us-us strategy, if widely adopted, would tend to radically reduce violence, it would not necessarily forbid violence. When facing a tyrannical adversary like Adolf Hitler, violence might be necessary, but it would be kept within prudent limits. There would be none of the primitive *bespredel* that we have seen in Chechnya, where noncombatants have sometimes been deliberately tortured and killed.[4]

Shared meaning, common goals, and cooperative effort are extraordinarily important for citizens in a democracy. But as in sports, this process must be guided by the advanced neural system. Otherwise, given the complexity and volatility of the human brain, this strategy can have unexpected and sometimes negative results. Although the ancient Greek Olympic games tended to enhance a common Greek cultural identity, it did not prevent Greek city-states from engaging in self-destructive wars with each other that led to the collapse of Greek civilization. Meaning systems that exalt aggression and power, for example, can override other forces that tend to establish us-bonds. If the primitive neural system completely takes over motivations such as patriotism, nationalism, party loyalty, or team spirit, it may establish a strong but intolerant sense of "us" but at the expense of a stereotyped "them." The Greek meaning system is demonstrated in their language, for example, as in the word *xenophobia*—fear or hatred of strangers—a word with Greek roots, and the word *barbarian*, which is derived from the Greek *barbaroi*—non-Greek foreigner. Even the immensely talented Greek physician Hippocrates is said to have written that the Scythians—a nomadic people who were part of the "barbarian" world—tended to look alike, while Greeks were heterogeneous in appearance.

The value of sports or any other form of us-bonding based on shared meaning, common goals, and cooperative effort is greatly diminished if lodged solely in the primitive neural system. Primitive bonding can lead to aggression, including excessive fighting among athletes, which is becoming much too common. Irrational soccer rivalries have resulted in fighting, killing, and even wars, especially when officiating is disputed and officials are demonized—a common limbic reaction in any sport ("kill the umpire"). The goal of creating an us-us relationship with all other human beings requires the constant supervision of the advanced neural system. Left to themselves, primitive bonding mechanisms simply create more powerful us-them divisions that can lead to fanaticism and jingoism. Strategies such as shared meaning and common goals, which activate primitive mechanisms that tend to erase us-them divisions, must be carefully employed under the direction of the advanced neural system, just as a psychotherapist will intelligently employ behavior therapy to reduce or eliminate a phobia. Behavior therapy, for example, can deliberately use the primitive neural system's tendency to learn through immersion to extinguish inappropriate fears.

NARCISSISM

Even when dormant, us-them divisions are enormously dangerous. Virtually without exception, the most horrific mass killings of the past century have been the product of unscrupulous leaders who have intentionally inflamed latent hatred. This was just as true of the Nazis as it was in the Balkan wars and ethnic cleansing that began in the early 1990s. "What we've seen is the engineering of these old hatreds for the benefit of the political aspirations of leaders whose greed for power and territorial gain led them to incite hate," said Gabrielle Kirk McDonald, a former U.S. federal judge who served as president of the International Criminal Tribunal for the Former Yugoslavia in The Hague, Netherlands. A prime example is Slobodan Milosevic, the ex-president of Yugoslavia, who was turned over to the international tribunal in June 2001 to face charges of genocide, war crimes, and crimes against humanity. Milosevic engineered his rise to power through skillfully manipulating Serb nationalism, which alarmed the other ethnic groups in the former Yugoslavia and led to a savage series of wars that culminated in the ethnic cleansing of Kosovo. This prompted the 1999 NATO attack that ultimately resulted in Milosevic being turned out of office. Throughout his reign, Milosevic's state-controlled media bombarded Serbians with a steady stream of inflammatory propaganda and used the nation's schools, according to Veran Matic, editor-in-chief of one of the few independent Yugoslav media outlets, to teach "nationalism, hatred, and xenophobia."[5]

Milosevic, who lost both parents to suicide, seems to represent another personality type that psychologists have found potentially dangerous because of their extraordinary lack of empathy: the narcissist. Social psychologist Roy F. Baumeister said narcissism is "characterized by inflated or grandiose views of self, the quest for excessive admiration, an unreasonable or exaggerated sense of entitlement, a lack of empathy (that is, being unable to identify with the feelings of others), an exploitative attitude toward others, a proneness to envy or wish to be envied, frequent fantasies of greatness, and arrogance." The irrationally high self-esteem of a narcissist makes it almost impossible to admit mistakes and be empathetic with others, no matter what the situation. In a December 2000 television interview, for example, Milosevic said, "I can sleep peacefully, and my conscience is completely clear." Narcissists are sometimes attracted to politics because it provides the adulation and power (another word for control) to which they believe they are entitled. But the narcissist can be hypersensitive and react violently to any perceived threats.

The primitive neural system tends to equate cultural attention with importance to survival and reproduction, which is one reason celebrities have such a disproportionate influence, even when they involve themselves in issues in which they have no particular expertise. Narcissistic leaders seem to intuitively understand this and try to monopolize the spotlight. They make themselves celebrities and tend to shower themselves with praise. The gigantic portraits of leaders such as Saddam Hussein that usually dominate public places are telltale signs of a narcissist.

Although its inner mechanisms are not well understood, narcissism seems to include a form of primitive self-love. Primitive love— as, for example, the instinctive love between parent and child— involves primal bonding. In the case of the narcissist, this may take the form of a powerful, primitive bond with his or her positive self-image. The strength of this self-centered bond may leave little psychic energy for bonding with others, even vicariously, which may account for the narcissist's inordinate lack of empathy. Not only does a narcissist feel no empathy for his enemies, he may have little empathy for his supporters. Adolf Hitler, who is often considered to be a classic narcissist, even as he was planning his own suicide, issued orders to destroy Germany's infrastructure which, if they had been carried out, would have meant suffering and death for millions of additional Germans. Leaders of the factions in the civil war in eastern Congo—which began in 1998 and at various times has involved forces from Rwanda, Uganda, Zimbabwe, Angola, and Namibia— have wantonly destroyed the infrastructure of the region, which has cost the lives of an estimated two and a half million people, primarily from disease and malnutrition. Many of these people were supporters of one or another of the factions that did the destroying. Narcissists such as Hitler often commit suicide rather than face the consequences of a devastating defeat. During the forty-hour armed standoff with police at his residence in Belgrade prior to his arrest, Milosevic reportedly put a gun to his head and threatened suicide.

Thus, the narcissist's bond with his own self-image resembles the instinctive bond between a parent and child. Just as a parent tends to react strongly, even violently, to a threat to his child, the narcissist seems to feel the same protective urge toward his swollen self-image. The narcissist's limbic system, through some psychic quirk that we haven't yet discovered, appears to regard the protection of his self-image as vital to his survival and reproduction. Bullies are sometimes narcissists, and narcissistic leaders often bully others—including other nations—to get their way. Thus, both individuals and groups, as Baumeister observed, "should beware of people who regard themselves as superior to others, especially when those beliefs are inflated, weakly grounded in reality or heavily dependent on having others confirm them frequently. Conceited, self-important individuals turn nasty toward those who puncture their bubbles of self-love." Narcissists make dangerous rulers.[6]

Studies of extremely violent criminals find that a high percentage believe themselves to be members of an elite group that deserves special treatment. This is a reasonably good description of Timothy McVeigh. A government psychologist who studied McVeigh at length concluded that he had strong narcissistic tendencies and that his desire to hasten his own execution was the result of "a combination of his narcissism and boredom. If you could get inside his mind, there would be a lot of grandiose fantasies. He was a sensation-seeker." McVeigh never expressed the slightest remorse for the 1995 bombing of the Alfred P. Murrah Federal Building in Oklahoma City, which killed 168 people and injured more than 500—the worst act of terrorism ever committed on American soil prior to September 11, 2001. He appeared to go to his death believing that this attack was appropriate revenge for the federal government's handling of the 1992 standoff at Ruby Ridge, Idaho, which resulted in the deaths of the wife and son of white separatist Randy

Weaver, and the disastrous confrontation at Waco, Texas, with the Branch Davidians, in which about eighty members of that religious group died when their compound caught fire and burned to the ground. McVeigh's execution by lethal injection on June 11, 2001, had an element of suicide. He voluntarily gave up his right to appeals that might have kept him alive for several more years. This calculated decision, coupled with the publication at the time of a book that included his explanation for the bombing, made the thirty-three-year-old McVeigh the center of a worldwide media frenzy. As McVeigh requested, his body was cremated and his ashes scattered at a secret location because, he said, "I don't want to create a draw for those who hate me or for those who love me." His obsession with control was reflected in his last statement, in which he copied out the 1875 poem "Invictus" by William Ernest Henley; the last lines are, "I am the master of my fate: I am the captain of my soul."

DEVELOPING EMPATHY AS A STEP TOWARD AN US-US PERSPECTIVE

McVeigh's shocking comment that the nineteen children who died in the Oklahoma City bombing were "collateral damage" that distracted from his act of vengeance raises an uncomfortable issue about the deeply ingrained nature of our us-them view of the world. For when we learned the truth about McVeigh's role in the bombing, the implicit question for most Americans was simple and straightforward: how could McVeigh, an American citizen and Gulf War veteran, have done that to *us*? McVeigh's twisted rationale reflected in part the military ethic that allows violence to be committed against "them"—the enemy—even when there is collateral damage in the form of civilian deaths.

There have been many civilian deaths as the result of American bombing campaigns in all modern wars right through the Afghanistan conflict. But this is the nature of large-scale aerial bombard-

ment no matter which nation carries it out. Jack Valenti, a former
Kennedy administration official who later became president of the
Motion Picture Association of America, described what it was like
to pilot a B-25 low-flying attack bomber on missions over Italy during World War II: "Each of us, from nineteen to twenty-four years
old, was frightened out of our wits on every mission as we took
heavy fire from the Nazis who manned the antiaircraft guns determined to blow us out of the sky. But scared as we were, we flew the
missions. We took out our targets. We never turned back even as we
rode through a curtain of fire. Getting killed was a daily possibility.
God only knows how many civilians, including women and children, we killed on those missions." Of course, nothing McVeigh
could ever have said would justify in the slightest his cowardly and
heinous attack. He intentionally targeted a building that he knew
would be filled with ordinary citizens. Although civilians were
sometimes targets of aerial bombardment in World War II by both
the Axis and the Allies, the American military in recent conflicts has
done everything possible to avoid civilian casualties. Yet the disturbing thought is how intensely we grieved for the victims in Oklahoma City ("us") and how comparatively little we felt for the
civilians who died in Baghdad, Belgrade, and Kabul ("them"). For
hundreds of thousands of years, the us-group was indispensable to
the survival and reproduction of our hominid ancestors. Each small
band of hominids formed an us-group that struggled to survive in
an unforgiving environment. Because of this, we have a primitive
tendency to emotionally identify only with those we consider to be
one of "us."[7]

Advanced empathy is the crucial ingredient for an us-us perspective that focuses on both the common humanity and uniqueness
of every individual as we seek to curb hatred, intolerance, and violence. But this will require a major leap in the quality of humanity's
creative imagination. It is through the power of our imagination that
we vicariously enter the minds of others beyond our immediate
group. A series of skillful media reports on a distant crisis—starvation in Somalia, for example—can bring the human suffering

home to us and lead to an outpouring of support. But we cannot simply rely on others to activate our sense of empathy. Every individual must find his or her own way to creatively resist the tendency to turn strangers into "them."

One major advantage of an us-us view of the world is that it also tends to inhibit rational, impulsive, and negligent violence, which are forms of aggression that may not be motivated by hate but usually have an us-them component that stereotypes or dehumanizes "them" and, thus, may exacerbate aggression. Rational violence includes the kind of push-button warfare that is becoming more and more common. This violence may be motivated by rational considerations rather than hatred—the need to end Al Qaeda terrorist activities in Taliban-controlled Afghanistan, for example. Even here, however, it is dangerous to treat one's adversaries as a generalized "them" (the enemy). Someone who fires, or orders the firing of, a cruise missile is usually a long way from those whose bodies will be torn apart by its terrible impact. Though we may feel no personal hostility toward the possible victims, it is always risky to dehumanize them or view them as abstractions. Maintaining our sense of empathy for these potential victims will tend to restrict our aggression to what is absolutely necessary and might motivate us more strongly to find ways to resolve conflicts without the need for aggression at all. Rational aggression may also be carried out by zealots, who in their misguided fervor lose sight of the consequences of their actions on others. This was an element in the assimilation policy of the Australian government, which forcibly removed thousands of Aboriginal children from their families and placed them with white families. The architects of this policy sought to rationally justify their actions and felt they were motivated by benevolence rather than hatred, but they failed to empathize with the families they were destroying because Aborigines were still being treated as "them."

Impulsive aggression—which includes the infliction of physical or psychological pain—may be the product not of hatred but of a quick temper and a lack of reflection. For someone with this problem, a determined effort to empathize with the possible victims of such impulsive outbursts may be enough to give the advanced neural system the upper hand in curbing this kind of emotional volatility. Negligent aggression or violence can occur when the welfare of others ("them") is ignored because of a complete lack of empathy. This is a common mind-set of drunk drivers, who fail to consider the lives they are putting at risk by their reckless action. Negligent violence is also a common feature of gang warfare. Gang members who engage in so-called drive-by shootings often fire at their targets without regard to the surrounding bystanders, who may be injured or killed. Although the gunmen may have no particular desire to injure bystanders, they don't care enough to refrain from shooting.

Like every other limbic response, empathy can be generalized, even romanticized, by the primitive neural system. If our affectionate empathy for our children becomes excessive, for example, we may overprotect and spoil them, which can have negative consequences for their development. We might also unrealistically idealize them, so that we lose sight of their real strengths and weaknesses. Although empathy must never be suppressed, it should be modulated by the advanced neural system and balanced against other considerations. Empathy, for instance, should be combined with specificity (we should try to understand other people's thoughts and feelings in all their complexity) and a sense of perspective.

In rare instances, empathy is impossible because of an underlying biological abnormality. You will recall the disorder called episodic dyscontrol syndrome—also known as intermittent explosive disorder—which appears to involve the limbic system and related areas of the frontal and temporal lobes. It is characterized by explosive and uncontrollable outbursts of violence that may be directed at people or objects and can involve either pure rage or rage mixed with hatred. One neurologist described the violence as often having "a primitive quality—gouging, kicking, clawing, biting, spitting. . . ." In one case, a twenty-one-year-old California man who held a steady job and was described as easygoing by his coworkers began to experience powerful suicidal and violent impulses. During these outbursts, he would sometimes attack his wife. His explosive anger was not mixed with hatred, however, and he would tearfully beg her for forgiveness after the episodes were over. A brain scan revealed a nonmalignant tumor at the tip of his right temporal lobe, affecting the right amygdala. When the tumor was surgically removed, the violent episodes disappeared. This disorder is also associated with deficiencies in serotonin and related neurochemicals. When there is a clear biological anomaly, cognitive behavior therapies are usually ineffective because a hyperactive primitive neural system overwhelms neocortical control. Instead, treatment must include medication, even surgery. Our rudimentary understanding of most mental disorders means that pinpointing the exact cause is usually not possible. Nevertheless, there are many effective treatments available. Untreated, many kinds of mental disorders can lead to violence against the self and others. Our prisons are full of people who have severe problems with aggression and indifference to the feelings of others.[8]

Reestablishing empathy in hardened criminals is difficult, though not impossible, and is more an art than a science at this stage in our understanding of the brain. Sometimes having the perpetrators of violence meet their victims can break through the wall of indifference and begin to produce feelings of empathy. Some programs require violent offenders to care for animals, which can establish sympathetic bonds with other living beings. As we have noted, lithium is sometimes useful in curbing impulsive violence. It seems to work by giving the individual's advanced neural system time to reflect on the wisdom of giving in to these impulses. One violent prisoner who was treated with lithium stated, "Now I can think about whether to hit him or not." Lithium itself does not seem to activate the empathy centers of the orbitofrontal cortex, but this additional time for reflection provides an opportunity to intentionally cultivate the capacity for empathy. Impulsive aggression is also treated with the class of antidepressants called selective serotonin reuptake inhibitors, which includes Prozac. These medications provide a greater supply of serotonin to the brain and seem to normalize an oversensitized stress response in some people.

For most people, however, there is no such obstacle to the kind of empathetic identification that is essential to an us-us perspective. And it is this perspective that is our best hope for avoiding the manifestations of hatred that have punctuated the twentieth century, including mass murder, war, and racial and sexual violence.

APOLOGIES ARE A STEP
IN THE RIGHT DIRECTION

One important strategy for defusing long-standing animosities is for individuals—especially leaders—to offer specific, heartfelt apologies as a first step toward reconciling and establishing mutual empathy. This form of apology tends to dissipate the primitive sense of threat, release the obsession with old wrongs, and create an atmosphere conducive to forgiveness and reconciliation. Pope John Paul II, in his efforts to heal the centuries-old rift between Catholicism and the Eastern Orthodox churches, has gone so far as to apologize for the sack of Constantinople by Catholic Crusaders in 1204, which remains a sore spot in the history of the Orthodox Church. He also apologized to Muslims for the Crusades themselves. As we have seen, Osama bin Laden and his fellow fanatics continue to tap into lingering resentment about the Crusades to fan anti-Western hatred. If the leaders on both sides of conflicts in places such as the Middle East, Northern Ireland, and the Balkans gave speeches that included heartfelt apologies for specific wrongdoings and mistakes, this would be an important way to begin reducing hostility and encouraging reconciliation. But the apology must be perceived as sincere, which is not always easy in a cynical and suspicious atmosphere.

Forgiveness, empathy, and understanding require not only reconciliation, but justice as well. This is why the conviction of Thomas E. Blanton Jr. for the Birmingham bombing and the trial of former Yugoslav leader Slobodan Milosevic for crimes against humanity may help bring a fresh start to two regions troubled by past hatreds. There are, of course, contemporary issues that create conflicts and must be dealt with intelligently. But lingering prejudice and hatred tend to make these problems intractable. A constant focus on the common humanity and unique individuality of rivals and adversaries, with a sincere attempt to understand their positions and feelings, is far more likely to lead to genuine solutions.[9]

Though she is regularly lionized by the Australian press, on one important issue Cathy Freeman made her displeasure with the national leadership quite clear prior to the Sydney Olympics. Like the United States, Australia has both a federal government and state governments. Several state governments have formally apologized to the Aborigines for the way they were treated after European colonization. But the national government argued that it has been trying to make amends through its policies and a formal apology would not be appropriate. "I was so angry because they were denying they had done anything wrong, denying that a whole generation was stolen," Freeman said. Australians began picking sides on this issue. "It obviously has become important symbolically," said Henry Reynolds, a professor at the University of Tasmania. "All the evidence from the various truth commissions and bodies around the world that have dealt with historical problems of injustice have been quite clear: recognition given in the form of leaders' apologies is among the key steps in healing." There is, however, reason to believe that Australia will find its way through this difficult process. In May of 2000, two hundred thousand people from all ethnic groups—inspired, in part, by Cathy Freeman—participated in a march for racial reconciliation across Sydney's magnificent Harbor Bridge.

16

AN ENLIGHTENED FUTURE

THE SEMAI PEOPLE OF MALAYSIA almost never fight and seldom hate. If two clan members have a disagreement, it is resolved through words, not weapons. A village elder will call a meeting where everyone is invited and anyone can venture an opinion—and most people do. The meetings can go on for days. When the participants have said all they have to say, the elder will make a ruling and order that the matter never be spoken of again. That is the end of the dispute.

The Semai represent one of a handful of human cultures that are almost completely peaceful. Murder and crimes of violence are rare among them. Anthropologist Robert Knox Dentan, who lived with and studied the Semai, reported that they have a highly developed sense of empathy. The Semai "do not often hit their children," he wrote. "A person should never hit a child because, people say, 'How would you feel if it died?' . . . Similarly, one adult should never hit

another because, they say, 'Suppose he hit you back?' . . . It should
be clear at this point that the Semai are not great warriors. As long
as they have been known to the outside world, they have consistently
fled rather than fight, or even than run the risk of fighting."

Are the Semai innately different from the rest of humanity? An
unplanned experiment, courtesy of the cold war, provided a startling answer. The Semai, wrote Dentan, "had never participated in
a war or raid until the Communist insurgency of the 1950s, when the
British raised troops among the Semai, mainly in the West. Initially,
most of the recruits were probably lured by wages, pretty clothes,
shotguns, and so forth. Many did not realize that soldiers killed people. When I suggested to one Semai recruit that killing was a soldier's job, he laughed at my ignorance and explained, 'No, we don't
kill people, brother, we just tend weeds and cut grass.' Apparently,
he had up to that point done nothing but grounds duty."[1]

Eventually, the Semai were introduced by the British into coun-
terinsurgency activity. They went into combat against the Communist rebels. "Many people who knew the Semai insisted that such
an unwarlike people could never make good soldiers," reported
Dentan. "Interestingly enough, they were wrong. Communist terrorists had killed the kinsmen of some of the Semai counterinsur-
gency troops. Taken out of their nonviolent society and ordered to
kill, they seem to have been swept up in a sort of insanity which they
call 'blood drunkenness.' A typical veteran's story runs like this. 'We
killed, killed, killed. The Malays would stop and go through people's pockets and take their watches and money. We only thought of
killing. Wah, truly we were drunk with blood.' "

Had the Semai been permanently changed by their immersion in
savagery? Dentan studied former soldiers who had returned from
the conflict. "Talking about these experiences, the Semai seem
bemused, not displeased that they were such good soldiers, but
unable to account for their behavior," wrote Dentan. "It is almost
as if they had shut the experience in a separate compartment, away

from the even routine of their lives. Back in Semai society they seem as gentle and afraid of violence as anyone else. To them their one burst of violence appears to be as remote as something that happened to someone else, in another country. The nonviolent image remains intact."

University of Michigan anthropologist Raymond Kelly reports one other striking characteristic of the Semai and similar cultures—they have very weak group identity. Their societies tend to be loosely organized, and being a member of a group of any kind is not especially important. They would find such concepts as patriotism and identity politics virtually incomprehensible. Thus, they tend to engage in very little us-them stereotyping and generally treat each other as individuals.

THE SIGNIFICANCE OF ENVIRONMENT

What does all this mean? It suggests something quite remarkable: the mechanisms that produce us-them distinctions, prejudice, hate, and violence—though they are genetically structured and lodged in the mind of each of us—*are largely activated by the environment*. This implies that it may be possible to design a relatively peaceful culture, like that of the Semai, which seldom activates these mechanisms. As long as the Semai were in their culture, these mechanisms that produce so much misery and destruction were inactive. But when they were immersed in a more warlike culture, the Semai became just as violent as everyone else, if not more so. Back in their own culture again, the mechanisms were no longer activated and the Semai returned to their peaceful ways. Although this idea raises exciting possibilities, it will require much more study before we have a full understanding of the relationship between genes, the environment, aggression, and hate. We already know of one complication.

This complication is that the term *environment* includes not only the culture that we are immersed in, and to which our primitive neural system is tuned, but also the unique experiences we undergo as we develop into biologically mature human beings. If these developmental experiences are unfavorable, then an individual with no particular genetic predisposition to violence may nevertheless become more violent than normal because of his or her upbringing.

One example of this is with babies of drug-addicted mothers. The explosion of drug abuse over the past thirty years has placed particular strain on addicted mothers and the rearing of their children. "An addicted mother's attention is focused on drugs, not her child, and her ability to cope with stress is compromised by the long-term effects of substance abuse," said neuroscientist Debra Niehoff. "Unfortunately, a drug-exposed baby who's slow to respond or learn and needs endless clinic visits to manage long-term health problems, doesn't pay attention, throws tantrums, and gets into everything as soon as he can crawl is just the sort of high-demand child guaranteed to outstrip her limited emotional resources. Emotionally disorganized child and overreactive mother egg each other on, each negative interaction adding to the chemical record of disaster, the perception of threat and the risk of violence spiraling higher and higher. The more impaired the relationship, the greater the risk it will become a violent relationship." Such mothers often become frustrated and neglectful.[2]

Experiments with laboratory animals indicate that the result of a neglectful or absent mother is a damaged threat response system, either overreactive or underreactive. And this may be compounded, particularly in human males, by the absence of something we can't test in lab animals: a father. No other species has our unique form of social organization in which a mother and father often work together for many years caring for and educating their dependent children. The presence of a father seems to contribute to tuning a child's nervous system in ways we don't yet fully understand. The explosive rise in absent fathers may have a damaging effect on some children; however, the mother-child bond seems to be central, even in humans. The absence of or neglect by a mother does serious and long-term damage to the preconscious alerting system. As we have seen, a damaged stress response can cause problems whether it is overreactive or underreactive. An overreactive response may lead to impulsive outbursts of hatred and violence. An underreactive response can result in violence that is colder, more calculated, and heartless. "Sluggish reactions to stress are a cardinal feature of anti-social aggression," said Niehoff. "Of course, that doesn't mean that all antisocial individuals grew up without the benefit of a mother or, conversely, that a mother's death or disappearance predicts a life of violence. But it may be more than an unhappy coincidence that the number of youthful 'superpredators'—children without a con-science—has grown in tandem with the drug-related disappearance of mothers." What some criminologists call "superpredators" are children under eighteen—overwhelmingly boys—who are believed to account for 25 percent of the violent crime in the United States. Between 1989 and 1994, the arrest of fourteen- to seventeen-year-olds for murder, rape, robbery, and aggravated assault increased by almost 50 percent, which was three or four times the increase in any other age group.[3]

All this appears to correlate with another finding of anthropology. The least violent societies, such as the Semai, tend to be those in which men and women live together, eat and sleep together, and raise their children together in a more or less equal setting. The most warlike societies are those in which men live in separate houses for eating and sleeping (the equivalent of army barracks), and in which boys are removed at an early age from their mothers and subjected to various forms of indoctrination, including stressful training for war. Tragically, many cultures create just such a warlike environment. Too often in American inner-city neighborhoods, fatherless boys are introduced into male-only gang activity at an early age.

TRANSFORMING THE
GLOBAL CULTURE

The Semai represent a traditional culture that has been relatively isolated from the rest of the world for centuries. But in the globalizing modern world, no culture can stay isolated for long. And more aggressive cultures can easily push less aggressive cultures into hatred and violence as a matter of self-defense. For there to be stability in the modern world, a peaceful, democratic global culture must be created. And if we can successfully modify world culture, we may well be able to substantially curb the problems of prejudice, hate, violence, and terrorism. This is a daunting but vital task in an age in which biological, chemical, and nuclear weapons are spreading and suicidal terrorism has become all too common. An unprecedented coalition of nations banded together to wage the war on terrorism that began as a result of the September 11 attacks—the first war of the new century. If this coalition also takes enlightened steps to transform the global culture by ensuring that there is an open dialogue among nations, their acts could lessen the likelihood of additional wars.

The task of the civilized world is not just to cease acts of terrorism but to curb and eliminate dehumanizing hate. We must expand the concept of "us" until it includes every human being and the idea of "them" falls into disuse as an obsolete stereotyping device. This can be achieved only through the constant and determined use of the advanced neural system when it has been bolstered by a first-rate education and supportive culture that protects the rights of all people. Although humans will continue to form separate us-groups, there must be a shift from an us-them to an us-us perspective that never suppresses our empathy for the common humanity and unique individuality of the members of all other groups. Individuals and groups will differ at times, even passionately disagree, yet they should never stereotype or dehumanize each other. Humanity must begin to embrace, both cognitively and emotionally, what modern genetics tells us—we are a remarkably homogeneous young species within which, scientifically speaking, there is only one race: the human race. As United Nations Secretary-General Kofi Annan said on receiving the 2001 Nobel Peace Prize, the lesson of September 11 is that humanity is indivisible.

To successfully cope with the enormous dangers of the globalizing world of the twenty-first century, we need to use recent breakthroughs in the understanding of the brain and behavior to address the problems of hatred and violence. It is imperative that we make a determined effort to solve the problem of hate as quickly as possible before hate-inspired violence again engulfs the world. And we must move as a species from limbic parochialism to neocortical inclusiveness, unequivocally discarding in the process all primitive stereotypes and generalizations that classify human beings as "them." Thus, we must slough off the discredited idea of human "races," which has no scientific basis and is a dangerous hangover of eugenics that does little more than feed racism by implying that there is a genetic basis for differences among "racial" groups. In the process, we must develop a new vocabulary for describing ourselves that emphasizes our uniqueness and individuality rather than some form of group identity. This effort appears to be gathering momentum. The American Anthropological Association, for example, has recommended dropping the term *race* in the 2010 census.

The idea of the American Dream symbolizes hope for a better future that tends to neutralize the tendency of primal emotions such as hate to trap us in the past. It continues to attract people to the United States from all over the world. To effectively combat hate, we must develop a Global Dream that involves stirring ideals, expansive hopes, and intelligent common goals that shift humanity's attention to the future, away from past hatreds and divisions. We need to develop both tolerance and new overarching meaning systems that constructively satisfy our drive for meaning. These new meaning systems should incorporate all of the strategies for curbing hate—be specific, empathize, communicate, negotiate, educate, cooperate, put things in perspective, avoid feeling trapped, immerse yourself, and seek justice rather than revenge—which are designed to neutralize the innate tendencies that make hate possible. Our goal should be to immerse our children in an environment that is as free as possible of hatred, prejudice, and demeaning stereotypes.

THE SCIENTIFIC VISION

In order to rid our nations of hate, we must use the precepts of modern science—largely the offspring of Sir Isaac Newton, René Descartes, and the Enlightenment, which also produced through the ideas of thinkers such as John Locke, Baron de Montesquieu, and Adam Smith the foundations of the market-oriented democracies within which the bulk of the modern scientific enterprise takes place. Science uses reason for both the discovery of general laws and the reduction of natural phenomena to their most fundamental constituents: elementary particles of matter, for example, and neurons within the brain. As Harvard biologist Edward O. Wilson put it, science "is the accumulation of humanity's organized, objective knowledge, the first medium devised able to unite people everywhere in common understanding. It favors no tribe or religion. It is the base of a truly democratic and global culture." Only science fully harnesses the human drive for meaning, control, tool-based culture, and our taste for novelty. Science and technology have enriched and will continue to enrich the arts and humanities. The models of the mind and the universe that they generate are infinitely stimulating. And they produce concrete innovations such as printing, electricity, photography, and communications technologies such as radio, television, computers, and the Internet. But the major obstacle to making science a universal meaning system is attaining a high enough level of education worldwide to allow the great bulk of humanity to vicariously share in the scientific vision—a vision that provides the kind of cognitive and emotional meaning that keeps scientists fascinated for a lifetime. The scientific community will have to do a far better job of explaining the importance of its work to the general public. There are enough mysteries and discoveries as we look within ourselves as well as look out—and eventually spread out—into the universe to keep the human race productively and peacefully occupied indefinitely. A scientific education, however, must be integrated with the principles of an us-us perspective so it will remain humane and empathetic.[4]

One major insight of modern neuroscience is that meaning comes in two forms: cognitive and emotional. Cognitive meaning is primarily mediated by the advanced neural system, emotional meaning by the primitive neural system. As with a snake phobic who learns cognitively that garter snakes are harmless but continues to react emotionally as if they are still dangerous, emotional meaning can lag behind cognitive meaning because of the limbic system's more primitive architecture. The limbic system tends to be slow to change a deeply ingrained assumption. This is a primary reason that traumatic shock is often accompanied by disbelief. After the 1963 church bombing in Birmingham, much of the nation felt a sense of disbelief that racial hatred could be so barbaric.

In some instances, the cognitive meaning we attach to a person, place, or thing can remain unchanged while the emotional meaning shifts dramatically. The events of September 11 radically transformed our emotional landscape. The deaths of so many heroic firefighters at the World Trade Center, for example, gave this profession a whole new emotional meaning, though our rational understanding of the firefighter's role in society remained basically the same. And consider the striking transformation in the emotional meaning of such things as skyscrapers, air travel, box cutters, anthrax, and Afghanistan. And then there was Osama bin Laden himself. For most of us prior to September 11, he was someone whom we cognitively knew was a terrorist but who seemed a distant threat. It was only after September 11 that we realized in the most traumatic way that for bin Laden and his collaborators, we were simply "them"—

the hated infidels—and the suffering and death of innocent American men, women, and children not only meant nothing to Al Qaeda but was even a source of perverse amusement.[5]

Our intellectual and cultural challenges are immense. Genetic engineering alone will pose the most difficult ethical problems imaginable. We must be prepared to employ our full intellectual and emotional resources. The language of cognitive meaning is organized around reason and logic and is expressed in the long sequences of words, ideas, and behaviors that only humans are capable of—language-trained great apes have difficulty constructing sentences longer than three words. The detailed rules of the language of emotional meaning, however, are not as clear. This lack of understanding has led to a tendency to deemphasize—even distrust—emotional meaning in many areas of modern thought, especially the scientific and technical fields. Whereas cognitive meaning involves complex temporal sequencing that is coordinated in the brain's left hemisphere (in most people), emotional meaning seems to engage the capacity for complex pattern recognition that is centered in the right hemisphere. We tend to detect emotional patterns almost instantly, without going through an explicit sequence of reasoning. When the language areas of the right hemisphere are damaged, we can lose the ability to understand prosody—the emotional content of speech. We can no longer tell, for instance, whether someone is being serious or sarcastic based on his or her tone of voice. The power and mystery of emotional meaning are on display in great teachers and great art. My most inspiring teachers were those who not only conveyed the cognitive content of a subject but who also communicated its emotional meaning through their passion and animation. Emotional meaning centers around the complex motivational values of things (what is worth doing and what isn't, for example) but is difficult if not impossible to convey in cold logic. How do you logically explain the aura of a great teacher or artist? Yet the concept of emotional meaning can help us understand the nature of phenomena such as music. We tend to interpret the singing human voice or the sounds of musical instruments not as noise but as a kind of speech, conveying forms of emotional meaning that, though often difficult to explain logically, may nevertheless be remarkably powerful. As we saw in the aftermath of the September 11 attacks, a new context can give enhanced emotional meaning to familiar songs such as *America the Beautiful* and *The Star-Spangled Banner*. An overemphasis on cognitive meaning alone can produce high cognitive intelligence but low emotional intelligence. This is especially worrisome because many of the issues we face—from cloning to terrorism—are intensely emotional and subject to primitive limbic distortion.

Emotional meaning is unquestionably a vital area for further scientific research. A better understanding of emotional meaning will help clarify the underlying therapeutic mechanisms of one of the most powerful techniques ever developed to treat psychological disorders: cognitive behavior therapy. This approach might be called meaning therapy because it affects both cognitive meaning and emotional meaning. It is not unusual for a skilled therapist employing this technique in a controlled setting to produce—in a single therapy session—significant and permanent reductions in lifelong fears. Cognitive therapy uses the advanced neural system to correct a patient's rational misconceptions and explain why the brain is generating an irrational response. Behavior therapy seeks to recalibrate the limbic system's emotional meaning to match the correct cognitive meaning by guiding the patient through carefully designed behaviors: handling a harmless snake, for example. Studies have shown that cognitive behavior therapy is exceptionally effective in treating mood disorders, which include depression as well as phobias and other anxiety illnesses. Its effectiveness equals that of the most powerful psychoactive drugs and is sometimes superior to them. This is not surprising because neural processing that alters our meaning systems—cognitive or emotional—simultaneously alters our brain chemistry and creates new neural circuitry. All this can establish permanent changes in brain function. Mood disorders involve inappropriate emotions, and hate can be classified as a mood disorder. And as we saw with Australian runner Cathy Freeman, the integration of sports teams might be viewed as one form of cognitive behavior therapy that helps break down stereotypes, diminishing racial hatred. The deeper our understanding of the riddle of meaning, the more effectively we can apply the methods of cognitive behavior therapy to the problem of hate.

We must also grapple with the mystery of consciousness, which goes to the core of our very nature. The human brain has three major association areas responsible for the highest level of neural processing. One is called the parietal-temporal-occipital association cortex and is located at the junction of these three lobes—roughly the area of the brain around the ears. The second is the prefrontal association cortex, which consists of the large expanse of the forward area of the frontal lobes, including the region of the cortex under the forehead. The third is the limbic association cortex, which is made up of older areas of cortex that line the inner face and bottom of the cerebral hemispheres and include the orbitofrontal cortex. Both the prefrontal association cortex and the limbic association cortex can be extensively damaged without destroying consciousness. This suggests to me that consciousness may be a product of the parietal-temporal-occipital association cortex. Note that this particular association region is adjacent to the somatosensory cortex, which contains the primary map of the human body. Consciousness may be a fantastic elaboration by the parietal-temporal-occipital association cortex of this and other brain maps, creating the model of the self acting in its environment that we perceive as our subjective sense of "me." It is noteworthy that Alzheimer's disease, unlike most other forms of dementia, is a disease that ultimately destroys consciousness, producing a condition that experts sometimes term "mental emptiness"—advanced Alzheimer's patients often cannot recognize themselves in a mirror. Where does Alzheimer's disease initially launch its attack on the brain? Imaging studies have shown that the parietal-temporal-occipital association cortex suffers one of the first assaults. Neuroscientists James Goldman and Lucien Côté reported that "low blood flow to the parietotemporal areas has been shown to occur early in the disease." Other sorts of damage to this region of association cortex can alter the very structure of consciousness. The spatial awareness exhibited by individuals who suffer a brain injury to the parietal-temporal-occipital association cortex may suddenly skew to the left, so that they neglect or ignore objects in the right half of their visual space, even the right half of their body. Equally strange is that victims of this kind of injury are often unaware that their perception has radically changed. It is as if their conscious mind has been reshaped seemingly without their knowing it. Consciousness may not even control our will. The prefrontal association cortex and the limbic system, including its preconscious alerting system, appear to be the decision-making centers of the brain. Our prefrontal association cortex, not consciousness, may be the seat of advanced neural choice. Consciousness does, however, seem to influence, though not control, decision making by keeping a record of previous decisions in autobiographical memory and creating meaning systems that the decision-making areas can refer to as they ponder future decisions. This helps explain experiments showing that brain activity signaling a decision (say, to move your finger) precedes conscious awareness by about a third of a second. As neuroscientist Benjamin Libet concluded, "The brain 'decides' to initiate or at least to prepare to initiate the act before there is any reportable subjective awareness that such a decision has taken place. . . . This evidence certainly constrains the way we may view free will—as a mechanism of self-control but not as an initiator of the intention to act." Libet's observation would be more accurate, it seems to me, if we substitute the word *consciousness* for *free will*. To summarize, consciousness seems to be centered in the parietal-temporal-occipital association cortex and may simply be one—extremely important—system that the brain has evolved to construct many of the elaborate models we use to discover meaning and guide our behavior: in this case, the system that creates the model of the self. Though we tend to equate self-awareness with the very essence of our being, consciousness appears to be only one component of a much larger and more elaborate neural system. The scientific study of consciousness may profoundly alter the way we perceive ourselves, but it could ultimately produce healthier strategies for harnessing the full potential of our brain. And the better we understand the brain, the more we will understand its complex capacity for self-hatred and self-destruction.[6]

Like any human enterprise, science is capable of being misused, and scientists are not above demonizing each other. An us-us global civilization incorporating strategies for combating hate should be based on an understanding of both our common humanity and our common frailties. And the us-us perspective can be extended beyond human beings to intelligently consider other species and Earth itself not as "them" or "it" but as part of "us," over which we must be responsible stewards. Clearly, general educational levels must increase dramatically. The globalizing information economy, which is wholly based on modern science and technology, is an important spur to upgrading education. Computer-based technologies such as the Internet are becoming powerful educational tools. All this can be assisted by the new brain imaging technologies, which will be able to directly and noninvasively explore how the brain learns and remembers and ways these processes might be optimized—ultimately, perhaps, identifying the unique learning styles of each individual.

WHAT A MORE ENLIGHTENED FUTURE WOULD INCLUDE

In a more enlightened world, hate would be treated as a medical disorder like other psychiatric problems caused by anachronistic features of our brain architecture: phobias, depression, suicide, and anorexia. These conditions can be treated by various forms of cognitive behavior therapy, including the strategies discussed throughout this book for combating hate, and medication, when that is appropriate. If there is an underlying biological disorder—a neurochemical imbalance, some type of seizure in the limbic system, brain damage, or tumor—additional forms of medical treatment may be required.

In order to create a more enlightened future, we must dispense with primitive stereotypes. The primitive neural system can literally warp our view of ourselves and others. When an eighty-pound anorexic looks in the mirror and sees someone who is fat, she is not delusional. The primitive neural system is preconsciously superimposing a stereotype of herself as overweight, prior to her rational perception. These sorts of limbic filters infest the prejudiced and hate-filled mind. Preconsciously superimposed limbic filters are the reason that a racist sees someone first as an Asian, Hispanic, or black and only later, if at all, as a unique human being. Unfortunately, such filters subconsciously affect not only bigots but also virtually everyone who grows up in a culture with strong racial, ethnic, or other forms of us-them divisions. In the 1920s and 1930s, African-American artists and intellectuals who traveled to Europe were amazed that most Europeans—raised in societies generally free of the racial tensions that plagued the United States—viewed them not through the stereotype of "Negroes" but as distinct individuals, whose skin color was no more relevant to their persona than their eye color. We must all begin the formidable task of seeing each other, first, as individuals, just as the Semai do.

We must also focus, as science does, on proximate meaning—that is, discovering the mechanisms and forces underlying natural processes. The ultimate meaning and purpose of the natural world are not directly addressed by science. Questions of ultimate meaning must be left to the individual. All systems of meaning, spiritual and otherwise, should be respected as long as they do not infringe on basic human rights. Our goal should be to develop a sense of meaning and purpose that provides a comprehensive model of the world's richness and complexity and orients us toward the future. A highly educated citizenry in an enlightened global system would be able to make the wisest possible decisions about powerful new technologies such as genetic engineering, which have the potential to clone human beings and genetically design children. Such technologies must be carefully monitored because, though human beings are genetically homogeneous today, genetic engineering has, in the long run, the power to change that and fracture our common humanity.

The problems of a worldwide consumer culture will also have to be addressed. Is this culture sustainable given global resources? Because consumerism has no core values other than the market itself, it can be shaped by the changing tastes and desires of the consuming public. Those tastes are now heavily manipulated by the propaganda of advertising, which generally appeals to the primitive neural system. An us-us global civilization could move from limbic self-absorption within a culture of materialism to a culture of enlightened meaning. And in a more enlightened age—if tastes shift away from overconsumption and acceptance of the lowest common denominator in cultural offerings—the market will shift as well.

Ultimately, a more enlightened future would be a reaffirmation of the optimistic faith in education and progress that was expressed by Denis Diderot, the chief editor and guiding genius of the greatest publishing project of the Enlightenment, the *Encyclopédie*, who believed that "our children, better instructed than we, may at the same time become more virtuous and happy."

THE IMPORTANCE
OF PERCEPTIVE LEADERS

Perceptive leaders throughout history have intuitively grasped the importance of each of the strategies for combating hate outlined throughout this book. The nonviolent campaigns against persecution and discrimination led by Mohandas Gandhi and Martin Luther King Jr. involved intense and sophisticated programs to prepare their followers to maintain a spiritual and principled state of mind in the face of naked anger and brutal assaults. Both King and Gandhi labored tirelessly to break the destructive limbic cycle in which hate breeds hate and violence breeds violence. Each complemented his public campaign of civil disobedience with equally brilliant campaigns in the courts of law, the court of public opinion, and the corridors of power. But make no mistake: hate is extraordinarily difficult and dangerous to overcome. Both men died at its hand, though their work was enormously fruitful.

Northern Ireland for decades has represented one of the most explosive cauldrons of hate in the world and a textbook example of limbic self-destruction. The fragile peace that was finally achieved in the 1998 Good Friday agreement was forged using strategies for curbing hate that have been discussed throughout this book. Credit for this breakthrough goes to many, including the governments of the United Kingdom and the United States, leaders throughout Northern Ireland and the Republic of Ireland, and thousands of ordinary citizens. One of the outstanding figures in this process was John Hume, an indefatigable spokesman for the Catholic minority in Northern Ireland. For his efforts, he shared the Nobel Peace Prize. Hume emphasized the vital role empathy has played. "We have to realize," he said, "that our common humanity transcends our differences." He stressed what a breakthrough it was just to get the two sides talking seriously. "There are many in Northern Ireland," Hume observed, "who say that if you took the word *no* out of the English language, the hard-liners would be left speechless." He tried to put things in perspective by remembering the sacrifice of the people who died during the many years of violence, resolving "that they will be the last generation that will have suffered that way." Rather than being trapped by hate, Hume sees a new Ireland in which north and south work together "to use our energies to build a new society that gives hope to the younger generation." As part of the healing process, Hume advocates programs that encourage Catholics and Protestants to live, work, and be educated together. "The real border is not between north and south," he said, "but in the minds and hearts of our people."

On January 18, 1999, at a ceremony in Atlanta marking the national holiday that celebrates the birthday of her husband, Coretta Scott King presented the Martin Luther King Jr. Peace Prize to John Hume.

NOTES

CHAPTER 1

1. For an overview of the events of September 11, see Editors of *New York* magazine, *September 11, 2001* (New York: Harry N. Abrams, 2001). See also Elie Wiesel, "We Choose Honor," *Parade* magazine (October 28, 2001), pp. 4–5.

2. Patricia King and Andrew Murr, "A Son Who Spun Out of Control," *Newsweek* (June 1, 1998), pp. 32–33. See also Marlene Cimons, "Surgeon General Aims Campaign at Rising Suicide Rate," *Los Angeles Times* (May 3, 2001), p. A16; "Profiles of School Shooters," *Orange County Register* (March 6, 2001), p. News 5. Although school shootings represent only a tiny fraction of the violence in this country, many experts see them as part of a larger

problem: the dramatic rise in the rate of homicides and suicides among young people. See Sasha Nemecek, "Forestalling Violence," *Scientific American* 279, no. 3 (September 1998), pp. 15–16.

3. Note how obscenities, to the extent that they apply to others or the self, invariably employ the coarsest and most indiscriminate kinds of stereotypes. Emotional sounds and language, including spontaneous obscenities, are associated with the cingulate cortex, which is part of the limbic association cortex. See R. Joseph, *The Naked Neuron* (New York: Plenum, 1993), pp. 243–45; Richard Restak, *Brainscapes* (New York: Hyperion, 1995), pp. 105–9. The complexity and, perhaps, individual variability of the human emotional system is indicated by the fact that some patients exhibiting episodic dyscontrol whose amygdalae were selectively altered using psychosurgery gradually regained their aggressive behavior. See Debra Niehoff, *The Biology of Violence* (New York: Free Press, 1999), pp. 24–25. See also Gregg D. Jacobs and David Snyder, "Frontal Brain Asymmetry Predicts Affective Style in Men," *Behavioral Neuroscience* 110, no. 1 (1996), pp. 3–6.

4. Robert S. McNamara and James G. Blight, "The Nature of the Danger We Face," *Los Angeles Times* (October 28, 2001), p. M2. McNamara is a strong advocate of seeking to empathize not only with one's allies but also with one's adversaries. See Robert S. McNamara and James G. Blight, *Wilson's Ghost: Reducing the Risk of Conflict, Killing, and Catastrophe in the 21st Century* (New York: Public Affairs, 2001).

5. Charles Darwin, *The Expression of Emotions in Man and Animals* (New York: St. Martin's Press, 1979), pp. 239–53. The book was originally published in 1872.

6. Antonio R. Damasio, *Descartes' Error* (New York: Grosset/Putnam, 1994), pp. 34–51.

CHAPTER 2

1. In a report to the president and Congress on January 31, 2001, a blue-ribbon commission on terrorism predicted that terrorists will probably attack the United States with weapons of mass destruction sometime in the next twenty-five years. See "New Anti-Terror Cabinet Agency Urged," *Los Angeles Times* (February 1, 2001), p. A4. See also Benjamin R. Barber, *Jihad vs. McWorld: Terrorism's Challenge to Democracy* (New York: Ballantine, 1995); Chalmers Johnson, *Blowback: The Costs and Consequences of American Empire* (New York: Henry Holt, 2000); Thomas L. Friedman, *The Lexus and the Olive Tree: Understanding Globalization* (New York: Anchor Books, 1999).

CHAPTER 3

1. "37 Days: A Special Report," *Los Angeles Times* (December 17, 2000), pp. V1–V9.

2. Joseph LeDoux, "Emotion, Memory and the Brain," *Scientific American*, p. 56. For a discussion of the binary instinct, see Edward O. Wilson, *Consilience: The Unity of Knowledge* (New York: Knopf, 1998), pp. 153–54.

3. A number of scientific theories of moral growth emphasize the importance of cultivating children's inborn capacity for empathy—the ability to vicariously experience the feelings of others. See William Damon,

"The Moral Development of Children," *Scientific American* 281, no. 2 (August 1999), pp. 72–78.

CHAPTER 4

1. Joseph, *The Naked Neuron*, pp. 20–29, 316–18.

2. Hilary E. MacGregor and T. Christian Miller, "Gunman Opens Fire, Wounds 5 at Day Camp," *Los Angeles Times* (August 11, 1999), p. A1; Terry McDermott, "Panic Pierces Illusion of Safety," *Los Angeles Times* (August 11, 1999), p. A1.

3. The case of Buford Furrow raises the issue of hate crime laws, which have been passed by the majority of states and the federal government as well as a number of other countries. These laws generally add additional punishment to crimes that are found to be motivated by certain kinds of hatred, including hate based on race, religion, color, national origin, and (sometimes) sexual orientation. The term "hate crime" did not come into general use until the 1980s, and this was the period when hate crime laws began to be passed. The U.S. Supreme Court upheld the constitutionality of hate crime laws in 1993. There are a number of rationales for such laws including deterrence, enhanced protection for certain vulnerable groups, and explicit societal condemnation of hate-based criminal activity. It is probably too early to measure the effectiveness of these laws. They do seem to reflect a greater sensitivity within the developed world to the problems of hate. Occasionally, they present technical legal problems. See Linda Greenhouse, "New Jersey Hate Crime Law Struck Down," *New York Times* (June 27, 2000), p. A19. And, like affirmative action, they have been

caught up in political controversies, including charges that
they are the tools of advocacy groups, they give too much
discretion to prosecutors, and they risk intrusion into
freedom of thought. See Fred Dickey, "The Perversion of
Hate," *Los Angeles Times Magazine* (October 22, 2000), p.
10. Because hate is obsessive, often develops early in life,
and is a problem of the primitive neural system (which is
resistant to rationality), society's first line of defense must
be to strategically buttress the advanced neural system
against the impulse to hate using education and other
means. The ten strategies I have proposed offer one such
approach. As with depression, the goal should be
prevention or early intervention. In the case of someone
such as Furrow, who suffers from a serious mental
disorder, aggressive medical treatment is called for. See
David Rosenzweig, "History of Mental Problems Spares
Furrow from Death," *Los Angeles Times* (January 25,
2001), p. B11; Henry Weinstein, "Furrow Gets 5 Life
Terms for Shooting Jews, Filipino," *Los Angeles Times*
(March 27, 2000), p. B9; Jocelyn Y. Stewart, "Lest Hate
Victim Be Forgotten," *Los Angeles Times* (January 25,
2001), p. A1.

4. Restak, *The Brain*, pp. 136–37.

5. Eric Halgren, "Emotional Neurophysiology of the
   Amygdala Within the Context of Human Cognition," in
   John P. Aggleton, ed., *The Amygdala* (New York: Wiley-
   Liss, 1992), p. 217; Eric R. Kandel, "Brain and Behavior,"
   in Kandel et al., *Principles of Neural Science*, 4th ed. (New
   York: McGraw-Hill, 2000), p. 15.

6. Joseph, *The Naked Neuron*, pp. 10–11.

7. Melvin Konner, *The Tangled Wing: Biological Constraints
   on the Human Spirit* (New York: Holt, Rinehart and

Winston, 1982), pp. 146–50; Joseph, *The Naked Neuron*, pp. 158–61.

CHAPTER 5

1. Maura Reynolds, "War Has No Rules for Russian Forces Fighting in Chechnya," *Los Angeles Times* (September 17, 2000), p. A1.

2. For a discussion of former U.S. Senator Bob Kerrey's alleged involvement in the killing of civilians during the Vietnam War, see Evan Thomas, "Coming to Terms with a Tragedy," *Newsweek* (May 7, 2001), pp. 38–41.

3. Roger Lewin, *The Origin of Modern Humans* (New York: Scientific American Library, 1993), p. 118.

CHAPTER 6

1. Chuck Philips, "Murder Case Spotlights Marketing of Violent Lyrics," *Los Angeles Times* (January 21, 2001), p. C1; and "Ruling Favors Band in Suit Over Girl's Murder," *Los Angeles Times* (January 25, 2001), p. C8.

2. Richard Leakey, *The Origin of Humankind* (New York: BasicBooks, 1994), pp. 101–3, 111, 118.

3. Ian Tattersall, "How We Came to Be Human," *Scientific American* 285, no. 6 (December 2001), pp. 56–63; Lewin, *The Origin of Modern Humans*, p. 168.

4. William H. McNeill, *The Rise of the West* (Chicago: University of Chicago Press, 1963), pp. 30–36.

5. Jared Diamond, *The Third Chimpanzee* (New York: HarperCollins, 1992), pp. 21–24.

6. Diamond, *The Third Chimpanzee*, pp. 35–56. See also Ian
    Tattersall, "Once We Were Not Alone," *Scientific
    American* 282, no. 1 (January 2000), pp. 56–62. Others
    argue that Neanderthals lost out in a more peaceful
    economic competition with modern humans. See Lewin,
    The Origin of Modern Humans, pp. 131–35.

7. Steven Pinker, "Facts About Human Language Relevant
    to Its Evolution," in Jean-Pierre Changeux and Jean
    Chavaillon, eds., *Origins of the Human Brain* (New York:
    Oxford University Press, 1995), pp. 263–85.

8. Richard Restak, *The Mind* (New York: Bantam, 1988), pp.
    7–8.

9. Irving Kupfermann, "Learning and Memory," in Eric R.
    Kandel, James H. Schwartz, and Thomas M. Jessell, eds.,
    Principles of Neural Science, 3d ed. (New York: Elsevier,
    1991), pp. 1002–3. See also Kandel, Schwartz, and Jessell,
    eds., *Principles of Neural Science*, 4th ed. (New York:
    Elsevier, 1999), passim.

CHAPTER 7

1. Nancy Gibbs and Timothy Roche, "The Tapes," *Time*
    (December 20, 1999), pp. 40–56. See also Matt Bai,
    "Anatomy of a Massacre," *Newsweek* (May 3, 1999), pp.
    22–31.

2. Roy F. Baumeister, "Violent Pride: Do People Turn
    Violent Because of Self-Hate, or Self-Love," *Scientific
    American* 284, no. 4 (April 2001), pp. 96–101.

3. David G. Myers, *The Pursuit of Happiness* (New York:
    William Morrow, 1992), p. 189. See also Martin E. P.
    Seligman, *Helplessness: On Depression, Development and*

Death (San Francisco: W. H. Freeman, 1975); and Martin
E. P. Seligman, *Learned Optimism* (New York: Random
House, 1991).

4. Frederick K. Goodwin and Kay Redfield Jamison, *Manic-Depressive Illness* (New York: Oxford University Press,
1990), p. 3; and Kay Redfield Jamison, *An Unquiet Mind*
(New York: Vintage Books, 1996), pp. 67–68.

5. Charles B. Nemeroff, "The Neurobiology of Depression,"
Scientific American 278, no. 6 (June 1998), pp. 42–49.

6. Benedict Carey, "Obsession with Perfection," *Los Angeles
Times* (December 17, 2001), p. S1; David Grossman,
"Waiting for a Miracle . . . or a Catastrophe," *Los Angeles
Times* (May 20, 2001), p. M1.

7. Elizabeth Mehren, "Negative Self-Image Starts Early," *Los
Angeles Times* (March 5, 2001), p. S1.

8. There is extensive ongoing research on the biochemical
basis of eating disorders, particularly serotonin imbalances
that may be associated with aggression toward the self and
others. The problem of eating disorders is expected to
only intensify with the epidemic of obesity in the
industrialized world. See Niehoff, *The Biology of Violence*,
p. 137.

9. Eating disorders are an example of the importance of
keeping meaning systems—which establish hierarchical
values for thoughts, feelings, and behaviors—under the
control of the advanced neural system. This includes the
capacity to rationally assess meaning systems, create one's
own meaning systems, and quickly modify one's meaning
systems based on rational considerations. Without this
capacity, the individual may tend to limbically absorb a
cultural or other meaning system (slim body image, for
example), even if it leads to irrational behavior. The

treatment for such a disorder of the primitive neural system involves a painstaking effort to reassert advanced neural control. See Kim Hubbard, Anne-Marie O'Neill, and Christina Cheakalos, "Out of Control," *People* (April 12, 1999), pp. 52–71.

CHAPTER 8

1. The lack of an instinctive us-group among humans based on kinship makes our kinship ties potentially fragile. And family feuds can create extremely bitter us-them hostility. See "Arab Honor's Price: A Woman's Blood," *New York Times* (June 20, 1999), p. A1.

2. Rita Carter, *Mapping the Mind* (Berkeley, Calif.: University of California Press, 1998), pp. 90–91, 197; Zaffar Abbas, "Pervez Musharraf's Extremist Dilemma," *Los Angeles Times* (December 16, 2001), p. M2.

3. Natalie Angier, "A Pearl and a Hodgepodge: Human DNA," *New York Times* (June 27, 2000), p. A1.

4. Francis S. Collins and Karin G. Jegalian, "Deciphering the Code of Life," *Scientific American* 281, no. 6 (December 1999), pp. 86–91.

5. Nicholas Wade, "Genetic Code of Human Life Is Cracked by Scientists," *New York Times* (June 27, 2000), p. A1.

6. Angier, "A Pearl and a Hodgepodge: Human DNA," *New York Times*, p. A1.

7. Collins and Jegalian, "Deciphering the Code of Life," *Scientific American*, pp. 86–91.

8. Thomas M. Jessell, "Neuronal Survival and Synapse Formation," in Kandel et al., *Principles of Neural Science,*

4th ed. (New York: McGraw-Hill, 2000), pp. 929–44; Richard Restak, *The Brain* (New York: Bantam, 1984), pp. 41–48.

9. Wade, "Genetic Code of Human Life Is Cracked by Scientists," *New York Times*, pp. A1, D1, D4; Marlene Cimons, "Decoding Raises a Double-Edged Sword," *Los Angeles Times* (June 27, 2000), p. A1.

10. Carol Tavris, "The Paradox of Gender," *Scientific American* 279, no. 4 (October 1998), pp. 126–28; Eleanor E. Maccoby, *The Two Sexes: Growing Up Apart, Coming Together* (Cambridge, Mass.: Harvard University Press, 1998).

11. Collins and Jegalian, "Deciphering the Code of Life," *Scientific American*, pp. 86–91; Wade, "Genetic Code of Human Life Is Cracked by Scientists," *New York Times*, pp. A1, D1, D4; Cimons, "Decoding Raises a Double-Edged Sword," *Los Angeles Times*, p. A1.

CHAPTER 9

1. Tracy Wilkinson, "Israel Mourns Victim, 16, of Cyber-Crime," *Los Angeles Times* (January 20, 2001), p. A2.

2. Lou Michel and Dan Herbeck, *American Terrorist: Timothy McVeigh and the Oklahoma City Bombing* (New York: HarperCollins, 2001).

CHAPTER 10

1. Barbara Bailey Reinhold, *Toxic Work* (New York: Dutton, 1996); "As Many as One in Four Workers Are Angry on

the Job, Report Finds," *Los Angeles Times* (August 11, 1999), p. A11.

2. Josh Getlin and John J. Goldman, "Shooter Kills 7 at Mass. Internet Firm," *Los Angeles Times* (December 27, 2000), p. A1; Josh Getlin, "A Private Man Accused of Great Cruelty," *Los Angeles Times* (December 28, 2000), p. A1.

3. Niehoff, *The Biology of Violence*, pp. 150–87.

4. Ibid., pp. 177–78, 183.

5. Restak, *The Brain*, pp. 315–33. Though neuroscientists are still unsure of the purpose or purposes of sleep, some studies link sleep to meaning, at least among advanced mammals. During normal sleep—with its regular stages of dreaming—the brain may organize and consolidate the information and experiences that are registered while awake. This could explain why sound sleep tends to improve memory and performance. Long-term lack of sleep, however, tends to produce a sense of fragmentation, meaninglessness, lethargy, and depression. See Dennis D. Kelly, "Sleep and Dreaming," in Kandel et al., *Principles of Neural Science*, 4th ed. (New York: McGraw-Hill, 2000), pp. 792–804.

6. Nemeroff, "The Neurobiology of Depression," *Scientific American*, pp. 42–44. See also Restak, *The Mind*, pp. 165–95.

7. Niehoff, *The Biology of Violence*, pp. 172–81. See also Paul Glue, David Nutt, and Nick Coupland, "Stress and Psychiatric Disorder: Reconciling Social and Biological Approaches," in S. Clare Stanford and Peter Salmon, eds., *Stress: From Synapse to Syndrome* (San Diego: Academic Press, 1994), pp. 53–73.

CHAPTER 11

1. Restak, *The Brain*, p. 169.

2. Carter, *Mapping the Mind*, pp. 72–76.

3. Jared Diamond, *Why Sex Is Fun: The Evolution of Human Sexuality* (New York: BasicBooks, 1997).

4. Diamond, *The Third Chimpanzee*, p. 87.

5. Carter, *Mapping the Mind*, pp. 68–72.

6. Walter J. Freeman, "The Lonely Brain," in Carter, *Mapping the Mind*, p. 146.

7. Niehoff, *The Biology of Violence*, pp. 1–2, 64–65, 259, 277–78. Mature love resists the primitive tendency to stereotype—for better or worse—the object of one's affection and seeks, regularly and deliberately, to deepen the ties of love through shared meaning, common goals, and cooperative effort.

CHAPTER 12

1. H. G. Reza, "'He Never Said a Word,' Guard Recalls," *Los Angeles Times* (March 9, 2001), p. A26. See also Scott Gold, Ken Ellington, and H. G. Reza, "2 Killed, 13 Hurt in School Shooting," *Los Angeles Times* (March 6, 2001), p. A1.

2. Greg Krikorian, "Rough Life of School Gunfire Suspect," *Los Angeles Times* (April 23, 2001), p. B9. See also Erin Texeira, Greg Krikorian, and Scott Martelle, "5 Hurt in Gunfire at High School Near San Diego; Student Is Held," *Los Angeles Times* (March 23, 2001), p. A1.

3. James L. Gould and Carol Grant Gould, *The Animal Mind* (New York: Scientific American Library, 1994), pp. 163–69.

4. Nemeroff, "The Neurobiology of Depression," *Scientific American*, p. 42; Carter, *Mapping the Mind*, pp. 99–102; Sharon Begley, "Why the Young Kill," *Newsweek* (May 3, 1999), pp. 32–35.

5. Media violence tends to influence those who are already aggressive. See Roy F. Baumeister, *Evil: Inside Human Violence and Cruelty* (New York: W. H. Freeman, 1999), pp. 277–81.

6. Richard M. Restak, *The Modular Brain* (New York: Macmillan, 1994), pp. 156–57.

7. Jeff Leeds, "Lawmakers, Parent Groups Laud Media Violence Findings," *Los Angeles Times* (January 18, 2001), p. C1.

8. Konner, *The Tangled Wing*, pp. 352–53; Myers, *The Pursuit of Happiness*, p. 86.

9. Tony Perry, "High School Shooter, 18, Hangs Self in Jail Cell," *Los Angeles Times* (October 30, 2001), p. B1.

CHAPTER 13

1. Michael Slackman, "Arabs See Jewish Conspiracy in Pokémon," *Los Angeles Times* (April 24, 2001), p. A1.

2. Salam al-Marayati, "Sheiks and Hollywood Are Two Sides of the Same Coin," *Los Angeles Times* (May 2, 2001), p. B11.

3. P. A. Russell, "Fear-Evoking Stimuli," in W. Sluckin, ed.,
    Fear in Animals and Man (New York: Van Nostrand
    Reinhold, 1979), pp. 86–124. In exceptional cases—as with
    the greatly increased threat level after the terrorist attacks
    of September 11, 2001—there may be a rational basis for
    extra vigilance with respect to certain groups. Just as this
    is a difficult line to draw constitutionally, it also poses a
    difficult problem neurally. The primitive neural system
    easily incorporates this kind of threat category, which can
    lead to instances of irrational behavior. In December 2001,
    for example, an Arab-American U.S. Secret Service agent
    who was on his way from Baltimore to Texas to join
    President Bush's security detail was barred from a
    commercial flight when the pilot of the plane became
    suspicious of his appearance. The agent was forced to take
    a later flight. See Megan Garvey, "Pilot's Concern Keeps
    Federal Agent Off Flight," *Los Angeles Times* (December
    28, 2001), p. A3.

4. Daniel Goleman, *Emotional Intelligence* (New York:
    Bantam, 1995), pp. 291–96.

5. Erika Hayasaki, " 'Pearl Harbor' Making Its Marks," *Los
    Angeles Times* (May 29, 2001), p. F1.

6. Carter, *Mapping the Mind*, pp. 23, 195–97, 202.

7. Tom Segev, "There Can Be No Peace Without Maturity,"
    Los Angeles Times (May 21, 2001), p. B13.

8. Grossman, "Waiting for a Miracle . . . or a Catastrophe,"
    Los Angeles Times, p. M1.

CHAPTER 14

1. McNeill, *The Rise of the West*, pp. 50–58; Martin Miller, "A Dish Best Served Cold," *Los Angeles Times* (May 11, 2001), p. E1.

2. "'He Never Said a Word,' Guard Recalls," *Los Angeles Times*, p. A26.

3. Jeffrey Gettleman, "A Racist Jailed, a City Healed," *Los Angeles Times* (May 3, 2001), p. A5.

4. Tracy Wilkinson and Mary Curtius, "Mideast Peace Prospects Unraveled as Acrimony Grew," *Los Angeles Times* (December 31, 2000), p. A10; Tracy Wilkinson, "Jews Cry for Revenge as Girl Is Buried," *Los Angeles Times* (April 2, 2001), p. A6.

5. Restak, *The Mind*, pp. 62–63.

6. Tracy Wilkinson, "One Israeli Who Lost a Son Fights for Peace," *Los Angeles Times* (April 17, 2001), p. A4. The anger and threats endured by Frankenthal and his supporters suggest an important characteristic of hate: it can be treacherous. When large groups of people are motivated by anger or hatred, they easily turn on each other. The primitive neural system tends to view dissent as a mortal threat. There was an element of this after September 11, 2001, when even mild questioning of the government's policies on terrorism was met by extreme anger in some quarters. Dissent and tolerance are sophisticated ideas that are the product of the advanced neural system and are difficult for the limbic system to comprehend. The Palestinians themselves have suffered terribly from this quality of hate. During the first *intifada*, which lasted from 1987 to 1993, an estimated nine hundred

of the two thousand Palestinians killed were slain by
fellow Palestinians—usually because of suspicion that
they were collaborating with the Israelis. Some of the
same kinds of killings occurred in the second *intifada*. See
Mary Curtius, "'Street Justice' for Suspected Informers,"
Los Angeles Times (March 8, 2001), p. A1.

7. "Prosecution Rests in Case of 1963 Church Bombing," *Los
Angeles Times* (April 29, 2001), p. A34; Jeffrey Gettleman,
"Ex-Klansman Convicted in 1963 Alabama Church Blast,"
Los Angeles Times (May 2, 2001), p. A1.

CHAPTER 15

1. Bill Plaschke, "Victory Laps," *Los Angeles Times*
(September 26, 2000), p. U1.

2. Diamond, *The Third Chimpanzee*, pp. 282–307.

3. The vital importance of cooperation to the survival of
early hunter-gatherer or scavenger-gatherer hominids
within a small us-group social organization was deduced
in part through the intensive study by anthropologists of
widely scattered hunter-gatherer cultures that persisted
into the twentieth century. See Lewin, *The Origin of
Modern Humans*, pp. 34, 147; Leakey, *The Origin of
Humankind*, pp. 60–61; William H. Calvin, *The River That
Flows Uphill* (New York: Macmillan, 1986), pp. 468–69;
and McNeill, *The Rise of the West*, pp. 5–6.

4. Each of the steps that contribute to an us-us approach
must be viewed in conjunction with all the others. For
example, the step "put things in perspective" refers to the
ability of the advanced neural system to shift its frame of
reference, often dramatically, by viewing experience
through a new meaning system. But this new perspective

or meaning system must be empathetic and free of prejudicial stereotypes. One striking example of perspective shifting is the case of Joseph Kovach, who as a fifteen-year-old Hungarian schoolboy was thrown into a Soviet prison. He lived a terrifying, mindless existence until he was transferred to a camp with a small library. "It was an altogether new world for me," he said. "I suddenly discovered an escape out of the starkness of the prison world into the beautiful world of words and poetry. But it was more than that. It marked the opening up of a whole new sense of thinking and of intellectual activity. From then on, I had an immense preoccupation and interest in anything relating to ideas, to language, to anything I could learn about. Although I had no way of doing anything about my physical condition, I was free." See Restak, *The Mind*, pp. 271–72.

5. David Holley, "Serbs Face Their Past, Dose of Truth at a Time," *Los Angeles Times* (April 17, 2001), p. A1.

6. Roy F. Baumeister, "Violent Pride," *Scientific American* 284, no. 4 (April 2001), pp. 96–101; Carol J. Williams, "Master Manipulator Rose to Power on Hatred—and Fell the Same Way," *Los Angeles Times* (April 1, 2001), p. A10. See also Baumeister, *Evil: Inside Human Violence and Cruelty*, pp. 136, 143–54.

7. Richard Serrano, "McVeigh Shows a Defiance Even as His Execution Nears," *Los Angeles Times* (February 11, 2001), p. A1; Jack Valenti, "Killing Civilians Goes With the Duty of War," *Los Angeles Times* (May 8, 2001), p. B15.

8. Restak, *The Mind*, p. 284; Restak, *The Brain*, pp. 135, 138.

9. Gerd Kempermann and Fred H. Gage, "New Nerve Cells for the Adult Brain," *Scientific American* 280, no. 5 (May 1999), pp. 48–53; Richard Boudreaux, "John Paul First

Pope to Visit Mosque," *Los Angeles Times* (May 7, 2001), p. A1.

CHAPTER 16

1. Konner, *The Tangled Wing*, pp. 204–6.

2. Niehoff, *The Biology of Violence*, pp. 236–39.

3. Ibid., pp. 221–24, 244–54.

4. Wilson, *Consilience*, p. 246.

5. Damasio, *Descartes' Error*, pp. 43–51, 245–46.

6. The parietal-temporal-occipital association cortex consists of a single contiguous region of neocortex in the right and left cerebral hemispheres located where these three lobes intersect. It is made up of the most sophisticated cortical areas of each of these lobes, capable of creating multifaceted associations through detailed analysis of input from many different brain areas. It is this particular association area of the neocortex that I believe is primarily responsible for generating consciousness as part of a system that also consists of several subcortical structures including the thalamus and reticular formation. In the early twentieth century, the human cerebral cortex was divided into about fifty different areas by the anatomist Korbinian Brodmann. These areas appear to have different kinds of neural architecture. The parietal-temporal-occipital association cortex corresponds to Brodmann's areas 39 and 40 as well as portions of areas 19, 21, 22, and 37. Irving Kupfermann, "Localization of Higher Cognitive and Affective Functions: The Association Cortices," in Kandel, et al., *Principles of Neural Science*, 3d ed., p. 824.

For a similar analysis, see Kandel et al., *Principles of Neural Science*, 4th ed., passim. Consciousness may have evolved, in part, through an expansion of the posterior parietal cortex. In monkeys, this cortical region includes Brodmann's areas 5 and 7, which are not part of the parietal-temporal-occipital association cortex. But in humans, this region has expanded to include Brodmann's areas 39 and 40, which are part of the parietal-temporal-occipital association region and adjoin the somatosensory cortex containing the primary sensory map of the body. Claude Ghez, "Voluntary Movement," in Kandel et al., *Principles of Neural Science*, 3d ed., p. 623. These two areas are also present in the great apes but in a much less well-developed form. Ghez summarized the function of this region: "By integrating information about the state of the animal with that of potential targets, the posterior parietal areas are thought to create a context or frame of reference for directing movement." Ghez, p. 624. I would argue that in the great apes and humans this "context or frame of reference" is consciousness. Consciousness combines an ongoing external model of the body moving in space and time with an internal model of ongoing neocortical processing, including memory, imagination, feeling, and analysis. This sophisticated neural model is the subjective "self" that we seem to inhabit. Consciousness is thus localized to a particular neural system, though extensively interconnected with other brain areas. The parietal-temporal-occipital association cortex lies on top of the thalamus, which is an important center of attention. Consciousness may be an extraordinary enhancement of thalamic attention. Damage to the thalamus severely degrades or destroys consciousness. Injury to the parietal-temporal-occipital association cortex, including the damage done by Alzheimer's disease, also impairs or

destroys consciousness. James Goldman and Lucien Côté,
"Aging of the Brain: Dementia of the Alzheimer's Type,"
in Kandel et al., *Principles of Neural Science*, 3d ed., p. 977.
One important function of consciousness is in the spinning
of complex scenarios involving the self. It is noteworthy
that the two most densely connected areas of association
cortex are the posterior parietal cortex and the dorsolateral
prefrontal association cortex, whose functions include
working memory, imagination, and planning.
Kupfermann, p. 828. Other evidence for the parietal-
temporal-occipital association cortex as the center of
consciousness includes the fact that consciousness is
normally preserved even with extensive damage to the
prefrontal association cortex and the limbic system. An
individual can remain self-aware even if the prefrontal
cortex, including the orbitofrontal area, is almost entirely
scraped away. Antonio R. Damasio and G. W. Van
Hoesen, "Emotional Disturbances Associated with Focal
Lesions of the Limbic Frontal Lobe," in Kenneth M.
Heilman and Paul Satz, eds., *Neuropsychology of Human
Emotion* (New York: Guilford Press, 1983), p. 86. If the
parietal-temporal-occipital association cortex is damaged,
however, through stroke or other injury, the structure of
consciousness often changes drastically—as with neglect
syndrome, in which patients may ignore half their visual
space or even half their body. In forms of brain injury that
do not involve the parietal-temporal-occipital association
cortex, patients usually remain consciously aware of their
infirmities; but in cases such as neglect syndrome patients
are often unaware that anything is wrong with them. Even
when confronted with the obvious and bizarre changes in
their behavior and functioning, patients often continue to
deny that there has been any change. Kupfermann, pp.
831–32. The flow of processing in the cerebral cortex is

roughly from the rear areas to the front. The primary visual cortex, for example, is in the occipital lobe in the very back of the brain. Generally, as information flows toward the front of the brain, it becomes more highly processed. This highly processed data is delivered to the prefrontal association cortex and the limbic system (including the limbic association cortex). These two areas, not consciousness, appear to be the actual decision-making centers of the brain, which compete—outside of consciousness—for control of behavior. The prefrontal cortex plays an important role in suppressing the impulses of the limbic system. Once a decision has been made (say, to raise one's arm), the command generally flows from these more anterior regions toward the rear of the brain. A movement command, for example, might originate in the prefrontal association cortex and then flow into the premotor and primary motor areas that lie just behind it and are responsible for activating the muscles of the body. It may be that only after the prefrontal cortex begins activating these motor areas is the movement command signaled to the parietal-temporal-occipital association cortex, which lies behind the primary motor and primary somatosensory cortices, and thus enters conscious awareness. Consciousness would, therefore, not directly control the will but only register the decisions made by the true command centers of the brain: most likely the prefrontal association cortex and the primitive neural system. Although consciousness would not exert direct control over these command areas, the context or frame of reference it creates would certainly be incorporated into the decision-making process and would thus be influential in shaping the final outcome. If this scheme is roughly correct, it might explain why careful studies by researchers such as Benjamin Libet and H. H. Kornhuber appear to show that the brain consistently makes its decisions a fraction of a second before consciousness becomes aware of them. Benjamin Libet, "Unconscious Cerebral Initiative and the Role of Conscious Will in Voluntary Action," *Behavioral and Brain Sciences* 8 (1985), pp. 529–66. See also Restak, *The Modular Brain*, pp. 115–16. Some researchers have suggested that certain cortical rhythms might also play a role in binding the moment-to-moment activity of the brain into the unified conscious experience that we perceive. One such rhythm sweeps from the front to the back of the brain at a rate of forty cycles per second (40 Hz) and appears to be generated by the thalamus. Rodolfo R. Llinás and Urs Ribary, "Perception as an Oneiric-Like State Modulated by the Senses," in Joel L. Koch and Christof Davis, eds., *Large-Scale Neuronal Theories of the Brain* (Cambridge, Mass.: MIT Press, 1994), pp. 111–24.

BIBLIOGRAPHY

Ader, Robert, David L. Felten, and Nicholas Cohen, eds. *Psychoneuroimmunology*. 2d ed. San Diego: Academic Press, 1990.

Aggleton, John P., ed. *The Amygdala*. New York: Wiley-Liss, 1992.

American Psychiatric Association. *Diagnostic and Statistical Manual of Mental Disorders*. 4th ed. Washington, D.C.: American Psychiatric Association, 1994.

————. *Violence and Mental Illness*. Washington, D.C.: American Psychiatric Association, 1994.

Barber, Benjamin R. *Jihad vs. McWorld: Terrorism's Challenge to Democracy*. New York: Ballantine, 1995.

Barzun, Jacques. *From Dawn to Decadence*. New York: Perennial, 2000.

Baumeister, Roy F. *Evil: Inside Human Violence and Cruelty*. New York: W. H. Freeman, 1999.

Bigler, Erin D., Ronald A. Yeo, and Eric Turkheimer, eds. *Neuropsychological Function and Brain Imaging*. New York: Plenum, 1989.

Calvin, William H. *The Cerebral Code*. Cambridge, Mass.: MIT Press, 1996.

———. *The River That Flows Uphill*. New York: Macmillan, 1986.

Calvin, William H., and George A. Ojemann. *Conversations with Neil's Brain*. New York: Addison-Wesley, 1994.

Changeux, Jean-Pierre. *Neuronal Man*. New York: Oxford University Press, 1986.

Changeux, Jean-Pierre, and Jean Chavaillon, eds. *Origins of the Human Brain*. New York: Oxford University Press, 1995.

Churchland, Patricia Smith. *Neurophilosophy*. Cambridge, Mass.: MIT Press, 1986.

Coles, Robert. *Children of Crisis*. Boston: Little, Brown, 1967.

Crick, Francis. *The Astonishing Hypothesis*. New York: Macmillan, 1994.

Damasio, Antonio R. *Descartes' Error*. New York: Grosset/Putnam, 1994.

———. *The Feeling of What Happens*. New York: Harcourt Brace & Company, 1999.

Darwin, Charles. *The Descent of Man*. London: Murray, 1871.

———. *The Expression of Emotions in Man and Animals*. New York: St. Martin's Press, 1979. The text is based on the 1872 edition.

———. *On the Origin of Species by Means of Natural Selection*. London: Murray, 1859.

Dawkins, Richard. *The Blind Watchmaker*. New York: W. W. Norton, 1987.

———. *The Selfish Gene*. New York: Oxford University Press, 1976.

Dennett, Daniel C. *Consciousness Explained*. Boston: Little, Brown, 1991.

Diamond, Jared. *Guns, Germs, and Steel: The Fates of Human Societies*. New York: W. W. Norton, 1997.

———. *The Third Chimpanzee*. New York: HarperCollins, 1992.

———. *Why Sex Is Fun: The Evolution of Human Sexuality*. New York: BasicBooks, 1997.

Donovan, Bernard T. *Hormones and Human Behavior*. Cambridge: Cambridge University Press, 1985.

Dozier, Rush W., Jr. *Codes of Evolution*. New York: Crown, 1992.

———. *Fear Itself*. New York: St. Martin's Press, 1998.

Drucker, Peter F. *Landmarks of Tomorrow*. New Brunswick, N.J.: Transaction Publishers, 1996. This book was originally published in 1957.

Editors of *New York* magazine. *September 11, 2001*. New York: Harry N. Abrams, 2001.

Frankl, Victor E. *Man's Search for Meaning: An Introduction to Logotherapy*. Boston: Beacon Press, 1962.

Friedman, Thomas L. *The Lexus and the Olive Tree: Understanding Globalization.* New York: Anchor Books, 1999.

Fritz, Charles E., and J. H. Mathewson. *Convergence Behavior in Disasters.* Washington, D.C.: National Academy of Sciences, 1957.

Gazzinaga, Michael S., and Joseph E. LeDoux. *The Integrated Mind.* New York: Plenum Press, 1978.

Goleman, Daniel. *Emotional Intelligence.* New York: Bantam, 1995.

Goodall, Jane. *The Chimpanzees of Gombe: Patterns of Behavior.* Cambridge, Mass.: Harvard University Press, 1986.

Goodwin, Frederick K., and Kay Redfield Jamison. *Manic-Depressive Illness.* New York: Oxford University Press, 1990.

Gould, James L., and Carol Grant Gould. *The Animal Mind.* New York: Scientific American, 1994.

Heilman, Kenneth M., and Paul Satz, eds. *Neuropsychology of Human Emotion.* New York: Guilford Press, 1983.

Jamison, Kay Redfield. *Touched with Fire: Manic-Depressive Illness and the Artistic Temperament.* New York: Free Press, 1993.

———. *An Unquiet Mind.* New York: Vintage Books, 1996.

Johnson, Chalmers. *Blowback: The Costs and Consequences of American Empire.* New York: Henry Holt, 2000.

Johnson, George. *In the Palaces of Memory.* New York: Knopf, 1991.

Johnson-Laird, Philip N. *The Computer and the Mind.* Cambridge, Mass.: Harvard University Press, 1988.

Joseph, Rhawn. *The Naked Neuron*. New York: Plenum, 1993.

Kagan, Jerome. *Galen's Prophecy*. New York: BasicBooks, 1994.

Kalivas, Peter W., and Charles D. Barnes, eds. *Limbic Motor Circuits and Neuropsychiatry*. Boca Raton, Fla.: CRC Press, 1993.

Kandel, Eric R., ed. *Molecular Neurobiology in Neurology and Psychiatry*. New York: Raven Press, 1987.

Kandel, Eric R., James H. Schwartz, and Thomas M. Jessell, eds. *Principles of Neural Science*. 3d ed. New York: Elsevier, 1991.

—————. *Principles of Neural Science*. 4th ed. New York: Elsevier, 1999.

Koch, Christof, and Joel L. Davis, eds. *Large-Scale Neuronal Theories of the Brain*. Cambridge, Mass.: MIT Press, 1994.

Konner, Melvin. *The Tangled Wing: Biological Constraints on the Human Spirit*. New York: Holt, Rinehart and Winston, 1982.

Kulka, Richard A., William E. Schlenger, John A. Fairbank, Richard L. Hough, B. Kathleen Jordan, Charles Marmar, and Daniel S. Weiss. *Trauma and the Vietnam War Generation*. New York: Brunner/Mazel, 1990.

Leakey, Richard. *The Origin of Humankind*. New York: BasicBooks, 1994.

LeDoux, Joseph. *The Emotional Brain*. New York: Simon & Schuster, 1996.

Levin, H. S., H. M. Eisenberg, and A. L. Benton, eds. *Frontal Lobe Function and Dysfunction*. New York: Oxford University Press, 1991.

Lewin, Roger. *The Origin of Modern Humans*. New York: Scientific American Library, 1993.

Llinás, Rodolfo R., ed. *The Biology of the Brain*. New York: W. H. Freeman, 1989.

————. *The Workings of the Brain*. New York: W. H. Freeman, 1990.

Maccoby, Eleanor E. *The Two Sexes: Growing Up Apart, Coming Together*. Cambridge, Mass.: Harvard University Press, 1998.

Mayr, Ernst. *The Growth of Biological Thought*. Cambridge, Mass.: Harvard University Press, 1982.

McGaugh, James L., Federico Bermúdez-Rattoni, and Roberto A. Prado-Alcalá, eds. *Plasticity in the Central Nervous System*. Mahway, N.J.: Lawrence Erlbaum, 1995.

McNamara, Robert S., with Brian VanDemark. *In Retrospect: The Tragedies and Lessons of Vietnam*. New York: Times Books, 1995.

McNamara, Robert S., and James G. Blight. *Wilson's Ghost: Reducing the Risk of Conflict, Killing, and Catastrophe in the 21st Century*. New York: Public Affairs, 2001.

McNeill, William H. *Plagues and People*. New York: Doubleday, 1976.

————. *The Rise of the West*. Chicago: University of Chicago Press, 1963.

Michel, Lou, and Dan Herbeck. *American Terrorist: Timothy McVeigh and the Oklahoma City Bombing*. New York: HarperCollins, 2001.

Myers, David G. *The Pursuit of Happiness*. New York: William Morrow, 1992.

Niehoff, Debra. *The Biology of Violence*. New York: Free Press, 1999.

Pagels, Heinz R. *Cosmic Code*. New York: Simon & Schuster, 1982.

Pais, Abraham. *"Subtle Is the Lord . . .": The Science and the Life of Albert Einstein*. New York: Oxford University Press, 1982.

Passingham, R. E. *The Frontal Lobes and Voluntary Action*. Oxford: Oxford University Press, 1993.

Pechura, Constance M., and Joseph B. Martin, eds. *Mapping the Brain and Its Functions*. Washington, D.C.: National Academy Press, 1991.

Plato. *The Republic and Other Works*. New York: Anchor Books, 1973.

Provine, Robert R. *Laughter: A Scientific Investigation*. New York: Viking, 2000.

Rachman, S. J. *Fear and Courage*. San Francisco: W. H. Freeman, 1978.

———. *Fear and Courage*. 2d ed. New York: W. H. Freeman, 1990.

Reinhold, Barbara Bailey. *Toxic Work*. New York: Dutton, 1996.

Restak, Richard M. *The Brain*. New York: Bantam, 1984.

———. *Brainscapes*. New York: Hyperion, 1995.

———. *The Mind*. New York: Bantam, 1988.

———. *The Modular Brain*. New York: Macmillan, 1994.

Rodgers, R. J., and S. J. Cooper. *Endorphins, Opiates and Behavioural Processes*. New York: John Wiley, 1988.

Savage-Rumbaugh, E. Sue, and Roger Lewin. *Kanzi: The Ape at the Brink of the Human Mind.* New York: Wiley, 1994.

Seligman, Martin E. P. *Helplessness: On Depression, Development and Death.* San Francisco: W. H. Freeman, 1975.

————. *Learned Optimism.* New York: Random House, 1991.

Shepherd, Gordon M., ed. *The Synaptic Organization of the Brain.* 3d ed. New York: Oxford University Press, 1990.

Sluckin, W. *Fear in Animals and Man.* New York: Van Nostrand Reinhold, 1979.

Snyder, Solomon H. *Brainstorming.* Cambridge, Mass.: Harvard University Press, 1989.

————. *Drugs and the Brain.* New York: Scientific American, 1986.

Solomon, Zahava. *Combat Stress Reaction.* New York: Plenum, 1993.

Stanford, S. Clare, and Peter Salmon. *Stress: From Synapse to Syndrome.* San Diego: Academic Press, 1994.

Warburton, David M. *Brain, Behavior and Drugs.* New York: John Wiley, 1975.

Wheeler, John Archibald, and Wojciech Hubert Zurek, eds. *Quantum Theory and Measurement.* Princeton, N.J.: Princeton University Press, 1983.

Wilson, Edward O. *Consilience: The Unity of Knowledge.* New York: Knopf, 1998.

Wilson, John P., Zev Harel, and Boaz Kahana. *Human Adaptation to Extreme Stress.* New York: Plenum, 1988.

Wolfenstein, Martha. *Disaster: A Psychological Essay.* Glencoe, Ill.: The Free Press, 1957.

INDEX